100 BEST FAMILY RESORTS IN NORTH AMERICA

100 Quality Resorts with Leisure Activities for Children and Adults

Sixth Edition

by

Janet Tice and Jane Wilford

Revised by Becky Danley

The Globe Pequot Press

GUILFORD, CONNECTICUT

Cover photos courtesy of TradeWinds Island Resort
Cover design by Lana Mullen
Text design by Nancy Freeborn/Freeborn Design

ISSN 1536-6170
ISBN 0-7627-1186-8

Manufactured in the United States of America
Sixth Edition/First Printing

The prices and rates listed in this guidebook were confirmed at press time. We recommend, however, that you call establishments to obtain current information before traveling.

To Fabiana and Sykes,
who first provided the inspiration,
and to Paul and Sarah,
who continue to share the adventure.
Our wonderful children
and our best family travel critics!

Contents

Preface

"Best" is a curious adjective, one that is entirely subjective. So let us define our sense of best—both what it does and what it doesn't mean.

Best is not necessarily the fanciest, the biggest, the most expensive.

Best is not always the sleekest, the poshest, or the newest.

Best, in the context of this book, is what is best for families.

Best is variety—in setting and atmosphere.

Best is variety in recreational interests and in prices.

Best is variety in geographical location. A broad selection allows you to have choices whether you want to travel far or near.

We searched for the most extensive children's programs, yet balanced this with an interest in presenting a good cross-section of North America. If we have overlooked your favorite, let us know. Please write to us in care of The Globe Pequot Press, P.O. Box 480, Guilford, CT 06437.

Also, many thanks to D. Sykes Wilford, who shared his travels and his travails during the production of this manuscript.

Janet Tice
Jane Wilford

Introduction

Although traveling with children is not a new phenomenon, many Americans these days are viewing the traditional family vacation in a different light. In past decades family vacations have most frequently been determined by the needs and wants of the children. Planning the entire vacation around the kids often left Mom and Dad feeling that they had not had a vacation at all but, rather, a trial by fire. The only option was to leave Junior behind in the care of grandparents or close family friends while the parents ventured off on their own. In an attempt to share experiences with their children, many parents, seeking middle ground, are adjusting the focus of their leisure-time plans.

Vacations these days often mean shorter and more frequent jaunts. Increasingly, they involve flying rather than loading up the family car and driving. Minivacations are becoming popular and are frequently planned to coincide with one or the other parent's business trips. On the philosophical side, current trends in child care emphasize the importance of a parent's presence, especially for the first three years, and many parents are reluctant to leave their infants and toddlers for extended periods.

The intent of this book is to identify those places where adults and children can enjoy interesting and age-appropriate activities. Baby-sitting services for infants, a ski school for three-year-olds, and a supervised recreational program for older children are some of the possibilities explored. In selecting resorts we have taken into consideration different styles, price ranges, and diverse geographic locations. It is a representative sampling rather than an all-inclusive listing. Often we have been limited by lack of space and lack of information. This book does not highlight every Disney World and Six Flags Over Somewhere establishment in the United States. While these certainly serve an important educational function in a pleasant and exciting atmosphere for children, therein lies the catch: They are directed primarily toward children. But parents deserve vacations, too—adult vacations with grown-up activities.

This is not, then, a book about vacations *for* kids. Rather, it is a book about vacations *with* kids, about family adventures in which adults can be adults and children can be children and in which there is common ground for sharing.

In general we are pleased with the progress we've noted in the resorts we have chosen from our previous editions. They are not resting on their laurels but seem to be enthusiastic and dedicated to making more and more improvements and providing better and better facilities and programs for families. In addition, new resorts developing exciting agendas are constantly entering this family-oriented market.

If we've left out your favorite family spot, or if you own a resort and feel slighted, please write to us in care of The Globe Pequot Press. We're always glad to know of places where families find special treatment.

Costs and Caveats

Prices are noted throughout the book in the accommodations section of each resort's description. They are current as of 2001. But, just like the new car that depreciates the minute you drive away from the showroom, prices have to be adjusted for inflation the minute they're stated. Keep this in mind if your travel plans do not materialize right away but instead are put on the back burner for a couple of years. Inflation takes its toll simultaneously and universally; however, the prices quoted here can serve as a basis for comparison among resorts regardless of the year in which you consult this guide.

The problem most commonly caused by prices is sorting out just what a given price includes. In the travel industry, various pricing schedules are frequently used to identify the relationship between lodging and meals. For example:

European plan means the rate quoted is for lodging only.

Modified American plan means two meals a day (usually breakfast and dinner) as well as lodging are included in the daily rate.

Full American plan means three meals a day and lodging are covered in the daily rate.

The extent of what else is included in the daily room rate, such as use of the recreational facilities, varies widely from one resort to another. Every effort has been made to identify the extras for which no additional charge is required. If "complimentary" or "free" is not clearly stated for a service or activity, you can safely assume that there is a fee.

Besides lodging and meals, prices are specifically noted for children's programs. As a well-seasoned traveler, you already have a ballpark idea of the prices of lift tickets for skiing and greens fees for golf. Emphasis here is on costs of the children's activities because now you're trying to become well seasoned as a traveling parent.

Planning Family Vacations

How This Book Can Help You

As your vacation rolls around, you start weighing the pros and cons of bringing the children along. You feel that you desperately need exclusive time for adult conversation with your spouse or other grown-ups. Yet you wonder if following through on that idea is fair to your kids. Vacations need not be an either/or proposition—either resigning yourself to a week or two of nonstop "Sesame Street" activities with no relief in sight or excluding the children from the few leisure weeks you have away from a demanding career. The former scenario almost always requires relinquishing your own interests, while the latter is complicated by worry and guilt over little Johnny or Susie left behind at Grandma's as you're off footloose and fancy-free. It is possible, however, to have a vacation that is fair to both you and your children.

So you're ready to plan a vacation with the kids. Though this sounds like what parents have been doing for generations, you're different from previous generations. You're better educated and fairly well traveled; you've delayed getting married and having children until your career was launched; and most likely you're older as you reach this phase of family life than were your parents. In addition, you probably have different expectations for both yourself and your children, expectations that influence how you want to spend your leisure time. While you're devoted to your children and conscious of the importance of your input into their intellectual, emotional, and social growth, you also realize that part of being a good parent is tending to your own physical and psychological well-being. You imagine that it must be feasible to share a pleasurable vacation experience with your children without denying your own interests and concerns. Well, it is!

When you've made the decision that the kids should come along this time and you know that one more carousel or one more pair of Mickey Mouse ears just might drive you crazy, then let this book help you discover the perfect vacation spot, where the whole family can be happy together.

Whether you are considering a few relaxing days at a country hideaway or a week of fun in the sun on a beach, rest assured that there are accommodations with facilities and activities that will delight both you and your children. A family vacation doesn't have to mean settling for renting the same house at the nearest beach each season for the next several years or the proverbial visit to Grandma's house year after year. Variety can be found, and if you're itching for a good game of golf, you don't have to fret over whether your three-year-old can manage walking eighteen holes or what antics he'll perform along the way. These concerns can be resolved by choosing the proper surroundings and conditions.

When a young parent once inquired about children's activities at one resort, the staff member gave her a bottle of bubbles. That would last about thirty seconds, right? Thank goodness many resorts are more enlightened, and those you'll find here.

Explore in the following pages a selection of hotels, condominiums, and resorts that offer conveniences to accommodate the needs and wishes of both adults and children. So that you can gratify your diverse and periodically changing geographical interests, you will discover that this guide includes establishments throughout the United States, with a few in Canada. The United States is at the forefront of the new approach to family vacations.

In compiling this collection several criteria were considered: attractive surroundings; good dining facilities, including comfortable lounges and bars; babysitting services; and recreational activities for both parents and children. Needless to say, some of the establishments listed here meet more of the criteria or meet them better than others. But then, your wishes and requirements may vary from one trip to the next: One year you may need just a competent baby-sitter to stay in your hotel room with your infant while you enjoy an elegant, leisurely dinner, and the next year you may need a complete day-care center/nursery school for your energetic toddler while you spend the day out on the slopes. This book does not rank resorts on how well the criteria are met; it simply describes them and all their available services. You can then pick and choose according to your personal preferences and current needs.

To make it easier to find your ideal vacation spot, the descriptive entries are grouped by geographical location, then alphabetically within these divisions; addresses and telephone numbers are included in the descriptions.

Following the descriptions is a standard alphabetical index of resort names to help you pull out the perfect place that a friend recently mentioned at a dinner party, the location of which eludes your recollective powers. This arrangement should afford you easiest access to the required information regardless of your perspective when designing your vacation.

Finally, a special categories index is given that lists resorts by type, such as seaside resorts or resorts with skiing. A resort may appear under more than one heading—it may, for example, shine for its golf course as well as for its beach. Conversely, a resort will not appear under every heading for which it has attractions, only for those that particularly distinguish it.

While probably the foremost concern for your next trip is simply to make that perfect match between your personal circumstances and the most suitable resort, you may occasionally feel a bit nervous about some of the practical logistics of traveling with kids. The section on helpful hints when traveling with children may forestall a few inconveniences that may arise when away from home; the medical information should allay some fears about illnesses and emergencies; and the segments on educating yourself and the advantages of a good travel agent may assist in ironing out the details of your vacation arrangements. In any case, they will stimulate you to analyze your own and your children's habits so that you can anticipate some of the problems and joys of traveling with youngsters.

So you're off. Good luck and happy vacation!

Helpful Hints for Traveling with Children

It can be a joy to travel with children. Sure, sometimes the preparations may seem exhausting and spurts of parental anxiety en route may be tiring as well, but the excitement and wonder of children as they encounter new experiences are worth the price of admission.

On the following pages you'll find some helpful hints for traveling with kids. Many of these suggestions may seem incredibly obvious, but stating the obvious is not always a disadvantage. And a little repetitive reinforcement may help you react more quickly or think better on your feet. An excellent resource book is *Trouble-free Travel with Children* (The Book Peddler, 1996) by Vicki Lansky, author of more than twenty books for new parents.

The first trick to traveling with kids is preparing them for the adventure. Talk to your child in advance; advise her where you're going and what you'll be doing. Infants (in spite of the mounds of disposable diapers you must tote) are very portable. Even toddlers whose whole world revolves around Mom and Dad are happy as long as familiar faces are near at hand. But as a child's world expands to include friends and a wider realm of belongings, verbal preparation becomes very important. Sometimes it's easy to assume that your youngster will pick up on things by osmosis, but children don't always assimilate information about vacation plans that floats around the house in chitchat. It's necessary to explain directly to them what is in store. Books and maps about your destination and route can be shared; even for very young children, maps translate the excitement of travel into a tangible form.

Besides detailing the fun of this new experience, reassure your child that you'll be returning home; that although your daughter may not bring along every Barbie doll and Raggedy Ann, her dolls will still be here when she gets back; and that even though your son may miss his best friends, they won't forget him. Even three- and four-year-olds can "write" postcards along the way as a means of staying connected with friends back home.

As an experienced traveler, you know the ropes of appropriate packing for trips. As a conscientious parent, you are most familiar with what your child will want or need away from home. The standard rule of thumb—don't overpack—applies just as well for children as it does for adults. The length of the trip adjusted for the dirt factor of your own child (how many outfits can he go through in a day?) should give you a reasonable handle on the amount of clothes to pack. Laundromats are never that far away, many hotels have laundry services, and kids' clothes (just by virtue of their size) are fairly easy to hand wash in a hotel bathroom. And don't take along what your child isn't happy with. No matter how much time dear Aunt Josie spent crocheting that sweet little dress, if your daughter doesn't like it, if it's uncomfortable, it will be nothing more than an unnecessary bulge in your suitcase.

If your child uses a bottle, a trip may not be the best time to nudge him out of it; a bottle may provide a bit of security in unfamiliar surroundings. Just be sure to pack a bottle brush: If a bottle gets lost at the bottom of a travel bag for a day or two, mysterious molds blossom, dispelled only by a little scrubbing.

Toys, too, have to fall under the "don't overpack" rule. Remember that for children, seemingly mundane objects in new surroundings often provide considerable amusement. It's a good idea to stash away a couple of new attention-getters, but don't forget the tried and true. A cuddly doll, even if it is beginning to look somewhat old and ratty, or a special pillow is often very comforting for a little one sleeping in a strange bed for the first time. Age-appropriate books, a small ball, crayons, coloring books, scissors, construction paper, a bean bag (remember them from when you were a kid?), and small games such as a pint-size checkerboard are all packable items. Even blocks like Duplos or Legos, if arranged in one compact cube, can be packed fairly easily. Some parents cherish a Fisher-Price tape recorder or a Walkman (with earphones, please) as something akin to a gift from the gods. Terrifically totable and accompanied by a selection of tapes (anything from Disney stories to old radio shows to historical accounts of George Washington and Benjamin Franklin are on the market now), a tape recorder can effectively hold a child's attention.

For the preschooler or older child, consider investing in a backpack. Set down the rules with your child when packing: He can bring along whatever fits in the pack, and he has to carry it. This way you give your child a sense of participating in the preparations and obviate the almost inevitable whine about something Mom didn't include. And practically unnoticed you can sneak in a little lesson in responsibility.

A "surprise box" is also a fun way to generate excitement about a trip. Without divulging details, clue your child in to your preparations of the secrets and mysteries of this cache. Then watch the fun as he delves into the goodies (snacks and small toys) when the vacation adventure begins. A surprise box can entertain your youngster anywhere from two minutes to two hours; if you're particularly circumspect and shrewd, you'll be on the latter end of the spectrum.

When making plane reservations, try to secure seat assignments at the same time. Indicate the age of your young traveler, and request the bulkhead seats. These seats afford a little extra leg room and can be padded with blankets and pillows if your child decides to snooze (lucky you!). It may mean that your feet will be struck by paralysis if little Janie nestles down on her pillow and curls up on your toes, but it is an improvement over having her elbow in your drink. Also, without passengers in front of you in this seating arrangement, you won't fret over a rambunctious child's kicks disturbing other people.

If two parents are flying with a lap child, try to reserve an aisle seat and a window seat. Regular air travelers never request a center seat, so if the plane is not full, you'll wind up with that third seat in which to spread out; if a stranger does venture into your row, it's simple enough for one parent to move over a notch.

Many airlines stock on-board activity packs for children, and some even prepare special meals for their younger travelers. Sometimes airlines have a limited amount of baby food; usually you need to pack your own. Inquire about these services.

If you plan to rent a car during your vacation, be sure to request a car seat for a child four years old and younger. While many rental agencies take this in stride, the number of car seats is usually limited, so it's important to make a reservation for this accessory in advance. Whether your mode of transportation is your own car or a rental, plan frequent stops. Cramped legs and fidgetiness set in fast for youngsters. These factors are not unknown in air travel either; even a walk down the aisle of the plane to the bathroom is a change of pace for a child.

Airplanes pose additional problems: Small children often have greater difficulty than adults in adjusting to altitude changes. During takeoffs and landings, infants should be encouraged to nurse or drink a bottle; the sucking action combats blocked ear and painful sinus problems. Older children can use the same techniques as adults—yawning and chewing gum.

In car travel, a small ice chest in the backseat can be a real boon. Filled with milk, juice, and fruit, it provides a source of ready refreshment and relieves frantic searches for a fast-food stop or a corner grocery. Even when traveling by air, if your luggage allotment permits, check a small ice chest (empty) along with your other bags. Once you arrive at your hotel, it can be filled with ice and drinks and can be taken along in a rental car on side trips. Many accommodations include small refrigerators in the rooms, and some are equipped with kitchens, but if not, you've solved a problem before it arises. It's much easier to dig into an ice chest for a drink than to track down juice somewhere in the hotel facilities at nine o'clock at night. But if this seems too cumbersome and your child desperately needs something late at night, remember the hotel bar— it is the best place to hit, for it always has orange juice (for Screwdrivers), tomato juice (for Bloody Marys), and milk (for White Russians). It may be more expensive, but can you really afford to count pennies when Johnny refuses to go to sleep without his nightly cup of milk? It's an investment in your peace of mind.

When stocking up on drinks, buy the variety in cardboard cartons. Since they are unbreakable and need no refrigeration, they can be squirreled away in a suitcase or even tossed into a purse. On an airplane, the flight attendants never seem to pass by soon enough or often enough to satisfy little ones.

For edibles, small boxes of raisins, granola bars, and individually wrapped cheese chunks such as La Vache qui Rit (what child can resist a silly laughing cow in a red net bag?) make good nourishing snacks. Good old clever Mom can rack up some kudos when she pulls one of these treats from her bag before Susie even thinks about getting antsy.

Once you arrive at your destination and settle into your hotel, turn over an area, even if just a corner, to your child. His own space filled with his own stuff may mean a lot to him in terms of a sense of belonging, and with a bit of prodding you may avoid having toys strewn all about.

Collecting souvenirs on a trip is at best a time-consuming process or maybe even a headache or two. Either Joey wants everything in sight or he chooses the most inappropriate piece of junk you've ever seen. Sure, certain limits on buying have to be set, but who cares if he chooses the made-in-Japan pencil sharpener in the shape of a cannon during a visit to Valley Forge? Just as a cookbook containing three wonderful meat-pie recipes from Nova Scotia or an artistic ceramic tile made in the Southwest is something that you can't possibly do without, there are special reminders of a trip that a child feels he needs. They're just different. A few neat rocks and a couple of sticks may be the only things he wants to show off to his best buddy back home. Or if your little girl wants to take home a shiny red coin purse to her best friend, she doesn't care (and neither does her friend) that the same item is on the shelves in every Wal-Mart–type store across the country, so why should you? A smattering of understanding and patience can go a long way.

Recreational activities in your new surroundings must be evaluated with a clear head and a sharp eye. Most of the resorts included here offer organized children's activities or baby-sitting services, so it may not be necessary to drag kids along on every adult event you want to investigate. Antiques hunting and museum visits are usually not first-rate attractions for members of the kiddie league. Plan on a baby-sitter or a group activity for an afternoon that you want to spend on a grown-up outing.

And for those days that are devoted entirely to being together, alternate grown-up pursuits with juvenile ones. Remember that a child's attention span is not as refined or sophisticated as an adult's; variety is more than the spice of life— it's the key to sanity in some cases. Climbing on the cannons at an old fort is much more fun for a child than reading every historical marker; a mixture of both keeps everyone happy. All day on the beach may be too much for a three- or four-year-old, and you can take ten-to-one odds that he won't be content following your lead to relax and soak up the sunshine. Bargain with your child: a run on the beach and a few splashes in the waves, then quiet time building a sand castle.

Many resorts have lodging with fully equipped kitchens so that you can cook family meals in a homelike setting. Many resort restaurants make an attentive effort to please children; a special dining hour for families or a clever children's menu certainly helps make life more pleasant. But when you grow weary of dining in restaurants, a picnic may be a reasonable alternative. Many hotels can prepare box lunches, or you can pick up some cold cuts at a small grocery for a do-it-yourself picnic. Ordering a meal through room service can be a special treat for a child.

As you skim the descriptive entries of the resorts, you'll realize that most are self-contained vacation spots. Each offers a place to sleep, a place to eat, and something to do. This is intentional, as children seem to function best staying in one place. Establishing a home base, exploring the setting, and taking afternoon side trips are often preferable to being on the road constantly. Besides negating all the packing and unpacking of a traditional road trip (remember, this is not the newest rock star promoting his latest album that you're traveling with!), having a home base helps a child develop a sense of security as the new surroundings become familiar.

With a few tricks up your sleeve and some understanding forethought, traveling with kids can be a fun-filled family adventure. Your well-considered plans make the whole process workable and buy a lot of happiness for both you and your child.

Medical Information

Unless you can take your own family doctor or pediatrician with you, the best advice to follow is the old Girl Scout motto "Be Prepared." Keep in mind: (1) This adventure you're about to embark upon is not a trek along the shores of the East Siberian Sea, and (2) you are not the sole custodian of Band-Aids. As amazing as it may seem, doctors and pharmacies do exist out there in that twilight zone called family vacations.

Before starting your trip, consult your pediatrician for advice; she/he may even be able to supply names of colleagues where you'll be visiting. If you fear that your child is coming down with something as you depart on your vacation, or if she's particularly accident-prone, you can check with the resort staff upon arrival about the location of the nearest hospital and pharmacy and the availability of doctors and nurses (many resorts have medical personnel on call). Sometimes the best recommendations come from other parents, wherever you may find them. If the need is immediate, don't hesitate to ask a likely looking parent working in a car rental agency, a restaurant, a shop, or the airport. And without seeming alarmist, look up the telephone number of the local poison control center; anticipating the slim chance of ever needing it, you'll be gratified that it's handy should your child ingest a handful of your brightly colored vitamin pills. It is also a good idea to check with your medical insurance provider before you leave home for out-of-state or -country authorization/billing procedures.

Pack a medical emergency kit and try to envision the unexpected. If your child scrapes a knee at a playground or develops an earache in the middle of the night, you won't want to take time tracking down a drugstore to relieve his discomfort. You can purchase a ready-made medical kit that fits compactly in a car's glove compartment or carry-on bag, or you may prefer the do-it-yourself variety. The following list is merely suggestive; review your own medicine cabinet to fill in the gaps.

vitamins and medications your child normally takes

a thermometer

children's Tylenol

children's cough syrup

adhesive strips

nose drops (though most kids hate them)

a decongestant such as Dimetapp

an aspirator

ear drops

suppositories and antidiarrheal medicine (change in water and altitude or sheer excitement can affect a child's system)

Desitin or A and D ointment

antibiotic ointment or spray such as Bacitracin or Bactine (for cuts and scrapes)

tweezers and a sterile needle (to remove splinters)

Ipecac (to induce vomiting if your child overdoses on peculiar substances)

Q-Tips and cotton balls

sterile gauze pads (for applying direct pressure to cuts)

insect repellent

Though this list seems long, the items take up very little space in a suitcase. Remember, you don't have to pack a lifetime supply of any of these things. A small box of adhesive strips and a small bottle of cough medicine will meet the immediate need and buy you time to find the drugstore.

Knowing What Questions to Ask

It seems as if there are almost as many pricing schedules, package plans, and special programs as there are resorts. There are EP, MAP, FAP, golf and tennis packages, weekend specials, and midweek discounts. Depending on geographical location, high season is winter at one resort and summer at another. Even the seasons are defined arbitrarily. Summer may be the end of June through Labor Day or, perhaps, Memorial Day through Labor Day. Christmas season starts December 15 at some places and a week later at others. All the jargon and variations on a theme can make you feel like a babe in the woods when contacting a resort about your plans. To avoid arriving someplace and getting halfway through your stay only to find out that you should have taken advantage of some special offer, you have to be savvy in the possibilities and the vocabulary. Even if you aren't familiar with the latest buzzwords, just knowing that different vacation configurations exist puts you a leg up; you can at least ask, "Are there any family discounts or package plans for _____ [fill in the blank—golf, tennis, skiing, etc.]?"

At some resorts, you walk in and pay one price. At others, every hour on the tennis court or every bicycle ride around the block is charged separately. Both approaches have redeeming aspects. To some folks, it's downright annoying to have to reach constantly for a wallet. After all, this is a vacation and they don't want to be troubled with mundane monetary matters. On the other hand, some people would rather pay as they go, laying down the cash for only the services they use. If you've had aquaphobia since childhood and don't care to be within 10 feet of a lake, much less out in the middle rocking a canoe, free boating privileges are worthless. As long as you're in the know as to a resort's practices and policies beforehand, you'll suffer no surprises and no aggravation or disappointment during your visit.

Much of a resort's terminology is self-explanatory, and for the experienced traveler, acronyms are no mysteries. The most commonly used abbreviations are

EP, for European plan, meaning lodging only; MAP, for modified American plan, which includes two meals a day in the room rate; and FAP, for full American plan, which includes three meals a day.

Knowing a resort's designation of low and high season is also crucial to your planning. If you're not absolutely wedded to certain dates and you can juggle your schedule on the home front, you might land in the low season simply by altering your plans by a week.

Moving to more detailed information, you may want to ask a resort certain specific questions. The questions outlined here can be used on the resorts described in this book for elaboration on particular points, or you can test them out on places that you discover on your own.

Lodging

Are the accommodations hotel rooms, condominium units, or cottages with kitchens?

If they are hotel rooms:

- Are there connecting rooms?

- Is there a refrigerator in the room? (This is handy for chilling juice and milk and keeping snacks fresh.)

- What is the range of prices, and is there a reduced rate for children?

- Is there a charge for a crib or rollaway bed?

Dining

What types of dining areas are there? Is there a spot to get Joey a hot dog and a place that tantalizes more refined taste buds?

Is there a dress requirement? (What a disappointment to venture into a tempting restaurant only to learn that gentlemen are required to wear jackets and you packed nothing but golf shirts!)

Is there a meal plan? Is it mandatory or optional?

Kids

Is there a supervised program for children?

- What are the planned activities, and what are the ages of the children who participate?

- When is it held—times of the year, days of the week, and hours of the day? (The level of specificity may seem a little overboard, but consider a Monday-through-Friday-morning program: It's not going to be much help if you pull in at 1:00 P.M. on Friday and leave at 10:00 A.M. Tuesday.)

What is the daily or hourly fee?

- Is there a playground or game room? (Even if you're doing the supervision, if there's something amusing for the kids, they can release some energy and you can sit on the sidelines and read the newspaper.)

Are baby-sitting services available?

- Who makes the arrangements—you or the resort staff?
- What is the average rate? (You may linger a bit longer over that fine Cabernet if your baby-sitter receives $3.00 an hour rather than $6.00 an hour.)

And if you're skittish about your kid's health or proclivity toward disaster, inquire about local medical facilities.

- Is there a doctor or nurse in residence or on call?
- Where are the nearest hospital and pharmacy?

For You

If you're investigating a resort or have chosen it as a vacation destination, you no doubt have an inkling as to its recreational facilities. You're looking at it *because* of its beach, golf course, tennis center, or ski mountain. Besides its main attraction, you'll also want to know what secondary diversions are possible. You can't play golf sixteen hours a day—not even Tiger Woods does that. So ask:

- Is there a jogging path? parcourse fitness trail? hiking trails?
- Is there a spa or exercise room? sauna, steam room, whirlpool?
- Does the tennis complex also house racquetball courts?
- For golf, tennis, and fishing—is it possible to rent equipment, or is it necessary to bring your own?
- Are there any concerts, lectures, or classes?

Your interests will determine which questions to ask. Once you get a handle on what to ask, you'll find planning a vacation a lot more fun and a lot less time-consuming. You don't have to have all the answers; just being able to pose a few intelligent questions sets the ball in motion and can generate maybe even more information than you thought you wanted. As a knowledgeable consumer, you can pursue plans on your own or you can work quite effectively with a travel agent. In either case, a little self-education can certainly enhance the preparation and the end product: your leisure time.

Information, Please

Travel, like so much else today, has become increasingly complicated. Since the deregulation of the airlines, the proliferation of airfares has been phenomenal. Any given pair of cities has up to one hundred different fares, with as many rules and regulations. While this ultimately benefits the pleasure traveler, it also creates a certain amount of chaos. On a trip from New York to San Francisco, for example, the same seat in the airplane can cost anywhere between $299 and $1,499, depending on how far in advance you book, how long you're staying, and the promotional needs of the air carrier. When one adds other factors such as the day of the week, certain airports, one-stop versus nonstop flights, or whether you're wearing polka dots, more complications arise. While airlines generally give you their own lowest fares, they do not necessarily tell you about a competitor who may have even lower fares or more convenient flights.

The Internet provides what seems like an unlimited amount of information, as well as a direct and efficient system for travel suppliers to market their wares. Airlines constantly evaluate their 'load factors'—how many empty seats remain on each flight. Once that airplane takes off, each empty seat is "dead" and has earned no revenue. The same is true of hotels—an empty room night cannot be profitable. Therefore, more and more, airlines are offering last-minute flights, particularly on weekends, in an effort to fill those seats. They are also offering lower fares, additional frequent flyer miles, and other incentives to encourage travelers to directly book on-line. Hotels and car-rental companies are following suit and wooing travelers with free nights, upgrades and special offers. Developing "brand loyalty" has long been a goal of travel suppliers; the advent of the Internet has intensified that process.

Incredible amounts of information exist in cyberspace. You can get lost for hours, sometimes pleasurably, sometimes not. Most airlines, hotels, car-rental companies, tour companies, and cruise lines have their own Web sites. Tourist offices in many states and countries offer virtual tours. Newsletters, chat rooms, and articles abound. A search for "travel with children" quickly gets you started.

Not comfortable with surfing the web? Ask your ten-year-old to help! Or let your children share their travel experiences at www.KidTravels.com, a site where kids contribute articles. It's an offshoot of www.familytravelforum.com, a comprehensive site for family travel information. The site offers lots of news, deals, and ideas for free; flexible membership plans range from $3.95 a month for "armchair travelers" up to $48.00 a year for an all-inclusive membership plan with $500 in travel savings.

Dorothy Jordon, one of the acknowledged pioneers of family travel, offers a quarterly newsletter, Family Travel Times, at www.familytraveltimes.com. The site is fairly simple, but Jordon's approach is straightforward and no-nonsense. As she says, "an honest publication—written by parents, for parents—based on first-hand research." Subscriptions are $39 per year.

This is the age of information overkill; managing this information, sorting through the myriad possibilities, can be mind-boggling. Working with a professional travel agent can add several dimensions to this information process. An agent is a bountiful source of books, brochures, and maps; but more important are the agent's personal experience, the client base that gives feedback on pros and cons of trips, and close contact with colleagues in the travel agency who have traveled extensively. Even something as seemingly straightforward as a hotel reservation can be complicated by weekend specials, golf or tennis packages, seasons, midweek, and family offers. A good agent is a whiz at interpreting brochures and deciphering the fine print. "Ocean view" does not mean on the beach; in fact, you may have to hang over the balcony with a pair of binoculars to see the ocean. "Secluded" may mean private, or it may mean you have to go 10 miles to find any other signs of life. Finally, you can capitalize on an agent's knowledge of the fares and facilities that each airline provides for children and of any special family-travel offers, such as "kids fly free" and discounts for spouses. A good agent can pull all of this together, analyze your needs, and help make your vacation dream become a coherent reality.

Travel agents provide a service. In the past there was no charge to the traveler for booking airline flights, or reserving hotel rooms and rental cars, as the travel suppliers paid commissions to travel agents. In recent years, the airlines have reduced the amount of commissions paid to travel agents by half, and placed a $50 to $100 cap on each ticket. While hotel and car rental companies still pay a 5 percent to 10 percent commission to travel agents, many agencies maintain they cannot survive without charging service fees. It has become an accepted practice for agencies to charge for each service they provide. The cost varies according to the services provided—from $10 for issuing an airline ticket to $100 per hour for planning and researching a more complicated trip. If you decide to work with a travel agent, it is vital to establish the charges up-front. If the agent books a hotel abroad, do you have to pay fax or phone charges? If you change your plans, what are the change or cancellation fees? Don't be afraid to ask.

Travel agents are dealers in dreams—in charge of that very precious event, your vacation. You should pick your travel agent as carefully as you would your doctor—or your auto mechanic! It's very nice to go to your Aunt Nelly or your neighbor's first cousin, but a smart consumer considers more substantial factors. A number of people prefer to go to the travel office and talk with the agent face to face. Others are comfortable with a telephone relationship, or even with booking on-line, perhaps with an agency that specializes in family travel. It's important to identify your own particular preferences and to honor them.

Regardless of which method you choose, certain considerations are basic. What are their policies on service charges, refunds, payments? Are they an appointed agency of the airlines, Amtrak, and the cruise lines? Airline appointments indicate a certain basic financial investment and preparation and the ability to write airline tickets. Agencies are computerized and have the capability to scan quickly for the best fares and most convenient flights, make seat assignments, and request special meals. Ask if they hold your money in an escrow account until your travel date. What insurance do they provide? What is their responsibility to you if the hotel/cruise/tour reservation is cancelled or not properly delivered?

Another consideration is whether the agency is a member of the American Society of Travel Agents (ASTA). There are good agencies that may not be members, but affiliation with this professional organization of the travel industry indicates that an agency has been in operation for at least three years. ASTA also acts as a ready resource for problems and possible complaints. In short, be proactive. This is your vacation; you should feel comfortable and ask questions—even the same one repeatedly and especially the ones you're afraid may sound dumb.

Whether you use a travel agent or "do it yourself," the higher your level of involvement in planning, the more satisfaction you stand to gain from your trip. A good agent should be able to determine the broad outlines of your trip, to respond and listen to your ideas and needs, and to fill in with specific suggestions. The agent should have an idea of your lifestyle, your ideal vacation, and your budget. Your agent should ask, or you should volunteer, what seems to be personal information: How do you like to spend your days? Is shopping important to you? If you have a beach, are you happy? Will you die if you have no evening entertainment, or do you prefer a quiet stroll and a good book? What are your hobbies or special interests? Again, do not be afraid to discuss financial expectations. This can avoid a few nasty surprises—such as having to ransom one of the kids to pay for the trip!

No one knows your expectations as well as you, so assume some of the legwork for detailed information yourself. Check with the tourist offices of the state or country you plan to visit for brochures and information on special events and attractions. The American Automobile Association (AAA) is an excellent resource for maps and detailed information if you're a member and are driving for part or all of the trip. Travel books and articles are fun for the family and often have good advice on extras or little-known attractions in the area; check your local library for these. (Chinaberry Book Service, in San Diego, California, 800–776–2242, www.chinaberry.com, has a catalog of well-selected books and tapes for various ages and interests.) Also, talk to your friends who have been there for those real inside tips.

Several tour operators specialize in family travel, working with both travel agents and individual clients. Call them for their brochures. In Chevy Chase, Maryland, Grandtravel does escorted tours for grandparents and grandchildren, both in the United States and abroad (800–247–7651). In San Francisco, California, Rascals in Paradise (800–U–RASCAL or www.rascalsinparadise.com) offers resorts with their own personally directed children's programs during school holidays as well as tours all over the world. Many local agencies are becoming aware of the family market and are beginning to specialize in this field; check your local parents' paper or the travel section of the local Sunday paper for agencies in your area. Several agencies are listed on Family Travel Forum's Web site, www.familytravelforum.com.

Finally, close your suitcase, lock the door, and take off—secure in the knowledge that your advance planning, plus professional help, will make this the best trip ever!

NEW ENGLAND

Maine

Massachusetts

New Hampshire

Vermont

The Balsams Grand Resort Hotel

Dixville Notch, New Hampshire 03576
(603) 255–3400, (800) 255–0600; (800) 255–0800 (in New Hampshire)
E-mail: thebalsams@aol.com
Web site: www.thebalsams.com

In the fine tradition of grand old hotels, The Balsams has been graciously welcoming guests since 1866. The three main buildings are interconnected and quite impressive, with their white facades and red-tiled roofs. Two date from the late 1800s—the Dixville House and The Balsams Inn—and the "new" wing, the Hampshire House, was added in 1917. At the foot of three very precipitous mountains—almost entirely surrounded by steep, 1,000-foot cliffs with the Notch Road the only way in or out—and overlooking Lake Gloriette, The Balsams offers a relaxed escape in a charming atmosphere. In summer Dixville Notch is a refreshing mountain retreat; in winter, a delightful getaway for skiers.

The Balsams adds all the amenities for a fun-filled vacation in a worry-free atmosphere. Golf, tennis, swimming, hiking, mountain biking, lawn games, children's day camp, fine dining, and nightly entertainment are available and—an increasingly rare practice these days—at no additional charges for use of any of the facilities. Winter activities include skiing, snowboarding, snowshoeing, and skating. Your needs are tended to, your interests can be pursued, and your cares can be dispelled. The resort is open from the third week in December until early April, reopening for the summer season from late May to mid-October.

Accommodations: There are 204 rooms at The Balsams, many with views of the mountains or the lake. Family suites with one or two bedrooms offer ample space for youngsters; these are quite popular. The Hampshire House is configured to provide convenient adjoining rooms for family accommodation. All the rooms have been restored, creating a comfortable ambience. Depending on the size of the room, its location and view, and the time of the year, prices range from $139 to $250 per person per night. Children's rates are on a graduated scale, calculated at $10 per day multiplied by the child's age, with a minimum charge of $40. So, infants to three-year-olds are $40 per day, and so on. These rates are based on a full American plan and include unlimited access to all the facilities. Cribs are provided.

Dining: The main dining room serves breakfast, lunch, and dinner during the summer season, breakfast and dinner only during the winter season. The summertime luncheon buffet is a sumptuous display of hot and cold entrees, cheeses, fruit, and desserts; you might sample the fried Maine shrimp or the Atlantic salmon. A menu luncheon is available at the Golf Clubhouse. The din-

Photo courtesy of The Balsams Grand Resort Hotel

ner menu offers an entirely different selection every evening, featuring seafood dishes as well as Long Island duckling, beef, and chicken. At the dinner hour jackets for men are appropriate. Parents are advised to bring appropriate dinner clothes for older children as well.

The Cafe is open for both summer and winter seasons, 10:00 A.M. to midnight, and is perfect for lighter meals (sandwiches and grilled items). In the summer you might try The Panorama Golf Clubhouse or the poolside bar for refreshments; both offer delightful views and a chance to soak up the beautiful scenery. In the winter warm up with a cup of cider or hot buttered rum in La Cave. Also in winter you'll be shuttling over to The Balsams/Wilderness Ski Area, where breakfast and lunch are served at the base lodge and an a la carte luncheon is served in the dining room. Evening entertainment means cocktails and floor shows in the Switzerland of America Ballroom or dancing in the Wilderness Lounge; both are in the hotel.

Children's World: The Balsams is interested in providing excellent service for its younger guests as well as its adult visitors. For children this translates into a busy schedule of fun activities. Camp Wind Whistle is available from the Fourth of July through Labor Day (seven days a week); here children ages five through thirteen meet with counselors in The Balsams Playroom for sports, games, picnics, swimming, nature walks, arts and crafts, fishing, farm visits, and movies. Outdoor activities are stressed. Children have lunch with their counselors and then, after linking up with Mom and Dad around 4:00 P.M. to share their day's experiences, they can rejoin their young group for dinner at 6:30 P.M. There is no charge for this service. Age groups are divided as follows: five to seven years, eight to ten years, and eleven to thirteen years. Camp Wee Whistle is a special program for younger children, ages three and four, at no additional charge; during July, call for specific dates.

The outdoor children's area features a state-of-the art fiberglass and stainless steel play structure. The indoor game room (supervised) has an array of board games, video games, and table tennis and pool tables. Open daily from 9:00 A.M. to midnight, the game room is a popular spot for youngsters to gather and make friends during both summer and winter seasons.

In winter children ages three to five can enroll in the Wee Whistle Ski School. Older children have their own morning and afternoon lessons. The cost is approximately $30 for two hours. Wintertime room rates for children at The Balsams include ski privileges.

A nursery at the base lodge takes nonskiing youngsters under six (who are out of diapers) while you're on the slopes. The experienced staff amuses children with a selection of games and toys from 9:00 A.M. to 4:00 P.M.; parents should join their children for lunch. This service is provided gratis to children of hotel guests. Individual baby-sitters (usually off-duty hotel employees) can be arranged at reasonable rates; sitters should be reserved when lodging reservations are made.

Recreation: At The Balsams you can spend busy days of back-to-back events from morning to night or just relax, set an unhurried pace, and enjoy the peace and beauty of the mountains. Two golf courses await golfers. The eighteen-hole championship course was designed by Donald Ross, an architect famous during the early twentieth century; set in the mountains, the undulating terrain can be challenging and the views truly stunning. The nine-hole course is just right for beginners or those who haven't tested their clubs in a while. There are pro shops at each course, putting greens, a practice fairway, and a pro staff on hand to help you polish your swing. The Centennial Golf School operates from May through early July and features a PGA professional for every four students.

Tennis enthusiasts can choose to play on either red-clay courts (three) or all-weather courts (three). Sign up with the pro for group or private lessons, and stop by the tennis shop to pick up those indispensable accessories.

Swim a few laps in the Olympic-size heated swimming pool overlooking Lake Gloriette. With the mountains in the background, this is an idyllic spot for sunbathing. You might try a refreshing dip in the lake or a relaxing excursion in a paddleboat, canoe, or rowboat. Fish in a crystal-clear mountain stream, hike in the wilderness (solo or with a guided group), or take a nature walk with the staff naturalist. The hotel's natural-history program combines tours, hikes, and discussions for a good introduction to the flora and fauna of the area. The mountain biking trails are well marked and offer fun at every level. Mountain bike rentals and repairs are available.

Lawn sports include badminton, horseshoes, croquet, volleyball, and shuffleboard; when you head indoors, there are billiards, table tennis, bingo, an aerobic exercise room, and a movie theater. Take to the library/card room to snuggle up with a good book or play a few hands of bridge. To track down that essential souvenir, drop in at the gift shop, craft shop, gallery, balloon store, and fashion boutique.

In the wintertime this wonderland is draped in snow, and The Balsams/ Wilderness Ski Area (located on the property) is just a short shuttle ride from the hotel. There are thirteen downhill trails and 95 miles of packed and groomed trails for cross-country. Wintertime also means ice skating, snowshoeing on dedicated trails, and riding in horse-drawn sleighs. Whether you're seeking an escape from city crowds or want an active sports-oriented vacation, The Balsams offers the attention and service to make it all possible. ≋

Highland Lodge

Caspian Lake
1608 Craftsburg Road
Greensboro, Vermont 05841
(802) 533–2647; fax (802) 533–7494
E-mail: hlodge@connriver.net
Web site: www.highlandlodge.com

Cross-country skiing in Vermont—it sounds so romantic and wholesome. You almost expect to see Bing Crosby round the corner of the inn. A lovely old white-frame building with a comfortable front porch, the lodge is set on 160 acres bordering Caspian Lake. Open from Christmas to mid-March, the lodge facilities make it easy to enjoy wintertime sports; open again from Memorial Day weekend until mid-October, the lodge is a perfect spot for enjoying the fall foliage colors or for enjoying a summer trip of swimming and boating.

Accommodations: Choose a guest room in the lodge or one of the cottages just behind the main building. Tastefully decorated with nice furnishings and old-fashioned wallpaper, these accommodations can house approximately sixty guests. The cottages feature a living room, porch, bath, and one to three bedrooms; nine cottages include kitchenettes. Cribs are provided for little ones.

Based on a modified American plan and double occupancy, rates are $97 to $128 per person per night. Children sharing a room or cottage with their parents are charged according to their ages, $25 to $80 a day.

Dining: Two connecting dining rooms in the lodge serve breakfast, lunch, and dinner. For entrees you may select fresh fish, lamb, duck, veal, or prime rib with vegetables from a local farm, and sample the homemade soups and breads, but be sure to save room for what the staff boasts are sinful desserts. You might sit near the fireplace in the dining room or by the large windows to take in the view; weather permitting, dining tables are set up on the porch. A modified American meal plan is offered, and there are children's portions and special items for youngsters.

Children's World: A swing set and a sandbox stocked with toys attract little ones. There are tennis and hiking for older children. For children of all ages, swimming at the supervised private beach is a great way to spend the afternoon. After a busy day kids may settle into the children's library, where they'll find books, games, and puzzles. In the mornings during July and August, youngsters ages four to nine link up with the Play Lady, who devises programs of crafts, swimming, and nature hikes; this is free of charge to guests. In addition, the staff can make arrangements for individual baby-sitters ($5.00 an hour).

Recreation: Thirty miles of groomed cross-country ski trails meander through fields and forests and across frozen lakes. You can line up a guided tour or pick up a little instruction. Bring your own equipment or rent the necessary para-phernalia at the ski shop. Snowshoe trails and rentals are also available.

Enjoy the sights and sounds of nature in both summer and winter with a res-ident naturalist on guided nature walks. In warmer weather hike or jog in the adjoining Barr Hill Nature Preserve, walk the lodge's nature trail, or take to the water; swim at the beach or head out on the lake in a canoe, sailboat, or pad-dleboat provided by the lodge. The lake also means good fishing, particularly in early summer and fall; set your line for salmon, trout, or perch.

Back on land, challenge another guest to a tennis match on the clay court and then round up a game of badminton, volleyball, or croquet on the lawn. The nearby Green Mountains and White Mountains lure guests into afternoon driving and hiking excursions. ≋

Killington Ski and Summer Resort

Killington Road
Killington, Vermont 05751
(802) 773–1330, (800) 621–MTNS
E-mail: Killington.com

Killington is the largest ski area in the eastern United States, and its vital statistics are indeed impressive: 212 runs on six interconnected moun-tains, plus Pico Mountain at Killington; more than 3,000 vertical feet; and a ski season that starts in mid-October and continues to June. Killington boasts an average annual snowfall of 250 inches. To ensure its earliest opening date and latest closing date in the East, sophisticated snowmaking techniques assist Mother Nature. Thirty-three lifts, including an eight-passenger heated gondola, get you quickly to the top.

A year-round resort, Killington is cradled in the Green Mountains of central Vermont, a setting whose beauty does not wane with the melting snow; in late spring and summer, the lush green landscape is the backdrop for tennis and golf holidays; in autumn the fall foliage colors take over.

Accommodations: There are almost 200 properties at Killington, ranging from small inns and lodges to condominium complexes. Killington Travel Ser-vices (800–621–6867) lists more than 115 of these and publishes helpful, descriptive information clearly outlining the many package plans available. Ski-in locations include Trailside Lodge, with standard rooms/bunk beds, and Trail-side Village, Sunrise Village, and Spruce Glen condos. Rates are lower in summer and higher at holiday periods. Call for the latest rates.

Photo by Bob Perry, courtesy of Killington Ski and Summer Resort

Killington Resort Villages (800–343–0762) offers hotel-style and one-, two-, and three-bedroom condos, some within walking distance of the slopes, plus several other condominium complexes. The Villager nightly rates range from $52 to $92 in summer, $49 to $196 in winter. Condo summer rates are $89 to $240, rising to $112 to $688 in winter. Condominiums not within walking distance but right at the base of Killington Mountain include Edgemont, Whiffletree, Highridge, Mountain Green, and Pinnacle. Studio to four-bedroom units have fully equipped kitchens and fireplaces. Some condominiums have special features, such as indoor pools or spa/exercise facilities (if you don't get enough on the slopes!).

Dining: In addition to the half dozen cafeterias at the bases of and on the mountains, The Clubhouse Grill is located across from Snowshed Base Lodge. In the area you'll find Italian, Chinese, Mexican, and German restaurants, or perhaps you'll sample French country dinners at the Red Clover Inn, typical New England dishes at the Vermont Inn, or Continental cuisine at the Pittsfield Inn. Pubs and nightclubs provide late-evening entertainment.

Children's World: Whether your child is six weeks old or twelve years old, a first-time skier or a veteran, he or she will find a niche at Killington's Children's Center. Open daily from 8:00 A.M. to 4:30 P.M., the staff orchestrates indoor and outdoor play for infants to six-year-olds. First Tracks Ski School, for four- to five-year-olds, includes ski lessons as well as supervised play; the Superstars Ski Program groups six- to twelve-year-olds by ability for a full day of ski and play. Full-day fees include lunch; half-day sessions are available for the nonskiing and introductory skiing groups. For teenagers there's a weekly under-twenty-one disco with DJ or live bands, soda, and pizza. In December and March special weeks for teens are scheduled as well.

The Alpine Adventure Summer Camp offers age-grouped activities for youngsters six weeks to six years. The child-care ratio is four to one. Call for current cost of youth activities.

Recreation: Start your visit with a Meet the Mountain tour; skiers are grouped by ability and guided through a complimentary two-hour introduction to Killington's mountains. All seven mountains are accessed by the same lift ticket. All have beginner runs from their summits so that even novices can enjoy top-of-the-mountain views. From long lazy runs (one beginner's trail is 10 miles long) to steeply pitched expert terrain, every skier finds the appropriate challenge. This goes for ski clinics too, from classes for the newest beginner to workshops in racing for the advanced skier.

Après-ski activities include sleigh rides in the country and movies in the village, but maybe most appropriate for the end of an active day is a quiet rest in a sauna.

Summertime brings golf on an eighteen-hole course; tennis at the Killington School for Tennis; fishing, hiking, mountain biking, and horseback riding (Sunrise Stables) in the mountains. ≋

The Lighthouse Inn

Lighthouse Road
West Dennis, Massachusetts 02670
(508) 398–2244
Web site: www.lighthouseinn.com

An old-fashioned country inn, The Lighthouse Inn sits on the shores of Nantucket Sound. The core of the main building is aptly named as the historic Bass River Lighthouse. The inn recalls an easier pace of past times. The classic Cape Cod–style main house provides a beautiful view of the ocean; sprawling out behind are nine secluded acres with additional accommodations and recreational facilities.

Accommodations: The main house offers individual rooms and suites. Alternatively, you might choose one of the cottages with one to three bedrooms. Prices begin at $258 a night (including breakfast) in the summer season, $198

Photo courtesy of The Lighthouse Inn

a night (including breakfast) in the spring and fall. Children sharing a room or cottage with their parents are charged a graduated rate depending on their ages: ages three to nine, $35 a day; ten-year-olds and older, $55 a day. For children the daily rate includes breakfast. Rates that include dinner are available.

Dining: The dining room in the main house entices guests with fresh fish and lobster dinners and lovely views over the water. Outdoors, the oceanside deck is the setting for lunch. A snack bar adjoins the pool. Once a week a poolside cookout is planned.

Children's World: Games, swimming, arts and crafts, sand-castle building, kite flying, miniature golf, and nature walks fill the days for InnKids. Three- and four-year-olds participate from 9:30 A.M. to noon, while children ages five and older carry on until 3:00 P.M. In the evening both groups are invited to get together from 5:30 to 8:30 P.M. for dinner and entertainment, perhaps a movie or a magician's show. The InnKids program runs from late June through August and is included in the fees for children noted above. Individual baby-sitting costs $6.00 an hour.

Recreation: Enjoying the soft ocean breezes may be all the activity you want during your first couple of days at Lighthouse Inn. Renewed and refreshed, you can then jump into the swimming pool, splash in the gentle waters of Nantucket Sound, and stroll along the beach. The outdoor tennis court awaits you when you turn energetic, and fishing can be a pleasant morning outing. You can also play table tennis, pool, and shuffleboard or pursue quieter interests in the library/game room. ≋

Mount Snow

Mount Snow, Vermont 05356
(802) 464–8501, (800) 245–7669
E-mail: info@mountsnow.com
Web site: www.mountsnow.com

A very popular New England ski resort, Mount Snow is situated in the beautiful Green Mountains of southern Vermont. Much of its popularity is, no doubt, due to its accessibility and proximity to major Northeast metropolitan areas; a four-and-a-half-hour drive from New York, two-and-a-half hours from Boston, makes this a very manageable weekend trip for residents of these cities. But Mount Snow's size and variety also account for its appeal. From gentle beginner and broad intermediate slopes to some of the steepest expert runs in the Northeast, 135 trails in all drop down from a 3,600-foot summit for 1,700 vertical feet. The average annual snowfall is about 157 inches. It is supplemented by sophisticated snowmaking that covers 85 percent of the skiable terrain; the ski season runs from about early November to late April.

Accommodations: Lodging runs the gamut of possibilities in atmosphere, style, price, and location. From modern condominium complexes to quaint country inns, more than fifty options are within 10 miles of the mountain base. The lodging bureau issues descriptive booklets to help you choose the right spot, and various package plans for lodging and lift tickets are offered.

A full-service hotel at the edge of a small lake, Snow Lake Lodge is very close to the base of the mountain; with its own restaurant, game room, and spa, a two-day weekend rate is $390 on a modified American plan; reduced rates apply for children. Seasons and Snow Mountain Village are condominiums near the base, where two-bedroom units start at $722 for a two-day weekend. These units have kitchens and fireplaces; some have balconies and mountain views.

The new 199-room Grand Summit Resort Hotel is located slopeside in Mount Snow's main base area and offers a variety of rooms, ranging from standard hotel-style rooms to three-bedroom condos. Amenities include ski-in/ski-out accommodations, valet parking, a health club, spa and fitness programs, a year-round heated outdoor pool, Harriman's Restaurant, and more. A two-day weekend starts at $450.

Photo © Jeff Baird, courtesy of Mount Snow

The many country inns around the area can add a distinctly New England flavor to a ski holiday. The charming Hermitage Inn, 3 miles from Mount Snow, maintains 40 miles of cross-country ski trails; a two-day weekend is $500, which includes breakfast and dinner.

Dining: At the base of Mount Snow are five cafeterias, six lounges, and six restaurants; at the Summit Lodge, views over the mountains complement cafeteria-style lunches. Also near the base is Walter's restaurant in the Snow Lake Lodge. Most of the inns and lodges of the area have their own restaurants and feature a variety, from hearty home-style cooking to the Continental cuisine typical of the Hermitage and the White House of Wilmington.

Children's World: Throughout the ski season, kids have a place at Mount Snow. Child Care, a quality program for ages six weeks to six years, is located in the heart of the main base area. The program is fully licensed by the state of Vermont and is designed to be interactive, fun, and developmentally appropriate for each child's needs. Child Care is open weekdays from 8:30 A.M. to 4:30 P.M.; weekends and holidays, 8:00 A.M. to 4:30 P.M. Reservations are required. A two-day package is $115; snacks and lunch are provided. A list of baby-sitters is available through Child Care.

For three-year-olds enrolled in full-day Child Care, PreSki offers an introduction to the fun sport of skiing through games and activities both on and off the snow. Cost per one-day clinic, including equipment, is $18. For children four to twelve, Mount Snow offers Perfect Kids ski and snowboard clinics. Snow Camp is for ages four through six; Mountain Riders or Mountain Camp is for ages seven to twelve. Children new to skiing or snowboarding can enjoy expanded, private learning terrain. All Perfect Kids programs are centrally located in the main base area.

Kids ages twelve and under ski/ride free when their parents purchase a five-day nonholiday lift ticket. During "Fun Factor Five" weeks (mid-January through mid-March), free family activities include an ice-cream sundae party with costume parade, grooming machine rides, and animal puppet theater. Summer Kids camp is offered June through Labor Day weekend.

Mount Snow also offers a new lift-served snow tubing park open both day and night. Free sledding is available on the Ski Baba slope under lights from 5:00 to 9:00 P.M. An outdoor ice skating pond is adjacent to the sledding slope and is open day and night. Snow tube, sled, and skate rentals are available. The Galaxy Arcade is open daily in the main base area and features video games, recreational games, a penny candy counter, and a lounge area.

Recreation: Almost 75 percent of the runs at Mount Snow are ranked intermediate. The rest are just about evenly split between beginner and expert. The Main Mountain has forty beginner and intermediate trails, the North Face with its steeper terrain and moguls attracts advanced skiers, and the Sunbrook area with sunny southern exposure supports a couple of long lazy runs. The teaching staff is prepared to show you the way to improved techniques, and you have your pick of packages for various combinations of lifts, lessons, and equipment.

For cross-country skiers, four touring centers are within 10 miles of Mount Snow at the Hermitage, Sitzmark, Timber Creek, and White House. Also within this distance are three stables—Beaver Brook, Flames, and Adam's Farm—where you can arrange sleigh rides.

When these mountains turn green, the big event is the Golf School, held on the championship Geoffrey Cornish course. Other warm-weather activities include swimming, fishing, hiking, biking, and horseback riding. ≋

The Mount Washington Hotel & Resort

Route 302
Bretton Woods, New Hampshire 03575
(603) 278–1000, (800) 258–0330

M ajestic Mount Washington presides over this resort, a massive complex of lodging, dining, and recreational facilities on 2,600 acres of wooded New Hampshire countryside in the White Mountains. Voted a *Better Homes and Gardens* "Favorite Family Resort," the architectural gem and focal point of this New England resort is the gracious and stately hotel. Built in 1902 by the industrialist and railroad tycoon Joseph Stickney, the hotel began welcoming visitors to a lifestyle of classic elegance and soon claimed its status among prime vacation retreats of the Northeast.

International fame came to Bretton Woods in 1944 when the hotel hosted financiers from forty-four countries who created the World Bank and the International Monetary Fund and set the gold standard at $35 an ounce (ah—the good old days). In 1978 this fine old structure—its wonderfully spacious veranda furnished with white wicker chairs and settees and its 150-foot-long lobby—was added to the National Register of Historic Places. Since 1986 it has held the distinction of being a National Historic Landmark.

A multiyear winterization project was implemented in 1991, with a goal of offering this world-class grand resort on a year-round basis by the end of the twentieth century. The goal has been realized with the resort's purchase of the popular Bretton Woods Ski Area in 1997 and the winter opening of The Mount Washington Hotel in 1999.

Accommodations: The 200-room hotel offers standard to deluxe lodging with a number of two-bedroom family suites. Nearly all have views of Mount Washington, the Willey-Rosebrook Mountain range, or the well-tended gardens. All guests in the hotel participate in a modified American plan, and prices range from $269 to $569 for double occupancy. Children under age four are free; ages five to twelve are $35; and over twelve are $70. A family chamber costs $449 to $609 a night and accommodates up to four persons. The Bretton Arms, also a National Historic Landmark, offers accommodations in the atmosphere of an English country home. Guests here enjoy all the facilities of the main hotel. Prices range from $109 to $249 per night. The Bretton Arms is open year-round.

Also open year-round, The Lodge Bretton Woods, located across from the hotel's entrance, offers contemporary accommodations at rates of $79 to $149 per night.

Photo courtesy of The Mount Washington Hotel and Resort

For an economical alternative, The Townhomes at Bretton Woods provide ample space for parties of two to twelve people; situated on the mountainside, these one- to five-bedroom units (with full kitchens) run from $169 to $479 per night, depending on the size of the unit and the season. All guests have access to all resort recreational facilities at established guest rates. Cribs are complimentary, and cots are available at $10 a night. Inquire also about special packages.

Dining: With all the different dining arrangements, your biggest problem will be deciding where to pick up your napkin. From casual, light meals to gracious, formal dinners, it just depends on how the spirit moves you. The main dining room of The Mount Washington Hotel is a large octagonal space (heaven forbid anyone should be relegated to a corner!) glimmering with crystal chandeliers and stained-glass windows. The menu changes nightly and features Continental cuisine and regional American dishes. In this elegant setting, with views of Mount Washington, guests are invited to regard dinner as a dress-up affair; jackets are required for men, and ladies and children should dress appropriately. Sumptuous breakfasts are also served in the dining room.

The Bretton Arms dining room is also open for breakfast and dinner; here the evening meal features classic New England cuisine. For lunch and dinner Stickney's Restaurant (located on the lower concourse of the hotel) has a cafe atmosphere and specializes in lighter fare—salads, sandwiches, and light entrees; afternoon cocktails are also served here. Darby's Restaurant in the lodge serves breakfast and dinner; here guests enjoy Continental cuisine, along with scenic views of the mountains and the hotel. For sandwiches, Italian fare, and seafood, Fabyans Station is open for lunch and dinner. A restored railroad depot from the Victorian era, Fabyans is near the base of the ski area about a mile from the hotel. The base lodge at the ski area offers full lunch and dinner at the Slopeside Restaurant and Lounge as well as quick breakfasts and lunches cafeteria-style for those eager to hit the slopes. The midmountain Top O' Quad restaurant serves lunch with spectacular mountain views in winter.

For sipping cocktails, you may want to linger at Stickney's, Darby's, or Fabyans. Or perhaps you'll discover the Cave Lounge; located in the lower lobby of the hotel, the speakeasy atmosphere and nightly live entertainment transport you to the days of Prohibition. The elegant Princess Lounge is perfect for before- and after-dinner cocktails. The Pool Bar offers refreshments on warm summer days.

Children's World: Mid-June through Labor Day, and on weekends in spring and fall, the hotel sponsors the King of the Mountain Kids Kamp for children five to twelve. Enroll your child for a full- or half-day program with adventures like hiking in the woods, treks to the stables, swimming, tennis, "Cooking with the Chef," "Putting with the Pro," and crafts sessions. The program is from 9:00 A.M. to noon and from 1:00 to 4:30 P.M. The cost is $40 for full day, $25 for half day. Lunch is available for $7.25. There's also an evening program ($15) from 7:00 to 9:00 P.M. so that parents can dine quietly. Guests not on the modified American plan pay an additional $10 for dinner. Baby-sitting can be arranged for $8.00 per hour, plus $2.00 for each additional child.

In the wintertime, the nursery at the ski area lodge takes children from two months to five years for an indoor program costing $55 full day or $45 half day.

Children ages three to twelve participate in the Hobbit Children's Ski and Snowboard School. Rates for lifts, lessons, equipment, and lunch are $75 a day. Those children under age five who are new to the slopes can join a snow play and ski-readiness program, also $55 a day.

Recreation: You'll never be at a loss for things to do at Bretton Woods; your only dilemma may be trying to fit in all the activities. You may start your day jogging on one of the many marked trails ranging from 1 to 11 miles in length and graded by levels of difficulty.

Then stroll over to the first tee for a match on the eighteen-hole Donald Ross–designed championship golf course or challenging nine-hole course and take in the rolling terrain and mountain views, or sharpen your skills on the putting green and driving range. The Golf Club Pro Shop can meet all your needs for equipment and accessories (including attire) and can assist in scheduling lessons.

There are two heated pools at the hotel (one outdoor and a smaller indoor one) and another indoor heated pool at the motor inn; both locations have a sauna, and the motor inn facility includes a Jacuzzi as well.

Tennis buffs can head over to one of twelve well-groomed red-clay courts or join the tennis program for instruction (group and private lessons) at all levels of expertise.

The horseback-riding stables mean good fun for those who want their exercise sitting down. Set in an old Victorian building, the stables offer lessons and guided trail rides on the 50 miles of picturesque trails in the woods and fields. The woods are captivating whether you choose horseback riding or hiking (maybe you'll link up with a guided tour or a nature walk).

If fishing is your pleasure, some mighty fine trout are found in the Ammonoosuc River, which winds its way through the hotel grounds.

For other diversions you might consider a game of badminton, croquet, volleyball, or horseshoes; an afternoon of bicycling; or an hour in the game room for billiards, table tennis, and video games (particularly big with the seven- to fourteen-year-old group). Your interests may take you to a night at the movies, a fashion show, an aerobics class, a bridge tournament, or a presentation of fine culinary techniques (these often include a bit of wine, sampling a dish, and a tour of the kitchen). The activities staff is on hand full-time to plan interesting and varied events. For some private, quiet time, wander into the library or relax under the nimble fingers of an expert massage therapist.

Music is special at Mount Washington. Chamber-music recitals are held frequently in the Conservatory; live music is featured in the Cave Lounge; the Mount Washington Orchestra will dance you off your toes nightly during dinner.

Kids love an excursion on the Mount Washington Cog Railway, the original "little train that could." Built in 1869, it was the world's first mountain-climbing cog railroad, and it remains the only one still powered entirely by steam. The (breathtaking!) round trip takes about three hours, and you can visit the mile-high park and observation center at the top.

Stickney Street, in the lower concourse of the hotel, is an array of shops featuring gifts, crafts, fashions, ice-cream delights, flowers, and the hotel's own post office.

Wintertime explodes in skiing events at Bretton Woods. The Bretton Woods Touring Center, housed in a Victorian-style building, is one of the finest cross-country skiing complexes in the East. There are approximately 100 kilometers (60 miles) of beautifully groomed trails among the firs and birches of the scenic countryside; three different trail systems are ranked in difficulty. Head out on your own, enroll for instruction, or join a daytime guided tour or a moonlight trek. Alpine skiers are delighted with the expansion done in the past decade. This once pleasant ski area of 1,100-foot vertical drop has added 400 vertical feet and now boasts sixty-six trails serviced by eight lifts. The ski season lasts from late November to mid-April; the average annual snowfall is 180 inches, and 95 percent of the trails are covered by snowmaking equipment to assist Mother Nature. In addition to the children's ski school, instruction for the more advanced is also available, accommodating all skiing levels in your family.

By the year 2003, the ski area will have tripled its skiable terrain, with the opening of the West Mountain in 1999 and Mount Stickney, scheduled for 2003. Three new lifts and expanded base facilities will ensure an optimal ski experience for all! ≋

Smugglers' Notch Resort

4323 Vermont Route 108 South
Smugglers' Notch, Vermont 05464-9537
(802) 644–8851, (800) 451–8752

The Green Mountains of Vermont are not just beautiful foliage colors in the autumn and skiing fun in the winter. Smugglers' Notch Resort makes sure there's much more to enjoy all year long. Tucked in the rolling hills and mountains of northern Vermont, Smugglers' Notch is a self-contained resort village with sports facilities and getaway relaxation potential for the whole family. In winter, when Mother Nature blankets the region in snow, skiing on the three interconnected mountains is the primary activity. Tennis, hiking, swimming,

Photo courtesy of Smugglers' Notch Resort

and horseback riding are favorite pastimes when the weather warms. Any time of year one can explore the natural beauty and charm surrounding this mountain village and experience family fun—guaranteed! (Yes, the resort guarantees families will have fun or it refunds the activity portion of their stay.)

Accommodations: Approximately 525 condominium units are arranged in clusters of two- and three-story, modern but rustic buildings. From these all the amenities of the village are accessible by foot. Most of the units have fireplaces and private balconies, and all have completely equipped kitchens or kitchenettes. Size varies from studios to five-bedroom apartments.

The Club Smugglers' package plans cover lodging and most of the recreational activities. For example, the summertime FamilyFest program for five days and five nights includes accommodation in a one-bedroom condo (which sleeps four), the children's day camp, guided walks and hikes, swimming and water sliding, and family game nights, from $1,325 (rates based on dates of stay and size of accommodation). A winter five-day package for a family of four in the same type of lodging runs about $1,930; this includes lift tickets, lessons (Nordic, Alpine, snowboard, cross-country, telemark, and shaped skis), outdoor ice skating, limited tennis, welcome parties, swimming pool, sauna, and après-ski activities. A crib or extra futon cot for two- to seven-year-olds can be provided for $20 for the entire stay.

Dining: Though you may opt to cook in your condo, there are several restaurants in the village when dining out seems better than facing a skillet. In winter The Green Mountain Cafe and Bakery serves home-baked breakfast treats and hot lunches with fresh-roasted specialty coffees. The Mountain Grille is open for all three meals, including light fare available well into the evening and a special buffet for children. At the Hearth & Candle parents enjoy nouveau cuisine, and at Riga-Bello's all ages savor the ever-popular Italian favorites—pizza, calzones, salads, and beverages—to eat in or have delivered to their condo. For summertime ice-cream treats, there's the Village Creamery, or choose refreshing drinks at the Sports Bar, with its big-screen TV.

The Poolside Cafe and Mountainside Cabana are relaxing summertime spots for lunch and cocktails. And teenagers even have their own clubhouse, The Outer Limits, open daily from 5:00 P.M. to midnight, serving juice and soda. For extras and snacks stop by the Village Grocery, with Deli and Wine Shop.

Children's World: The Little Smugglers' Discovery Dynamos Camp operates from early December to the beginning of April. Three- to five-year-olds join their ski host for morning and afternoon ski lessons, sleigh rides, movies, and arts and crafts. Skiers and boarders ages six to twelve meet with the Smugglers' Adventure Ski and Snowboard Camp for lessons, snow soccer, and races. Après-ski activities include a daily bonfire at 3:30 P.M. with storytelling and hot chocolate for parents and children. With lunch included, the daily rate for these programs, 9:30 A.M. to 4:00 P.M., is $67. The program, however, is included in the FamilyFest packages.

For teens ages thirteen to seventeen, the Explorer Ski and Snowboard Program offers challenging instruction and techniques, racing development, and a great way to make new friends. With the Outer Limits teen center and scheduled daily activities at 7:00 and 9:00 P.M., teenagers have plenty to do.

For younger, nonskiing children (newborn to three years), Alice's Wonderland is just that. Located in a quiet, sunlit corner of the resort, Alice's is 6,900 square feet or ten rooms of real state-of-the-art facilities. There are kid-size bathrooms, a complete kitchen, an infant "crawler room" equipped with mirrors and soft-sculpture gym, a separate crib room for naps, a closet of costumes, and an indoor jungle gym. Open from 9:00 A.M. to 4:00 P.M. (8:30 A.M. to 4:30 P.M. during ski season), staffed with professionals, and boasting a ratio of one to four, it's a steal at $15 an hour ($55 for a full day).

During the summer season, from the end of June through Labor Day, the Discovery and Adventure Day Camps offer daily activities for three- to twelve-year-olds. Fun events include outdoor games, fishing, arts and crafts, hiking, treasure hunts, and swimming. At the playground are swings, climbing equipment, and a sandbox. Tennis, movies, hayrides, dances, and scavenger hunts/overnight hikes are scheduled for teenagers. The day camp is included in the price of the family vacation. For the really wee ones, individual baby-sitters can be booked for $8.00 an hour. A really nice feature is Parents Night Out, when children ages three to twelve are invited to dinner and a fun evening from 6:00 to 10:00 P.M. The cost is $20 per child. A similar program is free with the FamilyFest program.

Recreation: A network of sixty runs on three interconnected mountains is the focus of wintertime play. The ski season runs from Thanksgiving to mid-April, and the average annual snowfall of 286 inches is supplemented by snowmaking equipment. The three mountains fall more or less into novice, intermediate, and advanced runs, but each mountain offers skiing for all levels of expertise. The total vertical drop is just over 2,600 feet. For the cross-country skier, 14 miles of trails roam through the mountains. Lessons in cross-country skiing, downhill skiing, and snowboarding can help you learn as a beginner or improve your skills. You might also try ice skating with the kids or a sleigh-ride adventure.

Turning indoors, you can enjoy the benefits of The Tub Club; with an exercise room and whirlpool and sauna facilities, you learn the proper regimen for a spa experience. With the resort's two indoor courts, tennis can be a wintertime sport; also in winter the large, heated swimming pool is covered with a bubble, so pack your swimsuit along with your ski sweater. In summer the bubble comes down. There's a water slide, called the Flume; a baby wading pool; and a seventeen-person outdoor hot tub. Free swimming instruction is provided as part of the day-camp program, and adults can join the Aqua Aerobics for a good workout.

Notchville Park, Smugglers' newest water playground, encompasses three acres with three pools in a unique, tiered hillside setting. In addition to 5,000 square feet of water, the park includes Raven's Roost Climbing Tower, Catbird's Croquet Court, Sand Swallow's Volleyball Court, Peregrine's Picnic Pavilion, and the Half-Moon Bath House.

The Family Water Playground is a third, separate water facility that includes a turtle slide (for children ages three to eight years), the Little Smugglers' Lagoon (a large splash pool with waterfall, tunnels, fountains, and a lazy river ride), a lap pool, and every parent's delight, the Giant Rapid River Ride—306 feet of twists and thrills on an inner tube beginning 26 feet up in the air. Bathhouse, snack bar, and lounging deck with gorgeous mountain views help one recover.

Also a favorite with families is Rum Runner's Hideaway, a beautiful swimming lake tucked in the mountains, a short hike or hay-wagon ride away from the Village. Access is free to resort guests for swimming, fishing, picnicking, and relaxing; canoes and paddleboats are available for rent. It's a great way to relive the old days and introduce your kids to the joys of summer days at the ole swimmin' hole.

In addition to the two indoor courts, there are eight outdoor clay courts; six are lighted for evening play. The Ten Pro Tennis School, which has videotape review, just about guarantees improvement in your game.

Hiking and biking are popular ways to enjoy the mountain countryside, or try jogging on one of the cross-country trails. Head to a mountain stream for perch, pike, and trout fishing. Outdoor lawn games include softball, volleyball, soccer, and shuffleboard. And reserve time for a session in the spa or a horseback ride at the Vermont Horse Park (services here are not included in the package plans). For those who can't possibly leave home without their golf clubs, courses in nearby Stowe and Morrisville are open to Smugglers' guests. ≋

Stratton Mountain Resort

Stratton Mountain, Vermont 05155
(802) 297–4137, (800) 843–6867, (800) STRATTON

Lessons, lessons, lessons! At Stratton Mountain Resort you can have instruction and training in several major sports. Whether your interests lead you to golf, tennis, swimming, racquetball, cross-country skiing, downhill skiing, telemark skiing, snowboarding, or snowshoeing, you can participate in classes for an introduction to a new sport or for polishing existing skills and techniques.

And where could you find a better place to get into shape and sharpen your sports expertise than in southern Vermont? Stratton Mountain Resort is set on 4,000 acres in the beautiful Green Mountains of Vermont. Since its opening in 1961, the resort has expanded a number of times to enhance the facilities and to attract sports-minded visitors to return again and again. Stratton Mountain is open year-round.

Accommodations: Choose a resort hotel, an alpine lodge, or your own villa. The Stratton Mountain Inn has 125 rooms and suites and also houses a restaurant, lounge, pool, sauna, and tennis courts. Stratton Village Lodge has ninety-one rooms and is in the heart of the village, just a few steps away from shops, and is considered ski-in/ski-out. The Birkenhaus and the Liftline Lodge offer more traditional accommodations, and each has its own restaurant. Winter rates at the Stratton Mountain Inn or Stratton Valley Lodge range from $119 to $169 a night; the Liftline Lodge is $85 to $135; the Birkenhaus, $99 to $149. Rates vary depending on date, midweek or weekend, packages, and so on. The Mountain Villas are one- to four-bedroom condominium apartments with fully equipped kitchens; many have fireplaces and private balconies. One-bedroom

Photo by Hubert Schriebel, courtesy of Stratton Mountain Resort

condos cost $90 to $230 per night, two bedrooms are $130 to $320, and three bedrooms are $170 to $400.

Two- to five-day/night Lifts and Lodging packages are available, from $49 to $99 based on a per person, per night rate. The popular Family Ski Week package includes five days' skiing and five nights' lodging, midweek (nonholiday), in a two-bedroom Valleyside condominium for families consisting of two adults and two children, all for $65 per person per night; children between the ages of four and twelve receive free KidsKamp. Call ahead for other available packages.

Summer rates at Mountain Villas range from $59 to $79 for hotel rooms, $90 to $150 for one-bedroom villas, and $110 to $170 for two-bedroom villas. Again, check for special-interest packages.

Dining: The Sage Hill Restaurant at the Stratton Mountain Inn serves hearty breakfasts, lunches, and New England cuisine dinners; savor cranberry duck or rack of lamb and pick up the recipe for your favorite dish, graciously shared by the chef. Also at the inn is The Tavern, a cozy spot to sip a hot toddy or your favorite cocktail. Tenderloins is the restaurant and lounge at the Clubhouse on the golf course.

In the winter start your day with breakfast at the base lodge, also fine for a quick lunch; the Mid-Mountain Restaurant (at 2,700 feet) is perfect for those who don't want to be off their skis long. Also at the mountain are the Birkenhaus Restaurant and the Liftline Lodge, which offer an old-world European atmosphere and cuisine, and the Partridge in a Pantry deli. Mulligan's Tavern is a great spot for families, with a good kids' menu, fireplaces, and live music. For terrific entertainment head back to the base lodge for live music at The Roost, a bar/restaurant.

Children's World: The ski season lasts from mid-November into April, and during this period youngsters are well cared for and find lots of entertainment. Seven- to twelve-year-olds join the Big Cub group for full-day supervision, lunch, and ski lessons, at $69 a day. Little Cubs take in ages four to six years for indoor games and fun as well as ski lessons (9:00 A.M. to 3:45 P.M. daily); the fee is $69 a day, including lunch; a half-day is $45. And real tiny tots gather at the Stratton Childcare Center, a certified day-care facility for children six weeks to three years old. It operates year-round from 8:30 A.M. until 4:30 P.M. and offers indoor and outdoor activities. The cost is $69 a day in winter. The Stratton offers night skiing trails and extended nighttime childcare. Contact the resort for details.

The fun continues in summer with day-camp programs offered seven days a week during July and August. Kids between six and twelve years old spend from 8:30 A.M. to 4:00 P.M. busily engaged in art classes, swim and gymnastics lessons, group games, and field trips. The cost is $37 a day. The child-care center entertains ages six weeks to five years during the same hours for $40, including lunch. An intensive tennis camp for ages seven to seventeen focuses on lessons and tournaments but breaks up the day with hikes, games, and swim time. Its cost is $60 per day.

Recreation: Skiing at Stratton Mountain is a big event. Thirty-seven miles of trails add up to ninety-two runs for all levels of downhill skiers. Mother Nature drops an average annual 170 inches of snow on this mountain—at 3,875 feet, the highest peak in southern Vermont—and is nudged along by rather sophisticated snowmaking equipment, covering 80 percent of the skiable terrain.

The Stratton Ski School holds classes for every level of ability. It prides itself on a full-day learning experience—five hours with an instructor. The Stratton Touring Center offers instruction in cross-country skiing for treks through the tall evergreens and across quiet meadows. Ice skating is another favorite winter sport.

If you're more inclined to warm-weather sports, enroll in the Stratton Golf School. Meet fellow students and your PGA instructors in a twenty-two-acre outdoor classroom where all playing conditions can be simulated, then head to the Stratton Mountain Country Club for a round on the twenty-seven-hole championship course.

Attend the Stratton Tennis School for private lessons or a group clinic. There are nineteen indoor and outdoor tennis courts at the Stratton Sports Center and two courts at the inn.

At the Sports Center are classes in swimming and aquacise in the 75-foot indoor pool, aerobics classes, Nautilus exercise, tennis, and three racquetball courts. During a recess from classes, sneak into the steam room or the whirlpool for some solitary relaxation. In addition, an outdoor pool, a sauna, and three whirlpools are located at the inn.

And don't forget to poke around the beautiful Vermont countryside. Hike in the hills and breathe that fresh clean air, jog or bicycle (rentals available) down country roads along fields of wildflowers, horseback ride on mountain trails, or try mountain biking from the summit. When you've had your fill of exercise, join bargain hunters at a local antiques auction or crafts fair. At the Stratton Arts Festival, in September and early October, you'll discover the fine wares of Vermont artists and craftspeople. Stratton Mountain Village, with the flair of an Alpine village, has lots of quaint shops, so finding the right memento of your trip will be an easy task. ≋

Sugarloaf/USA

RR 1, Box 5000
Kingfield, Maine 04947
(207) 237–2000, (800) THE–LOAF
E-mail: lodging@sugarloaf.com or info@sugarloaf.com
Web site: www.sugarloaf.com

Traditional New England reserve seems to be missing at Sugarloaf/USA. The prevailing attitude is friendly, upbeat, casually welcoming. While mainly associated with skiing and winter, Sugarloaf is fast becoming a four-season destination. All access is via Portland or Bangor, and once in western Maine, just about all roads lead to Sugarloaf. Route 27 is the main road to the ski area, and from the Carrabassett Valley, Sugarloaf literally stands out. You can distinguish the peak from 20 to 40 miles away, and once you leave the valley floor and start to climb, the panorama just gets better and better. Locals and repeat visitors have dubbed one particular spot "Oh-my-gosh corner," because it is so stunning as you round the corner and suddenly see the front of this impressive mountain with its seventy trails and an Alpine village set on the slope.

Accommodations: Sugarloaf has the capacity to sleep approximately 7,000 people on the mountainside. Condominiums, 912 of them, are set in various clusters of two to twenty-eight units and offer a wide selection of design. Styles include hotel rooms, studios, lofts, and up to five-bedroom, three-bath complexes. The thirty-six room Sugarloaf Inn and the Sugarloaf Mountain Hotel complete the lodging options. Custom packages are planned for each family's

needs. Packages always include a health club pass, and a complimentary shuttle system gets you around the resort with ease.

Rates range from $100 to $220 for a hotel room, from $153 to $241 for a one-bedroom unit, and from $292 to $447 for a four-bedroom condominium. Cribs and rollaway beds are provided at a daily charge of $5.00.

Sugarloaf was one of the first ski areas to introduce the ski-in/ski-out concept; in fact, every accommodation is ski-in/ski-out. This is great for older children, as it gives them a sense of independence and it gives everyone a sense of freedom. If you want to sleep late or linger over coffee, others in your party need not delay their skiing. Gondola Village is the largest condominium and the heart of the development, and here you will find the nursery.

Dining: Dining in the Sugarloaf area is a fun adventure that is taken quite seriously. With fourteen on-mountain restaurants, you can have everything from burgers to bouillabaisse to haute cuisine.

Gepetto's is a slopeside restaurant with a greenhouse addition and a gourmet menu for lunch or dinner. The Seasons Restaurant at the Sugarloaf Inn offers innovative American cuisine in a relaxed atmosphere. A highlight of the Seasons' menu is fresh Maine lobster. For après-ski the Widowmaker Lounge advertises "comfort with class," cocktails, and music you can hear yourself talk over. Upstairs at the base lodge, Avalanche provides a nonalcoholic teen center with lots of action. One of the more recent additions to Sugarloaf/USA is the

Shipyard Brewhaus, located just at the base of the Birches slope. It serves fine Maine microbrews on tap, lunch daily, and pub fare after 2:00 P.M. During the summer six restaurants remain open, so there's still a wide choice.

Children's World: Sugarloaf has a terrific child-care program. A state-licensed child-care center at the base of the mountain accepts children from six weeks to six years of age. Hours are from 8:30 A.M. to 4:00 P.M. Advance reservations are a must. The charges are $42 for a full day or $27 for a half day. The night nursery is available from 6:00 to 9:00 P.M. on Thursday and Saturday for $15, $10 per additional sibling. Reservations are required. A fenced-in outdoor play area adds to winter fun, and inside are toys, movies, storytime, circletime, and arts and crafts—a developmentally appropriate program provided by caring professionals. The nap area is separate, with individual cribs, cots, and mats. A hot lunch is served, and snacks are given during the day. Introduction to skiing lessons for three-year-olds originate from the child-care center. For $54 a full day or $39 a half day, your child has the option of a thirty- to forty-minute private lesson or two-hour group experience. Price includes lifts, rental equipment, and all the components of the child-care program.

Evenings offer free supervised activities for five- to twelve-year-olds, six nights a week. Included in the offerings are game nights, Movie Night, Wild Card Night, and Turbo-tubing. Reservations are required.

Mountain Magic teaches skiing to children ages four to six years and stresses independence, safety, and fun. The system teaches walking on skis, wedge stops and turns, side-stepping, falling, and, of course, getting up. Mountain Adventure is a program for ages seven to sixteen, where skills are perfected. These programs run from 8:30 A.M. to 3:00 P.M.; the costs start at $54 a day and include lift ticket, lessons, lunch, and equipment rentals.

Summertime brings flowers and traditional July and August day camps. A five-week program provided by Carrabassett Valley begins in the second week in July. Kids ages four to fourteen enjoy lessons in swimming, tennis, golf, and fly-fishing, and an extensive arts program. At $65 a week, with daily rates also available, it's a great deal. On the mountain, Sugarloaf offers summer child-care for little ones, six weeks to six years. The facility is open daily from 8:00 A.M. to 5:00 P.M., and the cost is $40 a day. Reservations are required.

Recreation: The most impressive aspect of skiing Sugarloaf is that you are skiing a big mountain. It is a traditional mountain in that it begins gently, goes to intermediate in the middle, and gets "durn hard at the top," as a local might say. Sugarloaf has the greatest vertical drop in the East. It is possible to come almost straight down the 2,820-foot vertical drop (and even do it in an upright position if you're good) having taken only two lifts. A good beginner or low intermediate skier can take Tote Road, a 3-mile trail from the top that follows the ridge and comes safely to the base, but gives that exciting feeling of skiing at the top of the world and surviving it. Cross-country skiers can explore 59 miles of trails, including some lighted for night skiing.

Other winter fun includes ice skating, snowshoeing, and cross-country skiing, with some scheduled night tours. The three Family Theme weeks offer additional family activities, and Holiday Weeks are chock-full of entertainment opportunities.

Come summer, when there is no snow on the ground, the Sugarloaf Golf Club opens. Designed by Robert Trent Jones Jr., this course is one of the best for wilderness golf and is one of the top twenty-five golf courses in the country, according to *Golf* magazine. Every tee has a spectacular view, and the mountain air is always cool. Tennis is limited to outside play, with two courts on the mountain and four in the town. The village has indoor racquetball courts, a sauna, hot tubs, a steam room, tanning beds, a climbing wall, and two swimming pools. But probably the most exciting summer sport is white-water rafting on the Kennebeck River. Sugarloaf also has a concentrated mountain-biking program. ≋

The Tyler Place Family Resort on Lake Champlain

P.O. Box 66, Old Dock Road
Highgate Springs, Vermont 05460
(802) 868–4000; fax (802) 868–5621
E-mail: tyler@together.net
Web site: www.tylerplace.com

Tucked away in the northwestern corner of Vermont, just minutes away from the Canadian border, Tyler Place Family Resort boasts of its beautiful setting and family-friendly atmosphere. The Tyler Place was one of the first resorts to devote itself entirely to families. The original owners, Mr. and Mrs. Edward Tyler, developed a concept that includes family time and time for parents to rejuvenate as a couple. The Tyler family (second and third generations) continues to carry on the resort's family philosophy. Open from late May to mid-September, it's the kind of place that families return to again and again.

Accommodations: The inn is the hub of activity, with its recreation rooms, main dining room, fireside lounge, deck, and glass-enclosed porches for visiting, relaxing, cocktails, and candlelight dining. Guest rooms—some are studios, some suites—are located in a separate wing. In addition, twenty-nine cottages, most with a fireplace in the living room and two or more bedrooms, are situated on and near the lake; these have kitchenettes and can sleep up to eight people. Many of the rooms include sleeping lofts or bunk beds; with these special attractions, it may not be difficult at all to get a youngster to go to sleep in a strange place. Cribs and high chairs for infants and toddlers are available at no extra charge.

In total, Tyler Place accommodates approximately sixty families. Based on a full American plan, the daily per person rate for each of the first two lodgers in a unit is $135 to $251 during July and August. Depending on the child's age, a rate of $45 to $92 a day applies; this covers lodging, meals, sports, and the activities program. Rates are 15 to 35 percent lower in May, early June, and September, during hands-on Retreats for the Whole Family. The resort is closed the rest of the year.

Dining: The main dining room in the inn serves a semibuffet breakfast, lunch, and dinner. New American country cuisine is the kitchen's specialty, and as a full American plan is in effect, you have only to decide which delicious entree to sample. Children have earlier dining hours with their counselors, allowing parents to relax over meals. A family breakfast room and family picnic lunch baskets are available.

Children's World: During the entire season there's an extensive program of events geared to eight different age groups, plus infant care. From the youngest Junior Toddlers (twelve to eighteen months) to Senior Teens (fourteen- to sixteen-year-olds), children are well entertained with morning and evening activities led by energetic and enthusiastic college students. Children take meals with their group leaders, and the hours between breakfast and lunch and after supper are filled with arts and crafts, nature walks, songs, games, storytime, volleyball, swimming, hayrides, fishing, movies, treasure hunts, sailing, tennis, sailboarding, kayaking, indoor pool parties—one gets out of breath just listing the activities! Busy and active, your child will no doubt be happy as well, with no chance of being "kid-starved." Afternoons are devoted to individual family time, with activities available if desired. If you can drag the kids away from friends and counselors, the staff will help you plan a day of sight-seeing or fishing and send you off with a picnic lunch.

For the very young (newborns to two and one-half years), the resort features one-on-one "Parents' Helpers" (from high-school-age to mature adult), who will care for your young child and even prepare meals. The standard fee is $4.00 to $6.75 per hour. This is a real vacation for Mom and Dad, a break from wet diapers and baby food.

Recreation: Beautiful Lake Champlain is the source of much of the recreation and relaxation of Tyler Place. Take off in one of the resort's sailboats, canoes, kayaks, or sailboards. Try waterskiing (with instruction), guided canoe and bike trips, yoga, aerobics (step and water), and the workout facilities. Or bait your fishing line for bass and pike. The outdoor and indoor heated pools and Jacuzzi on the lakeshore provide hours of fun.

Retreats for the whole family, a popular addition, started in 1998. They feature hands-on activities for all ages, including such topics as gardening, nature and outdoor skills, lakeshore studies, rural and farm life, and family wellness.

On land, six tennis courts and a fleet of bikes (one-speed, mountain, children's, tricycle, and child seats, all with helmets) are at your disposal, and the nature trails beckon hikers and joggers. For a change of pace, challenge another guest to an old-fashioned game of horseshoes, or try your hand at archery. Maybe you'll join a soccer game or start up a tennis round-robin with the folks in the neighboring cottage. Golf privileges are available at three golf courses within a fifteen- to forty-five-minute drive of the resort. Recreation fees are applied only for golf, outboard motors for fishing, waterskiing, lake cruises, and mountain bikes.

Nighttime brings other events, from dances and live jazz to guitar sing-alongs and Monte Carlo nights—pick your pleasure. What many guests like most is the hospitable atmosphere of the many and varied activities, with never any pressure to participate. ≋

Whitney's Inn

Box 822
Jackson, New Hampshire 03846
(603) 383–6886, (800) 677–5737; fax (603) 383–6886
E-mail: info@whitneysinn.com
Web site: www.whitneysinn.com

A holiday at a classic country inn does as much for the mind as it does for the spirit and rejuvenating the body. Located in the beautiful White Mountains of New Hampshire, the inn sits on fourteen acres of open fields and wooded hills, with a mountain pond and a brook. Drive into town across an old covered bridge, point your car toward the mountain, and at the end of the road, you'll find the welcoming charm of Whitney's Inn. Open year-round, this is a family operation, and the owners, the Bowmans, appreciate the special interests of families.

Accommodations: Standard and deluxe rooms are in the main inn, and family suites, particularly suited to parties with children, are close by in a separate building. The rate structure is a little complicated, as you have a choice between bed-and-breakfast or a modified American plan, with breakfast and gourmet dinner. Few standard rooms will accommodate families. B&B in deluxe rooms and family suites (more motel than inn style, but with more space also) cost $51 to $82 per person, double occupancy; children twelve and under are $15, and older kids are $28. MAP rates are $74 to $107 per person; children are $25. A good deal, and very popular, is one of the freestanding cottages (there are only two, so reserve early) with fireplace and two bedrooms: $146 to $210 per night, including breakfast. Weekend and holiday times are the higher rates. Children twelve and under stay and eat free during summer months in a Family Suite.

Dining: Breakfast and dinner will satisfy the best appetites. Breakfasts feature hearty fare, preparing you for an outdoor, athletic day. Dinners are relaxing affairs where you'll find such tasty items on the menu as pecan chicken topped with a tangy raspberry glaze or Veal Felix with asparagus, lobster, and Bernaise sauce. The children's table at dinner offers grown-ups their much-needed quiet time and youngsters their favorite dishes, such as pizza, broiled chicken, and fried fish. Try The Shovel Handle for lunch fare of salads, sandwiches, and hearty soups. Or stop by at the end of the day for a little après-ski.

Children's World: On weekends and holidays children between the ages of three and twelve can participate in any one of Black Mountain's Ski and Snowboard Schools. Package costs range from $40 to $90 and are available for "Never Ever" skiers and riders to advanced intermediates. Lessons and programs begin at 10:00 A.M., and parents are encouraged to sign up their children at least forty-five minutes in advance. Call the Black Mountain Ski and Snowboard School at (603) 383-4490 for more information.

Recreation: Skiing at the inn's back door is the primary winter activity. Of the forty downhill trails, 34 percent are ranked intermediate. The vertical drop on this sunny side of Black Mountain is 1,100 feet. From the summit, skiers look out to Mount Washington and across picturesque New England farms. Snowmaking facilities on 98 percent of the mountain complement Mother Nature's efforts.

The Betty Whitney trail, named in honor of a longtime resident, provides a 2-kilometer groomed loop connecting Whitney's Inn and the village of Jackson. This is a great starting point for families who ski both cross-country and downhill.

For cross-country skiers, the Jackson Ski Touring Center is located just 2 miles from the inn; some of its 150 kilometers of trails crisscross the inn's property. Also on the wintertime calendar, the inn has sledding, ice-skating parties, sleigh rides, and movies. The activities room offers games for the whole family, and the library is a peaceful hideaway.

In summer, mountain biking, hiking, and jogging in these beautiful mountains are favorite activities. You also can fish, swim, join a cookout, and play a bit of tennis, badminton, croquet, volleyball, and shuffleboard. ≋

EAST

New York

Pennsylvania

Golden Acres Farm and Ranch

South Gilboa Road
Gilboa, New York 12076
(607) 588–7329, (800) 847–2151, (800) 252–7787 (in New York)
E-mail: farmresort@aol.com
Web site: www.goldenacres.com

Old MacDonald had a farm, ee-i-ee-i-oh. And on that farm he had a cow." Well, the Gauthiers have a farm also, with at least as wide a variety of animals as Old Mac did—horses, goats, sheep, ducks, chickens, and a number of baby animals for cuddling and petting. If you like, you can begin your day by milking a cow, collecting eggs from the henhouse, or feeding the animals. The farm has always been family oriented and prides itself on a genuine "down-on-the-farm" experience with modern comforts. This 800-acre farm/resort is located on top of a 2,000-foot-high knoll in the Catskill Mountains and is open Memorial Day to Labor Day only.

Local sites of interest include Howe Caverns, Secret Caves, Hunter Mountain, game farms, and bird sanctuaries. Cooperstown, home of the Baseball Hall of Fame, is nearby, as is the Oneonta Soccer Hall of Fame. Golden Acres is in the center of numerous auction barns, flea markets, and roadside vegetable stands.

Accommodations: In the main house are the dining room, the nursery, an indoor playroom, and a teen lounge. Next door is a motel complex connected to game rooms, lounges, and the indoor pool and hot tub. Across the road (a short city block away) is Gilboa Ridge, with a farmhouse and farm cottage. There are ten connecting rooms and suites. Most rooms contain a double bed and a single bed, with space for rollaways or cribs ($25 per week per crib). Also at Gilboa Ridge are twenty-six "you cook" vacation apartments with kitchenettes and a campground area with water and electric hookups. The farm pays particular attention to single parents and has nondiscriminatory rates based on one adult traveling with a child. Rates are $60 to $110 daily, with children paying $20 to $35, depending on their age.

Dining: A modified American plan is optional and includes two meals for adults and three for children. Children and adults have a joint menu and dining room for breakfast and dinner, but no adults are allowed at lunch; then the children and teens and their counselors eat all those things that are so dear to their hearts—pizza and hamburgers, along with a few fruits and vegetables. Jewish dietary laws are observed. Two snacks daily are included for the young set, and the selection at the Snack Bar hits the spot between meals. Food is fresh and hearty, and you can eat all you wish. The evening menu includes appetizer, salad, soup, choice of two meats or one fish entree, side dishes, and desserts. All breads and pastries are freshly baked daily in the farm bakery.

Evening activities center on the Skylite Room and the Ragtime Lounge and include happy hour, bands, and entertainment; folk and square dancing; night at the races; and other activities—some for everyone, some for adults only, and a teen lounge for special programs. After the early evening entertainment, live music and dancing continue in the Ragtime Lounge.

Children's World: The program for children varies by age, takes advantage of the farm surroundings, and is offered from the end of May through the first week of September. For the under-four set, a complete nursery service is scheduled from 10:00 A.M. to noon, 1:30 to 5:00 P.M., and 6:30 to 7:45 P.M. Parents collect their children for mealtimes.

For four- to twelve-year-olds, it is nonstop action throughout the day. For teens, informal activities emphasize meeting others and sharing things while maintaining freedom of action. The rec room, with its jukebox and video games, is popular with this group. Experienced and enthusiastic counselors (most of whom are studying to be teachers) supervise the events. The staff is international, with thirty-eight countries represented. It's great exposure for the children, who learn games and activities from around the world.

A typical day starts at 10:00 A.M. with a tour to feed the animals, collect eggs, or visit the gardens. Then come horseback riding (teaching beginners is a specialty here), swimming, lunch, and a rest period. Afternoon activities are geared to the children's interests—berry picking, frog hunts, hayrides, crafts, games, and perhaps an excursion to the caves or a hike and cookout in the woods. A snack of milk and cookies is followed by rounding up the cows for milking.

After a break for dinner and a quick hello to the parents, evening activities such as bonfires, talent shows, or cartoons start at 7:45 P.M. Kids have another snack, then head for bed about 9:00 P.M.—and well deserved it is! Parents can go out if they want, as a night patrol is on duty from 9:00 P.M. to 1:00 A.M., with a sign-in sheet on each room door. If you prefer, you can hire a baby-sitter from either the staff or local listings at approximately $4.50 an hour, with a three-hour minimum.

Recreation: There is no charge for any of the activities. After catching your limit of fish, you might take off to one of the two tennis courts, the archery field, either of the two swimming pools, or the exercise room. The boats and floating docks at the lake make for a relaxing afternoon, or join a group for softball or volleyball. And grown-ups, too, can partake in the farm activities—feeding the animals, horseback riding, hopping aboard a hayride. A less active afternoon might include a class in macramé, copper enameling, pottery, or stained glass, or a stop by one of the recreation rooms for table tennis and pool. If the weather is uncooperative, there's an indoor riding arena, five playrooms for rainy-day activities, and a complete workout room for adults. One nice feature at the Golden Acres is the policy of allowing an early check-in and late use of the facilities when checking out. ≋

Mohonk Mountain House

Lake Mohonk
New Paltz, New York 12561
(845) 255–1000, (800) 772–6646
Web site: www.mohonk.com

The wholesome peace and serenity of Mohonk Mountain House are not merely by-products of its setting in 2,200 acres of the Shawangunk Mountains, 90 miles north of New York City. The resort was founded in 1869 by twin brothers, Albert and Alfred Smiley, who, following their Quaker upbringing, regarded drinking, dancing, smoking, and card playing as unacceptable activities. Rather, they emphasized spiritual renewal as evidenced by the nature walks or prayer meetings planned for their proper clientele.

The times have indeed changed, but the gracious, quieter way of life of a bygone era still prevails at Mohonk. No discos swing until dawn here. In fact, no bar is on the premises, though guests may order cocktails with the midday and evening meals. Instead, you'll find cozy conversation lounges furnished with Victorian antiques, verandas lined with rocking chairs, miles of hiking trails, and extensive gardens. Open year-round, the rambling wood-and-stone Victorian structure appears almost like a castle, complete with turrets and towers, and sits on the edge of a clear mountain lake a half mile long.

Accommodations: The 261 guest rooms are spacious and tastefully and simply decorated with period furnishings. Most have private balconies overlooking the lake or looking across the valley to the mountains. Many have fireplaces. Some connecting rooms share a bath. On a full American plan (mandatory), daily rates are from $310 to $495 for a standard double guest room. The special Victorian and tower rooms command higher rates. For children occupying a room with their parents, the charge is $115 a day for those over twelve and $70 a day for four- to twelve-year-olds; children under age four are accommodated free. There is no charge for cribs or rollaway beds. Weekly rates and package plans are available. Ask about the "kids stay free" events held throughout the year.

Dining: The main dining room where breakfast, lunch, and dinner are served is a large and elegantly simple room with highly polished woodwork and pan-

Photo by Matthew Seaman, courtesy of Mohonk Mountain House

eling rising 30 to 40 feet. The kitchen specializes in American cuisine, empha-
sizing the use of game and ingredients indigenous to America. Wholesome
foods prepared with the freshest ingredients are the hallmark of dining at
Mohonk, and the spectacular natural setting is the crowning touch to this
wonderful dining experience. Jackets are standard attire for gentlemen at the
evening meal. Cookouts and clambakes are occasionally planned. Afternoon
tea is served daily at 4:00 P.M. Refreshments are also available in the Ice Cream
Parlor and Soda Fountain and the Tee Room on the golf course.

Children's World: On weekends and holidays throughout the year and daily
from mid-June through Labor Day, children are divided into two age groups:
two- to three-year-olds, and four- to twelve-year-olds. Both groups have daily
activities in the morning and again in the afternoon, after lunch with the family.
Typical events on the agenda are hikes, nature walks, scavenger hunts, shuffleboard contests, swimming, pony rides, rock scrambles, and frog hunts. Movies,
square dances, and campfires are frequently planned for evenings. This is a
complimentary service for hotel guests. Baby-sitters can be hired for younger
children, with advance notice.

Recreation: Discovering nature's beauty is at the core of many of Mohonk's
recreational activities. More than 85 miles of hiking trails wind through the
woods and along the lake; dotting the paths are one hundred gazebos where
you can sit to take in the views. Explore the grounds on horseback (Western
and English style) or in a horse-drawn carriage ride, and leisurely meander

through the award-winning gardens. Mohonk Lake has a small sandy beach at the west end and is stocked with trout; it is the location of swimming, fishing, and boating.

Traditional sports are tennis (lessons available) on the six courts (four clay, two Har-Tru) and the two platform tennis courts and golfing on the nine-hole Scottish-design course and the eighteen-hole putting green. There are tennis and golf pro shops for equipment and apparel. The fitness center offers exercise equipment, and saunas. Spa services are available in Mohonk's Massage Center. Lawn games include shuffleboard, croquet, and lawn bowling.

During the winter months, when the lake freezes, ice skating is a favorite sport. New in 2001, Mohonk's Victorian Skating Pavilion is host to skating parties on a refrigerated ice rink in fall and winter. And Mohonk maintains more than 35 miles of marked trails for snowshoeing and cross-country skiing.

Throughout the year lectures, concerts, and slide shows are scheduled in the evening. Several three-day to weeklong programs are planned, covering topics such as bird-watching and identification, gardening, photography, foreign languages, cooking, music, mystery and sleuthing, and stargazing; professionals in the respective fields conduct these programs. ≋

Rocking Horse Ranch

Highland, New York 12528
(845) 691–2927, (800) 647–2624
E-mail: ranchrhr@aol.com
Web site: www.rhranch.com

"Giddy-up, ole paint" and, with a tip of your ten-gallon hat, off you ride into the sunset. Located only 75 miles from New York City and recently awarded a three-diamond rating by AAA, Rocking Horse Ranch has been owned and managed by the Turk family since 1958. They take pride in treating their guests as family; in fact, more than 80 percent of the guests are repeat clients. The 500 acres easily accommodate up to 350 guests while permitting a feeling of "wide open spaces." With a stable of 120 horses, mainly quarterhorse stock, Rocking Horse stakes a claim to being one of the best dude ranches around.

Accommodations: Rooms (120 in all) are located in either the main lodge or the Oklahoma Annex (motel-style units). The twenty-four connecting rooms and the ranchettes may be appropriate for large parties. The latter are similar to minisuites, with sitting areas and convertible sofa beds. Eighteen rooms have

Photo courtesy of Rocking Horse Ranch

refrigerators. Daily rates based on double occupancy and a modified American plan are $100 to $235 per adult; children are charged at 50 percent of the adult rate, and weekly stays offer savings.

Dining: A modified American plan is mandatory at the resort and includes two meals for adults but three full meals for children. The three dining areas are the main dining room, an indoor coffee shop, and, during summer, an outdoor snack area by the pool. Meals are five to six courses, prepared by graduate chefs from the nearby Culinary Institute of America. Dinner selections include roast prime rib, barbecued steaks, or fillet of sole brought in fresh from a local market, complemented by a huge salad bar. At the dessert bar the chocolate blackout cake is not to be missed. The Round-Up Room Nightclub has floor shows and a live band. Two other cocktail lounges, each with a fireplace and a conversation area, are also quite inviting.

Children's World: The Fort Wilderness playground area, with swings and climbing equipment and the animal farm where Tony the Llama lives, is a favorite with kids. Year-round, children have a planned, supervised program seven days a week. The 9:00 A.M. to 5:00 P.M. schedule is filled with horseback riding, swimming, waterskiing, crafts, and games. In the evening the fun continues with pizza parties, dances, and cookouts. On weekends during the winter, kids turn to skiing and snow tubing.

There is no charge for the day's events, which include lunch and snacks with the counselors, or for the "nite patrol," set up to make rounds of corridors and, upon request, to check inside the room when parents are out. Baby-sitting can be arranged at $6.00 per hour.

Recreation: You might start your day with an early-morning horseback ride; invigorated by the sweet mountain air, lead your horse down a quiet trail through the woods. You can try both English- and Western-style riding. If you're a novice, you can link up with the experienced ranch staff for some basic instruction.

The rest of your day may be filled with waterskiing (instruction is free), enjoying more than 150 feet of water slide, swimming, fishing, and boating (paddleboats and rowboats) on the ten-acre lake. Play a game of tennis and hike or jog along the nature trails. A relaxing swim in one of three heated pools (two are outdoors, with one just for kids) can revive your spirits for a workout in the exercise room or a rousing game of volleyball, softball, basketball, or badminton. For an easier pace try a round of croquet, shuffleboard, or horseshoes. An archery field and an indoor shooting range are available for aspiring marksmen, and the eighteen holes of miniature golf are fun for kids and their parents.

In the fall the social director plans apple-picking trips, hayrides, and cookouts. In winter add cross-country skiing, snow tubing, and horseback riding in the snow; the 300-foot vertical ski slope is modest but has two new trails. At Rocking Horse all activities are free; the horseback riding, the use of all the sports equipment and facilities, and the entertainment are covered in the lodging rates. ≈≈≈

The Sagamore

Lake George at Bolton Landing, New York 12814
(518) 644–9400, (800) 358–3585
Web site: thesagamore.com

The notion of an island hideaway usually involves images of thatch-roofed huts or oceanside condominiums, palm trees waving in a gentle breeze, miles of sandy beach, and golf, tennis, sailing, and swimming. The Sagamore will take you by surprise, for it is an island resort, and it grants its guests opportunities for golf, tennis, sailing, and swimming—and then it deviates from the traditional image. You see, The Sagamore is on a seventy-acre island in Lake George in upstate New York. Surrounded by clear lake waters and the Adirondack Mountains, the tall evergreen trees and the clean mountain air set the stage here.

The Sagamore itself is different. Originally opened in 1883, it is part of another era, gracious and elegant. The main hotel building dates from 1930 and is listed on the National Register of Historic Places. After an extensive multimillion-dollar renovation, The Sagamore reopened as a year-round resort in 1985 and is a member of Preferred Hotels and Resorts Worldwide. The wings radiate from the main lobby and its semicircular, white-columned porch and seem to embrace the lawns, gardens, and lake views. Down the wings are more porches for sitting, strolling, and catching a different view of the lake. In the center, topping off this Victorian showplace, is the bell tower.

Accommodations: Of the 350 rooms and suites, 100 are in the main hotel and another 240 are distributed among the island's seven modern lodges (don't worry, modern does not denote a disturbance to The Sagamore's ambience). The remaining ten suites are part of a business executive complex. You will find attention to detail and historical accuracy in the decoration of the rooms and throughout the hotel. You'll think "charming, quaint, elegant, reserved" when you see Adirondack Stick or American Country furniture. Perhaps your room will be in mahogany and you'll draw a Queen Anne–style chair up to the desk when writing postcards. Rocking chairs and quilted bedspreads complete the picture in some rooms. In others fireplaces or balconies capture a guest's eye. Even the bathrooms are special and true to a grand era, with their pedestal-base sinks and mahogany towel bars.

Rates vary within the main hotel and the lodges, ranging from $120 to $630 depending on the season. While The Sagamore's European plan includes no meals, you are invited to dine on an a la carte basis. For added convenience and value, choose the modified American plan, priced at $49 per person per day, and enjoy a full breakfast and four-course dinner daily at any of The Sagamore's restaurants. Children five and younger dine free when the rest of the family is on the meal plan.

Dining: For a casual afternoon by the pool, you can have a light lunch and beverages at the Terrace. For a truly elegant and memorable dinner, the Trillium can transport you back through time in style (coats and ties required for gentlemen). Recipes for this restaurant have been carefully researched so that you can have an adventure in history as well as in dining. In between these options are the Sagamore Dining Room, where regional favorites are served at breakfast and dinner, and the Club Grill on the mainland, where views stretch out over the golf course and the lake. At the Verandah, in the lobby, guests can have continental breakfast in the morning, tea and finger sandwiches in the afternoon, and nightcaps before retiring. Mr. Brown's serves light meals in a publike setting. The touring vessel *Morgan* cruises the lake during lunch and dinner, offering its diners constantly changing scenic views. It is suggested that you make your dinner reservations when you book your room.

Children's World: Under the cheerful and watchful direction of the activities counselor, Sagamore kids take swimming lessons, play lawn games, dance, do face painting, go on boat rides, see clown shows, and unveil their hidden talents in crafts classes. In this one area The Sagamore does not follow nineteenth-century practices, which were somewhat restrictive when it came to children. Instead, in keeping with modern philosophies, The Sagamore wants its energized children to have a fun, athletic, and creative visit. The authentic 22-foot tepee gives the program its name: The Tepee Club. It runs from 8:00 A.M. to 4:00 P.M. daily during the summer and on major holidays and winter weekends for ages four to thirteen. The cost is $25 for each child, including lunch. From 5:00 until 9:00 P.M., four- to thirteen-year-olds can have dinner, play, or enjoy dress-ups and clown parties. A game room includes table tennis, a pool table, video games, and a television. For children under age four, baby-sitting is offered at $7.50 an hour, with a three-hour minimum. Children ages three to five can join the evening program with a baby-sitter for $10.

Recreation: Just across the bridge from The Sagamore's island, Donald Ross designed an eighteen-hole championship golf course in the Adirondack foothills near the lake's edge, complemented by the restaurant and pro shop facilities at the course's attractive Tudor-style clubhouse.

The indoor swimming pool, tennis courts, and racquetball courts help guests stay busy and active year-round. The complete health spa offers its own form of indoor workout with its Nautilus equipment and then pampers with saunas, whirlpools, and massages. Spa packages include special diets, herbal wraps, and aromatherapy.

In warm weather swim in the beautiful, clean, freshwater lake; skim across its surface sailing, waterskiing, and sailboarding; or gently stroke the waters in a rowboat or fishing boat. Jog on the trails around the island or hike the foothills around the golf course. Take a horse out for an hour-long jaunt or stay close to home for a Sunday afternoon concert on the lawn.

In the wintertime Lake George freezes; hearty souls go ice fishing, while others snuggle together during a horse-drawn sleigh ride. Ice skate over the frozen lake or go tobogganing and cross-country skiing on the snow-covered golf course. Downhill skiers can take advantage of nearby Gore Mountain and West Mountain, ski areas to which The Sagamore provides free bus transportation.

Saratoga is about 30 miles away and in summer shares its Performing Arts Center with interested visitors. ≋

Skytop Lodge

One Skytop
Skytop, Pennsylvania 18357
(717) 595–7401, (800) 345–7759
Web site: www.skytop.com

The Pocono Mountains have long had a reputation as a romantic honeymoon destination. While this is certainly warranted, the Skytop Lodge will convince you that this area of northeast Pennsylvania is just right for a family vacation as well. Set on 5,500 acres of rolling hills, lakes, and rivers, the lodge is a large, rambling, stone building with a welcoming circular drive. Just 100 miles from either New York or Philadelphia, Skytop attracts many visitors with its relaxed atmosphere, hospitable charm, and recreational activities. It is open year-round.

Accommodations: Most of the rooms have views of the gardens and grounds; some will accommodate a family of four. If a large-enough room is not available, or if parents prefer, children are given their own room at $100 off the regular rate. Based on double occupancy, full American plan high-season (May through October) rates are $445 to $545 weekends and $395 to $485 Sunday through Thursday. Children under seventeen sharing the parents' room pay $30. In November to April, special off-season rates and packages are available; weekend and holiday rates, however, are more comparable to those in summer.

Dining: All meals are served in the main dining room, where gentlemen are requested to wear jackets in the evening. The Tea Room serves light fare such as soups and sandwiches, and the seasonal Golf Shop Grill is an alternative luncheon spot in warm weather. The Pine Room, an elegant and inviting area of the lobby with floor-to-ceiling windows, is the site of afternoon musical entertainment in the summer and cozy gatherings near the fireplace in the winter. The Tap Room serves cocktails and features dancing several nights a week.

Children's World: Camp-in-the-Clouds is in session for four- to twelve-year-olds daily from July 1 to Labor Day. The morning program runs from 9:30 A.M. to noon, the afternoon program from 2:00 to 5:00 P.M. Each session is $18, or $25 for the full day, and covers a program of swimming, boating, hiking, games, and crafts. Young children also enjoy the playground and the kiddie pool, while the older ones make the most of pool, table tennis, and video games in the Recreation Room. The weekly Saturday night "Grand March" has become a tradition at Skytop. A combination parade, quadrille, and snake dance, it becomes hilarious at times, and guests and staff alike anticipate the fun. At holiday times during the rest of the year, the activities staff plans dinners and movies for children. Individual baby-sitters can be arranged for evenings only at $5.00 an hour.

Recreation: The Poconos make a lovely setting for sports activities. The eighteen-hole championship golf course is a combination of lush fairways and beautiful old trees on a rolling terrain. Putting greens and a pro shop round out the golfing facility. Tennis players are invigorated by the clean mountain air; of the seven outdoor courts, five are Har-Tru and two are an all-weather surface. Private lessons and clinics are offered.

Fishermen like the trout-filled stream and the three lakes full of bass and pickerel; novices will appreciate the fly-fishing instruction. Others take to these waters for swimming, boating, and canoeing. There's an outdoor swimming pool, and in cool weather swimmers enjoy the large indoor pool in its solarium setting.

You can work out in the exercise room, but outdoors you can have beautiful scenery *and* all the exercise you want. Try lawn bowling on well-tended greens (tournaments are held during the summer), or practice more conventional sports like badminton, croquet, archery, shuffleboard, softball, and miniature golf. The trails through the woods are perfect for hiking, biking, and jogging, and the gardens are suitable for relaxing strolls. Naturalists conduct tours of the local wildlife and vegetation. In the evening you might find a bridge game, play a little pool or billiards, take in a movie, or relax in the library.

In the winter Skytop has a few gentle slopes for downhill skiing. Two poma lifts and seven trails with a vertical drop of just 275 feet make it ideal for learning. A ski pro can help with lessons. Several well-groomed trails cover acres of attractive territory for cross-country skiing. Rental equipment is available for both types of skiing, and larger ski areas are nearby at Alpine Mountain (8 miles) and Camelback (15 miles). Tobogganing, sledding, and ice skating are also wintertime favorites. ≋

MID-ATLANTIC

North Carolina

South Carolina

Virginia

West Virginia

Fairfield Sapphire Valley

70 Sapphire Valley Road
Sapphire, North Carolina 28774
(828) 743–3441, (800) 533–8268
Web site: www.fairfieldsapphirevalley.com

The rolling foothills of the Blue Ridge Mountains provide the backdrop for Fairfield Sapphire Valley, a year-round resort community. The 5,700 acres, filled with the scent of pines and fresh mountain air, encompass three lakes, a golf course, a horseback-riding stable, and picturesque scenery for nature lovers and hikers. The serenity of a canoe ride on the lake, relaxing afternoon fishing from the dock, or the rigors of a tennis clinic attract vacationers to this mountain setting tucked in the southwestern corner of North Carolina.

Accommodations: Hotel rooms, efficiencies, one- to three-bedroom condominiums, and three- and four-bedroom houses boast spectacular mountain views or are nestled among tall pines. Most of these lodgings have kitchens, and all have sundecks or balconies where you can sit to watch the sunset. Condominium rates begin at $90 for a room and go to $265 for a deluxe three-bedroom with view. Off-season (November through March) rates are $10 to $35 less.

Dining: Many families prepare meals in their villas, but if your idea of a vacation does not include cooking, the restaurants can relieve you of this chore. The Library Restaurant offers fine dining in a casual atmosphere, while Mica's Restaurant has an old-world charm and serves lunch and dinner daily. The club for the Sapphire Mountain Golf Course also houses a restaurant, which is open for lunch. There's no meal plan, so you're free to pick and choose as you please. The resort is located in a dry township; while no liquor, beer, or wine can be purchased on-site, brown bagging is permitted and setups are available in the area restaurants.

Children's World: The children's program operates Monday through Friday from 9:00 A.M. to 4:00 P.M., mid-June through mid-August. Enroll your child for a full-day session of events supervised by an enthusiastic staff. A full day with lunch is $31. The program is offered for ages three to twelve.

Swimming, boat rides, tennis, nature walks, fishing, and arts-and-crafts classes are on the agenda, as are an occasional puppet show and scavenger hunt. Video games are offered for the young computer whiz in your group. The recreation staff assists in making individual baby-sitting arrangements.

Recreation: The Sapphire Mountain Golf Course is an eighteen-hole championship course. Views of the beautiful Blue Ridge Mountains provide ample

diversion if your game is not up to snuff. Water hazards on nine holes, including a waterfall, make it a memorable experience. If you're really serious about your performance, seek private instruction at the pro shop, which also accommodates your fashion and equipment needs.

Tennis enthusiasts enjoy the Tennis Center, which includes eight Har-Tru courts and two all-weather courts (two courts are lighted for evening play), as well as a well-stocked pro shop. The resident pro can assist in improving your swing in either private lessons or clinic programs.

For hikers and nature lovers, several trails wind around the lakes and through the woods; along the Fairfield Lake Trail, information plaques describe the plants and wildlife of the area. At the Equestrian Center you can engage a mount for a group escorted trail ride.

For an unusual afternoon outing, you might consider gem mining. In the late 1800s the land was mined quite successfully, and while you probably won't bring home a sapphire or a ruby, you'll no doubt have a good excursion. Check with the Recreation Department for mining tips and equipment.

Swimmers can opt for a dip in one of the lakes or in the indoor and outdoor heated pools located at the Recreation Center. Lake Fairfield is also the setting for boating expeditions; canoes, paddleboats, rowboats, and fishing boats can be acquired on a rental basis. Fishermen head to the lakes or a quiet mountain stream for fine trout fishing.

At the Recreation Center you'll also find basketball, volleyball, table tennis, miniature golf, swimming pools, a weight room, Jacuzzi, and a sauna. In winter the Recreation Center becomes the focus of ski activities. Three main trails are covered by snowmaking and lighted for evening skiing; group and private lessons are taught at the ski school. Many visitors reserve time for sight-seeing in the area. The Biltmore House and Gardens, along with its winery, certainly warrant a side trip. Local mountain crafts can be purchased in Cashiers and Highlands. ≋

The Greenbrier

300 West Main Street
White Sulphur Springs, West Virginia 24986
(304) 536–1110, (800) 624–6070

The Greenbrier is a 6,500-acre estate in the beautiful Allegheny Mountains. Its history dates back to just after the Revolutionary War, when early settlers discovered the sulfur springs of this area. The grand Georgian architecture of The Greenbrier with its white columned porticoes, elaborate formal gardens, and friendly atmosphere set the scene for a memorable experience of fine dining, recreation, and relaxation.

The only problem at The Greenbrier may be deciding what to do first. With a list of recreational and social activities a mile long, you may need a personal secretary to help you get organized. When planning events for your stay, though, save time for an escape to discover nature's charms along the enticing woodland trails, well marked for joggers and walkers alike. And pause among the twelve acres of formal gardens, tended meticulously from spring through fall. With a reputation that has attracted presidents and royalty, The Greenbrier provides a level of elegant service and comfort that ensures an unforgettable vacation. It is open year-round.

Accommodations: With rooms and suites in the hotel as well as guest houses and cottages, you have a wide choice of accommodations. The rooms are large and bright, with comfortable, elegant furnishings. Based on a modified American plan, daily rates for a standard room start at $203 to $260 (depending on the season) per person, double occupancy; larger rooms and prime locations command slightly higher rates. There is no charge for children occupying the same room as their parents. The guest cottages include one to four bedrooms, a living room, and a porch or patio; many have fireplaces. The daily per person rate, based on an occupancy of two to eight people, is $286

to $395, modified American plan. The Creekside Cottages are available to guests visiting for a minimum of one week. Golf, tennis, and family package plans are offered. Cribs are provided at no extra charge.

Dining: The Greenbrier boasts exciting culinary experiences. Regional Southern specialties, such as spoon bread and fresh trout from the nearby mountain streams, as well as Continental dishes, make dining a special part of a visit here. The sumptuous breakfasts, featuring homemade biscuits and country ham, are a real treat. A modified American plan is required for all guests. A coat and tie are standard attire for gentlemen at dinner in the main dining room.

The main dining room serves breakfast and six-course dinners; for a la carte dining April through October, the Tavern Room and Lounge provides a sophisticated setting. Sam Snead's at the Golf Club and Slammin' Sammy offer dining and entertainment during the summer season. At these spots diners enjoy views of the beautiful golf courses. Drapers Cafe—especially popular for its homemade ice cream—is convenient for light meals, snacks, and pastries throughout the day. Afternoon tea is served daily with musical accompaniment. In the elegant and warm Old White Club, guests gather at 5:00 P.M. for cocktails and complimentary hors d'oeuvres and later for music and dancing until closing.

Children's World: From Memorial Day through Labor Day and at the holiday times of Thanksgiving, Christmas, and Easter, the children's program more than fills the days of three- to twelve-year-olds. During the summer, experienced counselors direct arts and crafts, picnics, nature hikes, croquet, shuffleboard, swimming, and games. Older children (six to twelve years) have tennis and golf instruction as well. The fee is $45 a day (10:00 A.M. to 4:00 P.M.) for your first child and $35 a day for each additional child.

From 6:30 to 10:00 P.M., children ages six to twelve years old can join their counselors for dinner and an evening bowling or going to the movies. So it's possible for grown-ups to arrange an evening or two for wining and dining. Baby-sitting services for younger children are also available at an average hourly rate of $5.00.

Recreation: Avid golf and tennis players are well served at The Greenbrier. The Allegheny hills provide the beauty and the challenge of three eighteen-hole championship golf courses, one of which was redesigned in 1979 by Jack Nicklaus. The Greenbrier Sam Snead Golf Academy provides golfers of all skill levels the opportunity to improve their game. The academy provides professional teaching staff and state-of-the-art equipment and services.

Of the twenty tennis courts, fifteen are outdoors and five are indoors. The staff at the tennis pro shop can assist in finding partners. You may also confront the idiosyncrasies of your swing during instructional videotaped replays of your performance.

Kate's Mountain is the picturesque site of the Gun Club, with its four trap and skeet fields. Group tournaments can be organized, or perhaps you'll take in the action from the sidelines in the Clubhouse lounge.

Fishing enthusiasts head for the well-stocked streams and lakes, while swimmers can work out in the indoor or outdoor pool or relax poolside. An exercise room is adjacent to the indoor swimming pool. The bowling center (eight lanes), table tennis, horseback riding, shuffleboard, horseshoes, croquet, bicycling, carriage rides, and movies offer additional diversions. The five hiking trails are graded by length and rise in elevation. One of the two jogging trails features twelve exercise stations. Winter sports include cross-country skiing and sleigh rides. Downhill skiing is ninety minutes away at the Snowshoe Ski Resort.

And when the body wearies and the spirits droop, the only respectable place to be is the Spa, which pampers guests with mineral baths, massage, steam, and sauna facilities. It was the sulfur water with its medicinal and recuperative powers that first attracted visitors to this region. For shoppers a fine selection of fashions, jewelry, handcrafts, and gifts is presented in the Gallery of Shops. ≈≈≈

The Grove Park Inn Resort

290 Macon Avenue
Asheville, North Carolina 28804-3799
(704) 252–2711, (800) 438–5800
E-mail: groveparkinn.com
Web site: www.groveparkinn.com

The scenery and climate of the Blue Ridge Mountains have long attracted visitors to Asheville. The Grove Park Inn, located on the western slope of Sunset Mountain, opened its doors to guests in 1913 and gives a feeling of pure country in the midst of the city, with grand vistas of mountains and green golf courses. Built of granite from the nearby mountains and dedicated to preserving a gracious turn-of-the-century atmosphere, the inn was named to the National Register of Historic Places in 1973. Its guest list over the years reads somewhat like a Who's Who: Thomas Edison, Henry Ford, Woodrow Wilson, Enrico Caruso, Béla Bartók, and President and Mrs. Franklin Roosevelt. History buffs will have a fine time wondering which room General Pershing slept in or if F. Scott Fitzgerald sat by the fireplace in the Great Hall sipping an after-dinner brandy. A fireplace there, by the way, is so huge that an adult can walk into it!

The resort's country club (originally the Swannanoa Hunt Club that began in 1893) and the Inn were renovated in the late 1980s. Two wings, which

Photo courtesy of The Grove Park Inn Resort

complement the architectural style and materials of the main building, were added. The four-diamond, four-star Grove Park Inn is open year-round.

Accommodations: Both the historic main inn and the wings house guest rooms; those offering panoramic mountain views enchant many a guest. There are twelve suites and an exclusive club floor if your entourage warrants the space or additional amenities. In the regular rooms you can request a small refrigerator to keep children's drinks and snacks chilled and close at hand. During the low season, from January to April, the deluxe room rate is $149 a night in the main inn and $159 in the wings per double room. In the high season a deluxe double room is $200 in the main inn and $220 in the wings per night. Children under sixteen stay free in their parents' room; cribs and rollaway beds are available at no cost.

Dining: A full range of refreshments, from snacks and sandwiches to full-course meals, is offered. In the Blue Ridge Dining Room, buffet and table d'hôte meals are served. At the Sunset Terrace enjoy mountain views from the veranda along with fine Continental cuisine. The Carolina Cafe fills the bill for early lunches or late-afternoon snacks; it, too, attracts guests with its lovely views. For a change of pace, sample the gourmet cuisine at Horizons, a four-diamond-rated restaurant. In the evening you can enjoy your favorite beverage in the Great Hall Bar or take in the entertainment at Elaine's Nightclub (weekends).

Children's World: The inn organizes children's activities throughout the year, tailor-made to the number of children visiting the hotel, for ages three to twelve years. The program is most active from Memorial Day to Labor Day, when a large number of families are vacationing at The Grove Park Inn.

From May through Labor Day, the resort offers Operation Kid-Nap, Monday through Saturday from 9:00 A.M. to 4:00 P.M. Saturday Operation Kid-Nap is offered year-round. The $27 fee includes lunch and a snack plus activities such as sports, arts and crafts, nature hikes, and swimming (yes, there is an indoor pool). Monday through Thursday, 6:00 to 9:00 P.M. during the summer, a Dinner Club offers dinner and great activities for kids (and a chance for Mom and Dad to dine alone) for only $20. Kid's Night Out is a year-round program, held on Friday and Saturday nights from 6:00 to 10:30 P.M., which costs $25. If you prefer, the concierge desk will provide a list of individual baby-sitters, with varying fees.

Recreation: An eighteen-hole Donald Ross championship golf course meanders down the gentle mountain slope. Practice your backhand on one of the nine tennis courts (six outdoors, three indoors). The staff in the tennis and golf pro shops can assist you with your playing and fashion needs. An indoor Sports Center has racquetball, squash, and tennis courts; whirlpool; weight and exercise rooms; saunas; massages; and a fully equipped aerobics room with professionally taught classes. There are also indoor and outdoor pools available for hotel guests. But don't forget to take a walk down the garden paths and nature trails (also suitable when the urge to jog hits you).

Nearby you can explore the lake or try your hand at fishing, horseback riding, cycling, mountain biking, white-water rafting, ballooning, or llama trekking. In the winter a day of skiing (cross-country and downhill) is a popular excursion. For souvenirs you'll discover the six gift shops at the resort as well as many crafts shops and potteries in the area. The Biltmore Estate is only 8 miles from the inn; an afternoon can be well spent discovering the art, antiques, winery, and formal gardens of this magnificent old estate. ≋≋

High Hampton Inn & Country Club

P.O. Box 338
Highway 107
Cashiers, North Carolina 28717
(704) 743–2411, (800) 334–2551
Web site: www.highhamptoninn.com

The verdant Blue Ridge Mountains provide a beautiful setting, and High Hampton Inn, located in the Cashiers Valley at an altitude of 3,600 feet, allows its guests an escape to clean, crisp air, clear mountain lakes, and tall pine trees. Some people like the ambience of a country inn—quiet, friendly, with rustic accommodations and good home-style cooking. Others like the atmosphere of a resort, with lots of activities and events and busy days and nights. Happily, High Hampton has managed to blend the best of both these worlds. Roam over the 1,400 acres and explore the beauties of nature in the southwest corner of North Carolina. Dating from the mid-nineteenth century, High Hampton was once the summer home of Confederate General Wade Hampton and remained in the Hampton family until the 1920s.

For more than seventy-eight years, under the continuing ownership of the McKee family, the inn has welcomed guests to an informal atmosphere for golf, tennis, swimming, fishing, and simple relaxing. The architecture of the inn is charming and rustic, blending with the natural surroundings. The wide porches filled with plants and the lobby's stone chimney with four fireplaces hint at the warmth and friendly spirit within. The inn is open only from mid-April to mid-November, with a famous Thanksgiving Houseparty to close the season.

Accommodations: The 119 rooms at the inn (some of which are suites) are simple, warm, and rustic; the knotty pine walls and mountain-style furniture echo the landscape and the crafts of the region. Many of the rooms have very pleasant

Photo copyright © 1991 by Lavidge & Associates, courtesy of High Hampton Inn & Country Club

views of the grounds. Based on a full American plan, daily rates are $89 to $100 per person midweek, $95 to $114 on Friday and Saturday; children under six are $49, while older children are $67. Cribs are available for infants and toddlers at no charge. A number of privately owned homes are also available; these are fully equipped, with fireplace, deck, laundry, and kitchen. Choose from two to four bedrooms with no meals, but with daily maid service, for $247 to $456 a day. If you choose not to cook, a full American plan is available for $40 per person per day, or $20 for children under six years. Golf package plans are offered as well.

Dining: The one dining room at the inn specializes in regional Southern cooking, and service is buffet style. Imagine down-home favorites like country ham, cream of peanut soup, homemade biscuits, and vegetables fresh from the garden. Afternoon tea is served daily in the lobby. Coats and ties are standard attire for men in the evening, as High Hampton clings to traditional ways.

Wine and beer only are served in the dining room, but mixed drinks are served at the Rock Mountain Tavern, a popular spot to gather, listen to music, meet other guests, and line up partners for bridge or tennis. Movies, lobby games, bridge, and mountain hayrides fill the evening. Small groups of guests may gather on porches to compare notes, sip their own drinks, and talk about the day.

Children's World: Kids have their own building at High Hampton, called Noah's Ark, where youngsters ages five to twelve meet with counselors for daily activities such as arts and crafts, games, tennis, nature studies, and hiking.

Offered from June 1 through Labor Day, the program runs from 9:00 A.M. to 2:00 P.M. and includes lunch. After a free afternoon children can rejoin their group at 6:00 P.M. for dinner (sometimes a hayride and cookout!) and games, movies, and stories until 9:00 P.M. The fee is $3.00 an hour per child. For wee ones and the hours after 9:00 P.M., baby-sitters are available.

The Play Group, for ages two through four, is a fun experience where little ones do donkey-cart rides, bubble blowing, games, and crafts. The ratio of children to counselors is small, with lots of attention for each child.

While there's no swimming pool, a restricted, shallow area of the lake with a sandy beach is especially designed for young children. The area includes a toddlers' playhouse, swings, seesaw, and jungle gym, keeping the little ones amused for hours.

Rather than a teen club, High Hampton has The Gathering Place for Young Adults. Here, the next generation can gather to socialize and enjoy the pool table, table tennis, and video games. Outdoor activities such as volleyball, boating excursions, and picnics or mountain hikes are planned and enjoyed by all.

Recreation: The mountain terrain and picturesque scenery make golf a challenge and a pleasure. The eighteen-hole course, designed by George Cobb, is carved on a gently rolling plateau, skirting lakes and weaving through white pine and hemlock. There are two putting greens and a practice range; lessons are available. A dining facility, The Overlook Cafe, is next to the pro shop. It features light lunches and snacks, with continental breakfast for early birds.

The tennis center encompasses six outdoor courts, a pro shop, and a practice area; clinics and private lessons are offered. You pay court fees and greens fees unless you are on a four- or seven-day golf or tennis package.

There are three mountain lakes but the thirty-five-acre Hampton Lake is the center of activity, where paddleboats, canoes, rowboats, and sailboats can be rented. These clear waters are not just for invigorating swims and peaceful excursions. When the fishing mood strikes, you'll be happy to know that one of the lakes has rainbow and brook trout; bass and bream can also be lured from the waters.

Discover the rich natural beauty of these surroundings on one of the eight hiking trails. Or take to the mountain trails—in one and a half hours you can climb to the 4,618-foot summit of Chimney Rock for absolutely spectacular views. Take the ten-station Fitness Trail to the base of Rock Mountain. In a more leisurely manner, lawn sports such as badminton, croquet, shuffleboard, and archery may attract you, or maybe you'll be drawn to the gardens for a stroll among the dahlias, mountain laurel, rhododendron, and azaleas.

The inn occasionally holds workshops in such diverse areas as bridge, fly-fishing, quilting, watercolor painting, and investments—what a pleasant way to glean helpful hints on a variety of topics! While proud of its facilities, the High Hampton Inn mostly boasts of its friendly atmosphere, its low-key pace, and the serenity and beauty of its natural setting. It is also proud that High Hampton "is not for everyone." But those who stay return year after year, and their children bring their own children. It's that kind of place. ≋

The Homestead

Hot Springs, Virginia 24445
(540) 839–1766, (800) 838–1766

A few classic institutions in the United States have captured the attention of vacationers for many years. With all its charm and grace, The Homestead ranks as one of these. Its fascinating history has roots in the 1700s, yet The Homestead has moved into this century with style, preserving an atmosphere of friendly elegance. As with several fine old resorts in this country, the medicinal quality of mineral springs first attracted people to the site of The Homestead. While The Spa is still a captivating diversion of many guests, many recreational facilities have been developed over the years, with golf being the premier sport here.

The current hotel was built in 1902, with additions continuing into the late 1920s. Despite those three decades of construction, The Homestead is a cohesive, majestic structure of red brick and white columns in Georgian style. At an elevation of 2,300 feet, the estate sprawls over 15,000 acres (yes—15,000!) of the Allegheny Mountains in western Virginia. It is open year-round.

Accommodations: The Homestead boasts more than 500 bright and spacious rooms. Sizes vary from traditional rooms to parlor rooms and suites; the rate is determined by the size of the room and its location. Based on a modified American plan, the rate for a standard double room during the April through October season is $220 to $272 per person per day. The rates are slightly lower November through March, except during the Thanksgiving and Christmas holiday seasons. Children over five sharing a room with their parents are extra; there is no charge for children under five and no additional charge for cribs and rollaways. The modified American plan rates include the room, two meals a day, swimming, afternoon tea, evening movies, and use of the supervised children's playground. Separate fees are charged for all other activities.

Open in fall 2001, the new ballroom expansion and meetings facility features a 14,000-square-foot ballroom, complete with an additional 6,000 square feet of pre-function space, composed of a reception area and spacious outdoor ter-

race. Dressed in the gracious decor that has attracted visitors to The Homestead since its beginnings in 1766, the new ballroom features classical columns and chandeliers, adding a touch of splendor and elegance to the traditional wood paneling and floors. The new center opens up to a magnificent setting of the surrounding Allegheny Mountains through its floor-to-ceiling windows, affording guests a memorable vista.

Dining: Dining at The Homestead is special. Executive chef Albert Schnarwyler ensures that every meal is a memorable experience. Imagine baked apples and kippered herring for breakfast; consider lunches and dinners that feature local favorites such as Smithfield ham, rainbow trout from nearby mountain streams, and fresh turnip greens, as well as fine international cuisine. A selection that includes bluepoint oysters, grilled Dover sole with almonds, roast baby pheasant, and tournedos Rossini makes for difficult decisions; it's almost necessary to spend extended time at The Homestead just to sample the specialties. The sublime creations of pastries, sorbets, and fresh fruit tarts should not be missed.

The dining room is open year-round. During the April through October season, the 1766 Grille serves dinner. Golfers enjoy lunch at the Cascades Club restaurant, and Sam Snead's Tavern is yet another alternative for dinner. Casual resort wear is expected for lunch in the dining room, and coats and ties are required for gentlemen in the evening. Picnic lunches can also be prepared if you choose to spend the day outdoors in the wooded mountains.

A time-honored custom at The Homestead is Afternoon Tea, served daily at 4:00 P.M. in the Great Hall. In an elegant setting graced by chandeliers and Corinthian columns, you can relax to soft piano music while sipping tea.

Children's World: Although The Homestead has traditionally catered to an older set, supervised children's activities are now offered year-round. Children are divided into groups—ages three to twelve years—to enjoy an active sports program of swimming, tennis, fishing, nature walks, and visits to the stables. The outdoor playground has been completely renovated, and children have their own fishing pond—great for kids of all ages. If bad weather precludes outdoor play, children move inside the KidsClub for creative endeavors, stories, and educational games. The program operates Monday through Saturday from 9:00 A.M. to 4:00 P.M., and Sunday from 9:00 A.M. to 1:00 P.M. The cost is $60 for a full day with lunch; $40 for a half day with lunch.

During the winter children can learn to ski on The Homestead trails through Bunny School. Individual baby-sitters can be arranged for at any time (with proper advance notice).

Recreation: Even golf and tennis have hundred-year-old histories at The Homestead. There are three eighteen-hole golf courses, and the fact that native son Sam Snead started his golfing career here adds a certain panache to the atmosphere and lends credence to the caliber of play. The Old Course was opened in 1892 and revamped in the 1920s when a second course, the Cascades, was added. Robert Trent Jones designed the third course, the Lower Cascades, which opened in 1963. All three courses weave through a picturesque wooded landscape. With a putting green, a practice fairway, a pro shop, and lessons available, you have all the necessary ingredients to improve your game.

Tennis also got under way here in 1892. Today The Homestead has eight courts, including four Har-Tru courts and four all-weather courts. Two tiers of courts are laid out to give your game privacy plus a spectacular view of The Homestead tower and the mountain valley. Tennis lessons can be scheduled, and the tennis shop is well equipped.

The facilities at The Spa include massage, aromatherapy, mineral baths, aerobics classes, and indoor and outdoor swimming pools. There may be no proven miraculous powers in the famous mineral waters, but the benefits of a spa regimen to both body and spirit are not questioned. The Spa Salon offers complete hairstyling.

For fans of trap and skeet, there are four fields; instruction is offered so that even novices can try this sport. Other outdoor sports include falconry, horseback riding in the wooded countryside, trout fishing in the Cascades Stream, and hiking in the mountains. Or you may prefer to enjoy the scenery during a carriage ride. You might take your skills indoors to the eight bowling lanes. Or you might opt for table tennis, billiards, or card and board games. In the evenings go dancing or take in a movie.

Winter sports are limited, but The Homestead does have nine downhill ski runs, open mid-December through March. With a vertical drop of just 700 feet, it cannot offer the diversity and challenge that a good skier seeks, but it may be a fun place for kids to learn, and it does provide an added dimension to a winter vacation. Near the lodge, which houses a restaurant, the ski school, and ski shops, is an Olympic-size skating rink; skating lessons are offered. Cross-country skiers can explore acres of mountain meadows and trails, weather permitting, of course. ≈≈≈

Kiawah Island Resorts

12 Kiawah Beach Drive
Kiawah Island, South Carolina 29455
(803) 768–2121, (800) 654–2924; (800) 845–2471 (South Carolina)

In climate and scenery, the islands off the coast of the Carolinas offer some of the finest resort living. At Kiawah Island Resorts the beauty of the natural setting has been carefully respected, while man-made amenities have been added to provide visitors with the best in comfort, relaxation, recreation, and fun. An island with 10 miles of beach on the Atlantic Ocean, Kiawah is actually two resort villages, each with its own lodging and recreational facilities; a shuttle bus connects the villages.

West Beach Village (which dates from 1976) consists of the Kiawah Island Inn, condominiums, restaurants, a racquet club, shops, pools, and a golf course. At East Beach Village (the younger by five years), there are condominiums, restaurants, shops, a golf course, a tennis club, and Night Heron Park, a twenty-one-acre recreation area that encompasses a pool, lake, playgrounds, and picnic sites.

All these conveniences and amenities, and yet you still have the opportunity to feel close to nature, as only half the land will ever be developed. The sound ecological planning at Kiawah has preserved the lagoons and marshes and ensured homes for deer, raccoon, egrets, and brown pelicans; you might even get to see a loggerhead sea turtle, alligators, dolphins, or an eagle. The drive from the Charleston Airport is about forty-five minutes. As you enter the main gates to Kiawah, you'll be given a car registration pass that reads "Please respect the wildlife that inhabits Kiawah Island. Alligators are potentially dangerous and extremely fast. They should never be fed or teased in any way." When you see alligators plying the lagoon waters, you'll understand the seriousness of this warning.

Accommodations: The Kiawah Island Inn, located in West Beach Village, is the right choice for those who want to be pampered. The 150 rooms, distributed among four lodges, all have private balconies overlooking the ocean, pools, lagoons, or picturesque wooded areas; the services and conveniences are typical of a fine resort hotel.

The condominium villas, cedar-shingled or natural-wood frame structures, are dispersed throughout the island in different settings appealing to all different interests. You may choose one with an ocean view or one next door to the tennis courts, one alongside the lush green fairways of a golf course, one on a lake, or one nestled among oaks and hickories and sweet gum trees. These one- to four-bedroom units have well-equipped kitchens, and most of them have sundecks or screened porches—terrific spots for having breakfast or just taking in the views. One- to seven-bedroom luxury homes are also available.

Rates vary depending on the season; the inn ranges from $89 to $259 nightly and one-bedroom villas are $75 to $250. Weekly rates for villas are $579 to $2,099. Cribs are free at the inn, $15 per day in the villas; rollaways are $15 at the inn and $25 in the villas.

Dining: You'll never have a problem here; there are enough restaurants to meet varied moods and tastes. Enjoy a spectacular view of the ocean at The Atlantic Room, located at the inn. The menu features a wide variety of deep-ocean fish and shellfish caught daily.

The West Beach Cafe and Bar is a casual dining spot in the Shops at the Kiawah Island Inn; it's open for lunch and dinner and features tempting focaccia-

Photo courtesy of Kiawah Island

crust pizzas and sandwiches to please any palate. Nearby is Scooper's, where the ice cream and pastries are hard to resist (who can pass up an ice cream flavor called Mississippi Mud?). Beside the inn's pool, Sundancer's serves salads, burgers, and other light fare for lunch and supper. At East Beach Village the restaurant is The Village Bistro, an "island bistro" featuring New Southern cuisine. Both the Ocean Course and Osprey Point clubhouses are home to excellent restaurants. The dining room at Osprey Point carries AAA's four-diamond rating.

On Monday and most Wednesday evenings families head to Mingo Point on the Kiawah River for an outdoor barbecue and oyster roast, followed by the down-home music of a bluegrass band. For evening cocktails and musical entertainment, try the Charleston Bar at the Inn or Sundancer's, popular places to sip an old favorite or an exotic tropical drink. A casual market is located in East Beach, offering a variety of quick meals.

Children's World: From early May through September and at Thanksgiving, Christmas, New Year's, and Easter, children and parents alike find Kiawah Island Resorts the perfect destination for a family vacation.

Energetic college students with training in sports and recreation supervise young visitors in four different age groups in activities designed to ensure happy, fun-filled days. In fact, there's much more to do than we have room to outline. In summer Kamp Kiawah is in swing from 9:00 A.M. to 4:30 P.M. Monday through Friday. The cost is $35.00 (half days are available); lunch is an extra $5.00. Divided into three groups—three to four years, five to seven years, and eight to twelve years—kids enjoy swimming, treasure hunts, crabbing, storytime, and crafts. Kids Nature Club is a special program for eight- to fourteen-year-olds that is limited to twelve participants. Twice-weekly three-hour excursions with a staff naturalist allow them to have a hands-on, fun experience with nature. Ocean seining with a huge 40-foot net, canoe trips through the marshes, pond exploration, night walks on the beach, bird-watching—with more than 10,000 acres of marshland and five staff naturalists, the possibilities go on and on. Costs range from $3.00 to $15.00.

Discovery Series, a free weekly program, features speakers accompanied by live snakes or alligators, storytellers, and more. Kiawah has found a successful blend of activities that includes teenagers' favorite things: sports, music, food, and loose structure. Volleyball and basketball tournaments, "teen splash" (pool time only for them), T-shirt graffiti, and a Friday-night dance with DJ are just a sample of the options.

Children also enjoy the playgrounds filled with wooden climbing equipment, swings, and slides; the largest one at Night Heron Park is built in and among the trees, hardly disturbing the natural vegetation. The Heron Park Center features video games, live animals, and nature wear and gear, as well as a recreation concierge.

When you want to be together and join other families, afternoon and evening hours are filled with bingo, games, nature films, family movies, and cookouts; most of these activities are free. Particularly fun is the "dive-in movie"—movies shown at the pool, with swimming allowed. Baby-sitters are available when you want to indulge in a strictly grown-up evening.

Recreation: With five excellent eighteen-hole championship golf courses, golfers think they've discovered a little bit of paradise at Kiawah. Host site of the 1991 Ryder Cup and 1997 World Cup of Golf, The Ocean Course, designed by Pete Dye, is known worldwide. The Cougar Point Golf Course was designed by Gary Player, the Turtle Point Golf Course by Jack Nicklaus, the Osprey Point Golf Course by Tom Fazio, and Oak Point by Clyde Johnston; talent like this ensures challenge in a beautiful natural setting. You can enroll in group or private lessons or in a clinic, then practice newly acquired skills on the driving ranges and putting greens. The pro shops are well stocked with equipment, apparel, and accessories to enhance your game.

For tennis enthusiasts the West Beach Tennis Club offers sixteen courts; the East Beach Tennis Club has twelve courts and a ball machine. Add a practice alley, resident pros, clinics, and group and private lessons and you have every opportunity to improve your game. Kiawah has been rated the fifth-best tennis resort in the nation by *Tennis* magazine. It offers free tennis clinics and one hour of free tennis daily to guests.

Swimmers take to the ocean from April through October or dip into one of the three pools at the inn (one for adults only, one for the family, and one a children's pool). Two 25-meter pools are located in Night Heron Park and East Beach Tennis Club. You can sign up for swimming lessons for yourself or your child (even an infant). Other water sports, such as sailing, canoeing, and sailboarding, are also popular.

Bicyclists have more than 10 miles of hard-packed beach and 30 miles of paved trails to explore (rentals, many with baby seats, are available). Joggers find a good workout on the 1.1-mile parcourse fitness trail with twenty exercise stations. Try your luck fishing in the lake or creek and surf casting in the ocean, or introduce your child to the fun of crabbing, where an old chicken neck can net beautiful blue-legged crabs. Adult exercise classes (aerobics and water exercise) are offered weekdays during the summer. Nature lovers can participate in numerous expeditions into wilderness areas and river tours for a close look at the Low-Country wildlife and vegetation.

If shopping entices you, The Shops at the Kiawah Island Inn and the Town Center at East Beach Village have stores offering clothing, books, stationery, games, toys, jewelry, and gifts. And nearby Charleston (only 21 miles away) can charm you with historic tours and antiques shopping. With all it places at your disposal, Kiawah may tempt you back for many return visits. ≋

Seabrook Island Resort

1002 Landfall Way
Seabrook Island, South Carolina 29455
(843) 768–1000, (800) 845–2475
E-mail: resort@charleston.net
Web site: www.discoverseabrook.com

Sunshine and sandy beaches; lazy strolls under moss-draped oaks, palmettos waving in the breeze; enough fresh crabs, shrimp, and oysters to make your mouth water; golf, tennis, horseback riding, marina, fitness center, and water sports—is this a little bit of paradise? Visitors to Seabrook believe so. All this is only about thirty minutes from beautiful, historic Charleston; it almost seems as though you can have your cake and eat it too. A vacation at Seabrook is not exclusively a golfing trip or just an opportunity to develop a spectacular tan. You can go crabbing, ride horses, or join an exercise class in the morning, then discover the history and charm of Charleston in the afternoon. Take a house tour, visit nearby plantations, or go shopping, then return to the resort for an evening of dining and entertainment. Activities and events for every member of

Photo courtesy of Seabrook Island Resort

the family support Seabrook's "something for everyone" philosophy. The resort is open year-round.

Accommodations: The one- to three-bedroom villas—all with fully equipped kitchens, many with sundecks or balconies—are distributed throughout the 2,200 acres of Seabrook Island property. Some are oceanside, with expansive views of the Atlantic and close to the Beach Club, some line the scenic fairways of the golf courses, and some overlook the racquet club, marshlands, and tidal creeks. Rates depend on size, location, and time of year. During low season, from November through early March, villa rates are $110 to $245. The weeks around Easter and mid-June through mid-August are high season, at $175 to $500, and the shoulder season ranges from $120 to $475. Rates are for villa accommodations only; most recreational activities have separate charges. Weekly rates (for five to seven nights) provide a savings, as do tennis, golf, honeymoon, or getaway packages. A family recreation package during June, July, and August is a good value, with 20 percent discounts on most things, including golf.

Dining: With three restaurants, you'll have no trouble finding the cuisine and atmosphere to satisfy your taste and whim. The Island House Restaurant is elegant and offers traditional Southern cuisine and tempting seafood specialties. Here you might choose a sweet-potato soufflé or prawns stuffed with crabmeat. Bohickets Restaurant is next door, with equally good food in a more casual atmosphere. For steak and seafood and an ocean view, head to the Sea-view Restaurant, more informal than the Island House and more family oriented. Poolside cookouts are offered daily during the weeks surrounding Easter and throughout the summer season. A friendly atmosphere in which to sip a drink and discuss the day's events is provided at the poolside Pelicans Nest, Half Shell Lounge, and Bohickets Lounge. Island House and Bohickets are open year-round; the others are seasonal.

Children's World: From Memorial Day to Labor Day, kids and teens have their own Monday-to-Friday Kids Club recreation program. Children ages three to eleven meet from 9:00 A.M. to 4:00 P.M. in the Kids Club, where activities include golf and tennis clinics, pony rides, crabbing adventures, swimming, treasure hunts, nature hikes, puppet shows, storytelling, and arts and crafts. The cost is $35 for a full day, or $20 per half day.

Older children from twelve to nineteen are invited to the basketball and volleyball units by day and to the Recreation Pavilion every night from 8:00 to 11:00 P.M. This is their own time for video games, pool, table tennis, Foosball, air hockey, and socializing. Special theme parties, teen casino night, and even teen cruises are planned. Special nights are also planned for the entire family at a small cost.

The fun keeps on rolling at holiday times like Christmas, Thanksgiving, and Easter. Added to the regular activities may be Christmas caroling and a visit from

Santa, The Little Pilgrims Program, or an Easter decorations crafts class and an Easter egg hunt. A day of adventures will give your child fond memories for years to come. With all of this, normal baby-sitters may seem a bit of a letdown, but they are available.

Recreation: Golfing's fine in the Carolinas, and Seabrook has two vastly different eighteen-hole courses. Crooked Oaks was designed by Robert Trent Jones Sr.; it meanders through majestic oaks and dips along the sea marshes. Ocean Winds, designed by Willard Byrd, catches some of the tricky ocean breezes that make the play challenging and interesting. A fine teaching staff can help you smooth out the rough spots of your game, and the pro shop can fill in the gaps for clothing, equipment, and accessories.

Enjoy one of fifteen clay tennis courts at the Raquet Club. The Raquet Club offers a pro shop and a staff of pros who can do wonders for your backhand in individual or group lessons, camps, and clinics.

With 3½ miles of glorious ocean beach, you might suspect that water sports tempt many visitors here. There are sunbathing, swimming, ocean fishing, and shelling. Canter along the beach at the edge of the surf or take a leisurely ride through the forests—both are possible at Seabrook, one of the few resorts with an on-site Equestrian Center. The center offers trained instructors who can give you tips to improve your technique. Six swimming pools more than accommodate serious swimmers and sun lovers. With their palm trees, gardens, and lovely surroundings, they also charm serious loungers in for just a quick splash. Perhaps you don't want to sing for your supper, but if you want to *catch* your supper, try fishing (in the ocean or the creeks) or crabbing and shrimping in the tidal marshes. Bicycle along the island's 10 miles of roads—many rental bikes come equipped with baby seats—or join the current craze for in-line skating.

The Recreation Pavilion takes care of a lot of your needs (rental beach chairs, in-line skates, bikes, and fishing and crabbing equipment) and is the focus of the Family Fun Program—activities that all the family members can enjoy together, like nature walks, family games, cookouts, bingo, and water volleyball. You may even challenge your child to an evening of video games.

Within 1 mile of Seabrook's gate, enjoy the Bohicket Marina for chartered deep-sea fishing, creek fishing, and three family-style restaurants and shops. For the essentials and the fun of shopping, Seabrook has several stores: the Village Market for groceries; the Seabrook Shoppe for gifts, clothing, souvenirs, and sundries; and the golf and tennis shops for the latest fashions and equipment. ≋

The Tides

Irvington, Virginia 22480
(804) 438–5000, (800) 2–4–TIDES

In eastern Virginia, peninsulas of land reach out like fingers between the many rivers heading into the Chesapeake. It is a region steeped in history, from the early seventeenth-century settlements of Jamestown and Yorktown to the family homestead of Robert E. Lee. Its people have always had close ties to the water, originally for commerce and travel and today for recreation.

The northernmost of these peninsulas, bounded by the Potomac River and the Rappahannock River, is known as the Northern Neck. On its southern shore, on one of the Rappahannock's inlets, sits The Tides Inn. The hotel is surrounded by water, and yachts literally dock in the front yard. A sense of happiness and pride permeates the resort. The Tides is small and very much a family affair. It emphasizes uncrowded luxury and informal elegance in a leisurely atmosphere that supports its motto: "The place where nice people meet."

Accommodations: With 121 rooms at the inn, almost all of them waterfront, you might choose a room in the main building or a semisuite (some with balconies) in the Windsor House or the Lancaster House. Cribs are available. Inn rates range from $178 in the main building to $960 for the Robert E. Lee Suite. Children under ten are free. The high season at The Tides is May to October; the inn is closed from January to April.

Dining: Breakfast and dinner are served in the main dining room. Breakfast is from 7:30 to 10:00 A.M., with an "early bird" continental breakfast or a "sleepyhead" breakfast later in the morning. Lunch can be taken in the main dining room, at the poolside Commodore's, at Cap'n B's on the Golden Eagle Golf Course, and on many days aboard the yacht *Miss Ann*. Imagine your fun and pleasure as you cruise the coves and waterways while enjoying a gourmet meal. Cap'n B's is a popular spot even with nongolfers, as the 400 rolling acres with lovely lakes and unspoiled woodlands add an extra dimension of pleasure to your dining. Adjacent to the main dining room is the Chesapeake Club, where expansive views, music, and dancing can relax and entertain you. Dress is casual during the day, with jacket requested for gentlemen in public rooms during the evening.

Children's World: In addition to the beach and swimming pool, a grassy playground with slides, swings, climbing bars, and Chesapeake Bay Lighthouse attracts young guests. From Memorial Day to Labor Day, The Crab Net Kids children's program is in session Monday through Sunday, from 10:00 A.M. to 4:00 P.M., with lunch at the pool and swimming twice a day. All activities are covered for $20 per child, per day. Crafts and games, scavenger hunts, sand sculpting, bicycling, boating, and crabbing keep youngsters from four to twelve years old

busy. On Wednesday, Friday, and Saturday evenings from 6:00 to 9:00 P.M., children meet as a group for a "coketails and pizza party," followed by a movie. Baby-sitting is available at $7.50 an hour for one child; add $1.00 an hour for each additional child.

Recreation: With water on practically all sides of the inn, boating is a natural sport here. You can take off in a small craft like a sailboat, canoe, or paddleboat or check out the yacht program and cruise the creek, the river, and the bay. The weekly routine schedules varied yachts for luncheon cruises, cove cruises, and bayshore picnics. No additional fees are charged for use of the sailboats, paddleboats, and canoes, or for the yacht program. In fact, rates include almost all activities—tennis, nine-hole par-3 golf course, bicycles to explore scenic Irvington, evening music and dancing, and the fitness and health facility.

Golf is also available, with twenty-seven holes that skirt the waterways and dip back into the trees. A nine-hole executive course is on the inn's property. A challenging course with more hilly terrain is the championship Golden Eagle, 2½ miles from the inn.

Many of the ponds along the golf courses are well stocked for the fisherman who may also, in search of a saltwater catch, line up a trip with the dockmaster. A saltwater pool overlooks a small sandy beach, and table tennis, pool table, video arcade, croquet, and shuffleboard are available in the activities cottage. For your evening entertainment enjoy dancing, movies, bingo, or a pleasant stroll.

Nearby sight-seeing excursions lead to Stratford Hall Plantation (the birthplace of Robert E. Lee), Christ Church, and Epping Forest, where George Washington's mother lived. Colonial Williamsburg is just an hour and fifteen minutes away and makes a nice day excursion. ≋

Wild Dunes Resort

5757 Palm Boulevard
Isle of Palms, South Carolina 29451
(843) 886–6000, (800) 845–8880
E-mail: reservations@wilddunes.com
Web site: www.wilddunes.com

Have you ever seen a three-year-old scamper across a sandy beach to the ocean? A biker pedal down paths through the marshes? A fishing boat return to harbor after a successful day's mission? A sailboat catch the sun and the wind in one skillful motion? An ace serve zing across the net? Or a golf ball soar over the fairway and over grand oaks on its way to a perfectly manicured green? Wild Dunes can package all of these images into quite a family vacation for you.

Wild Dunes has garnered some of the best features of the Carolina coastal islands and wrapped them up into a fine year-round resort. It is recognized by *Better Homes and Gardens* as one of thirty "Favorite Family Resorts." This relaxed and gracious community occupies 1,600 acres of the northern part of the Isle of Palms, just thirty minutes from historic Charleston. Bounded by the Atlantic Ocean on the east and the Intracoastal Waterway on the west, Wild Dunes delights in mild temperatures, soft ocean breezes, and fresh salt air. Relax and rejuvenate your spirits here in South Carolina's Low Country.

Accommodations: Wild Dunes offers AAA four-diamond accommodations with the new Boardwalk Inn. The ninety-three-room inn is located in the heart of the resort. These luxurious accommodations provide amenities of the finest full-service hotels and access to world-class recreational facilities. Until mid-June and after Labor Day, daily rates for the Boardwalk Inn are $139 to $339. From mid-June until Labor Day, daily rates are $149 to $339. Wintertime (November to mid-March) nightly rates are $109 to $259. Rates are based on double occupancy. The one-, two-, and three-bedroom villas are grouped in two- to five-story buildings. Many are arranged along the beach, some border the tennis center, others look out on the fairways of the golf course, and still more enjoy the seclusion of the woods and marshland scenery. Inside decor ranges from dramatic, bold interiors to soft pastel furnishings that reflect nature's seaside

colors; a fully equipped kitchen is standard in every unit. Cribs can be provided for infants and toddlers.

The high season at Wild Dunes is mid-March through mid-November. Spring and fall rates for a one-bedroom villa range from $125 to $312; three-bedroom villas range from $213 to $458. From mid-June to mid-August rentals are on a weekly basis only, ranging from $1,404 for a two-bedroom near the beach to $3,420 for a four-bedroom oceanfront. Wintertime nightly rates are $105 to $215 for a one-bedroom and $145 to $325 for a three-bedroom.

Private homes are also available. The location of a rental property will determine the price; an oceanfront location commands the highest rate. Included with all rentals are local phone calls, on-property transportation, and one hour of tennis court time per bedroom per day. Golf, Town and Country, and Winter Extended Stay packages are available.

Dining: It is not surprising that seafood is highlighted on the menus of Wild Dunes' restaurants; gumbo and she-crab soup are favorite Low-Country dishes. But beef eaters can find tasty, tender selections here, too. With the opening of The Boardwalk Inn, Wild Dunes also gained a luxurious restaurant. The Sea Island Grill, serving breakfast, lunch, and dinner, features the freshest seafood available, prepared in a myriad of ways. Edgar's, located at the Links Clubhouse, features Southern cuisine; a children's menu is available. The Grand Pavilion, open only in summer, has early-twentieth-century architecture, an old-fashioned boardwalk, Coney Island–style food, and an airy gazebo. If you have a hunger attack on either golf course, you're in luck. Hot dogs, sandwiches, and drinks are to be found at the Half-Way House, on the Links, and on the Harbor Courses year-round. The Dunes Deli & Pizzeria features light fare for breakfast and lunch, as well as grocery items. At least twelve restaurants offer a variety of dining on nearby Sullivan's Island and the Isle of Palms.

Children's World: Ranked one of the top five by *Tennis* magazine for having the "Best Kids' Program," Wild Dunes knows just how to make your little ones' vacation special. Wild Dunes' summer program for kids runs from the end of May through Labor Day and is complimentary for guests. Toddler Time provides structured sessions with two full-time staff members. Parents are welcome to drop in, as kids enjoy tumbling, storytime, and arts and crafts. Babysitting is also available by the hour or day for a fee. Older children, from five to twelve years, are part of the Wild Adventure Club, held Monday through Friday from 9:00 A.M. to 4:00 P.M. Kids enjoy beach games, swimming, crabbing, scavenger hunts, putt-putt golf, and other "wild" adventures.

Li'l Dune Bug Club allows the kids (ages five to twelve) to leave the parents at home for a night out to play games, watch movies, and munch goodies. These sessions are held three days a week from 6:00 to 10:00 P.M.; the cost is $23 for the first child (the second is only $18), and kids get a T-shirt to wear and keep. Space is limited, so reserve in advance.

Activities for teens include beach volleyball, psychedelic tie-dye, dances, pizza parties, and cookouts. There is generally a $7.00 to $10.00 fee for materials, food, and so on. Video movies and special pool games allow teens to socialize and "hang out."

Recreation: A day of golf can begin on one of the two eighteen-hole golf courses designed by Tom Fazio. The older course, the Wild Dunes Links, is on the resort's ocean side and provides interesting play, with its many water hazards. Two holes edge by the sand dunes of the beach and are dramatically beautiful as well as challenging. The newer Harbor Course is across the island, surrounding the marina and harbor, and has its own fair share of demanding water hazards. A practice range, professional instruction, and a pro shop can help you over the hurdles with improved style and equipment.

In addition to golf, Wild Dunes offers tennis facilities, which have been ranked in the "Top 10 Greatest U.S. Tennis Resorts" by *Tennis* magazine. Guests receive one hour of free court time per day per bedroom. With a total of seventeen Har-Tru courts, including seven lighted for night play, tennis players might not want to go home. Tennis instruction can take the form of private or group lessons, clinics, and camps for a week, a weekend, or an intensive one-day session. Along with its well-stocked pro shop, this tennis facility leaves you very few excuses for not improving your game.

The IOP Marina has 200 boat slips. Here you can dock your own vessel or rent a boat for fishing in the Gulf Stream. Join a charter if you need an experienced captain's guidance in snagging the big ones, or finish off a day with a cruise in Charleston's harbor. Besides taking deep-sea excursions, fishermen can cast their lines in the ocean's surf, the creek, and the lagoons.

Swimmers have pools at most of the villa complexes, the main pool at the Swim Center, two oceanfront pools on the Grand Pavilion, the pool at the Boardwalk Inn, and, of course, the beautiful Atlantic Ocean. Joggers and bikers share the nature trails, where pine, oak, and magnolia trees grow; the hard-packed sand beach is also suitable for running and biking. Along the 2-mile stretch of beach, you'll find sunbathers, strollers, and seashell collectors, and just offshore, sailors and sailboarders. At the beachfront picnic area, the kids' playground consists of natural-wood climbing equipment under the trees. For a close look at the egrets, herons, and pelicans of Wild Dunes, take the canoe trip through the creeks and marshes.

Many family events, such as a sailing class, bingo, and an afternoon ice-cream party, are planned each week. Be aware, however, that there are charges for most of the activities. And when you decide to take a break from the fun and recreation, don't forget how close Charleston is. In a day of sight-seeing, you can enjoy a historic Charleston tour of antebellum houses, fine restaurants, and shopping for antiques or at more modern boutiques.

Nighttime comes alive at Wild Dunes. Featured entertainer Ronnie Johnson heats it up at Edgar's Bar five nights a week with his style mix of rock, country, and Jimmy Buffett. From mid-June to mid-August the resort features a Sunday welcome party, "Shaggin' at the Beach" on Tuesday and Friday, karaoke on Wednesday, and steel calypso music most afternoons. ≋

SOUTHEAST

Alabama

Florida

Georgia

Amelia Island Plantation

P.O. Box 3000
Amelia Island, Florida 32035-3000
(904) 261–6161, (800) 874–6878
Web site: www.aipfl.com

L ike many of its counterparts along the coasts of the Carolinas, Amelia Island Plantation is a well-planned and carefully executed development that combines resort living with an appreciation for natural beauty. Similarity to its sisters is no surprise, for this land was purchased in the late 1960s by Charles Fraser of Sea Pines in Hilton Head, one of the first resorts to blend nature's beauties with gracious amenities. In many ways Sea Pines set the standard for resort communities that followed.

Amelia Island Plantation, which opened in 1974, occupies 1,350 acres of the southernmost island in the Golden Isle chain along the Eastern Seaboard of the United States. Open year-round, it is on the coast of northeast Florida, about a forty-five-minute drive from Jacksonville. Besides palmettos and oak trees, a 4-mile sandy beach, marshlands, and lagoons, this corner of paradise is blessed with mild temperatures year-round and balmy ocean breezes. Amelia Island Resort is a two-time winner of *Family Circle* magazine's "Best Family Beach Resort" award.

Accommodations: You can lodge in oceanfront hotel rooms—many with private decks or balconies—or in a villa overlooking the ocean or a lagoon, bordering the tennis complex or one of the fairways of three golf courses. These one- to three-bedroom villas have complete kitchens; many have private patios, balconies, or screened porches. Architecturally, the multilevel accommodation buildings arranged throughout the property are of various contemporary styles, with stucco or natural-wood facades.

Rates depend on the size and location of the unit and on the number of people occupying it. For four people in a two-bedroom ocean-view villa, rates vary between $273 in winter, $459 in spring, and $408 in summer and fall. The off-ocean price range is $219 (winter), $358 (spring), and $309 (summer/fall). Cribs are provided for little ones at $10 per night or $40 per week (four to seven days). Weekly rates are available, and package plans such as six-day/five-night family vacations are offered. All lodgings are connected to the recreational and dining facilities via a complimentary shuttle bus.

Dining: When cooking in your villa seems just too strenuous after a day of sunbathing, gather the family at the Verandah in Racquet Park. Located in a building tucked among old oak trees, the dining room has large windows over-

Photo courtesy of Amelia Island Plantation

looking the tennis courts. Sample such fresh seafood from the Atlantic as sea bass, flounder, shrimp, and crab in the family-style atmosphere.

More elegant dining is available in the Amelia Inn dining room. With expansive views of the ocean, this restaurant features escargot, quail, and roast duck and desserts like Southern pecan pie. In addition to dinner, breakfast and a sumptuous brunch on Sundays are offered.

The Coop is a come-as-you-are breakfast and lunch spot where the menu includes salads and sandwiches, hamburgers and hot dogs. Also appropriate for breakfast and lunch is the Golf Shop Restaurant at Amelia Links or the Longpoint Clubhouse. At the Beach Club Grille, burgers, wings, and ribs are served; TVs add action to a meal. Seaside Sweets, at poolside (seasonally), will satisfy your sweet tooth, while the Dunes Club Bar serves light lunches and tropical drinks poolside (seasonally) between Sea and Turtle Dunes.

Children's World: Kids Camp Amelia children's program entertains kids three to twelve years old year-round. Activities include swimming, crabbing, and arts and crafts. Take nature walks and enjoy many activities with the resident naturalist. As additional activities are too numerous to mention, contact the resort directly for age, cost, and time specifications.

At Aury Island, a tree house and a dock for fishing and crabbing are reserved just for the twelve-and-under set. At the Beach Club little ones have their own wading pool and a playground filled with wooden climbing equipment. To find a baby-sitter, you can pick up a list of names and numbers at the main registration desk.

Recreation: The Amelia Links, thirty-six holes of golf designed by Pete Dye and Bobby Weed, offer variety in play, as each course has its own personality. Oak Marsh weaves through groves of oak, palmetto trees, and marshlands, while Ocean Links skirts the Atlantic Ocean, with five holes along the sand dunes and sea oats of the beach. The eighteen-hole Long Point Golf Course was designed by Tom Fazio. Lessons can be arranged through the pro shop, where you will also find equipment and fashions.

Racquet Park is well situated among beautiful live oaks, a lovely setting for twenty-one courts. Some are lighted for evening play. The site of the Bausch and Lomb Women's Championships, this tennis complex offers adult and junior clinics, ball machines for solo practice, and a pro shop for equipment and apparel.

Also part of Racquet Park is the Health and Fitness Center. Complete with racquetball, indoor heated lap pool, exercise equipment, steam room, sauna and whirlpool facilities, aerobics classes, and the soothing techniques of a masseuse, it fills the bill for a good workout or relaxing rejuvenation.

Swimmers can choose the ocean or pools for their hours of fun in the sun. In addition to the Olympic-size pool at the Beach Club, each of the groups of villas (except the Lagoon Villas) has a swimming pool—twenty-one pools in all.

Along the 4-mile beach, you can collect shells, sunbathe, play volleyball, ride horseback (the Seashore Stables are just 2 miles away), and fish in the surf for whiting, sea trout, and bluefish. Surrounding the island in bays and sounds and the Gulf Stream are tarpon, flounder, trout, redfish, red snapper, and king mackerel. The waters in this area give up some beautiful prizes, and for advice, insider's hints, tackle, and information on charters, head to the Amelia Angler.

Bicycle along 7 miles of trails (rental bikes with baby seats and children's bikes are available), jog along the wooded paths and down the beach, or maybe even challenge the kids to a half hour of video games at the Beach Club Game Room.

For an outing of a different sort, browse through The Shops at Amelia Island Plantation, or discover the Victorian district of Fernandina Beach at the north end of the island. The Amelia Island Plantation Resort Guide is worth checking upon your arrival; here you'll learn of classes, movies, hayrides, and cookouts. 〰〰

Bluewater Bay Resort

1950 Bluewater Boulevard
Niceville, Florida 32578
(850) 897–3613, (800) 874–2128
Web site: www.bwbresort.com

Imagine the serenity of a safe harbor, a lush wooded landscape bordering clear blue waters, a sunset over the bay, and a blue glow that settles over still waters and docked boats at dusk. You feel light-years away from the office, staff meetings, and business lunches. In northwest Florida, Bluewater Bay is nestled on the northern shore of Choctawhatchee Bay and can certainly provide that get-away-from-it-all feeling. You'll relax in the peaceful surroundings of Bluewater Bay, but you'll never be bored. The resort is open year-round.

Accommodations: The hotel accommodations overlook the marina at Ward's Cove and include one- and two-bedroom suites as well as the more standard single and double rooms. At the other end of the spectrum are the Villas of St. Andrews, freestanding homes with two and three bedrooms, tucked in among oak and magnolia trees. The name itself alludes to the fine old golf course in Scotland, so it's no surprise that from these homesites you have lovely views of the golf course.

In between these extremes, you may choose a Mediterranean-style town house on the water or surrounded by gardens, a bayside villa featuring one- and two-bedroom apartments, one of the golf villas bordering the first and second fairways, or a two- to three-bedroom patio home near the swim and tennis center.

Cribs are available for a nominal charge, and the rooms have refrigerators for your toddler's milk and juice as well as your own refreshments. Rates range from $65 to $165 a night during the low season (November through February) and from $85 to $225 a night in the high season. Weekly and monthly rates are also available.

Dining: The Clubhouse Restaurant serves breakfast, lunch, and dinner. Seafood from the local waters is always a good choice from the varied menu. Children have a special menu.

Children's World: In June and July the Golf Club at Bluewater Bay offers a Junior Golf Clinic to children ages nine through fifteen (call the Golf Shop at 850–897–3241 for dates and times or for more information). The price for the clinic is $50 per student. Each clinic consists of six one-hour sessions, a range card for the summer that allows students to purchase a bag of range balls for $1.00, and an end-of-the-clinic Golf Tournament and Cookout. Sign-up for the

Golf Shop begins on May 1; payment is due at the time of registration (telephone registrations cannot be accepted).

Recreation: Although the atmosphere is relaxing and laid-back, you'll never be wanting for something to do. The thirty-six-hole championship golf course shows the imprint of its designers, Tom Fazio and Jerry Pate. Respecting the natural setting, they've brought nature and the golfer together in a congenial blend. At the tennis center twelve of the nineteen courts are lighted for nighttime play. Investigate the tennis and golf pro shops for your equipment and fashion needs.

And if water sports are your true love, there are oh so many to entice you. Swim in one of four Olympic-size pools, or splash in the waters of the bay. The 120-slip marina provides full services for your days on the water. Bring your own boat, or rent a catamaran, sailboard, or powerboat. Line up a sportfishing charter to the nearby Gulf of Mexico, leisurely fish in the bay, join a canoe trip down the Blackwater River, or take in a round of shuffleboard. Whether you're active or relaxed, Bluewater Bay accommodates everyone from the young to the young at heart. ≋

The Breakers

One South County Road
Palm Beach, Florida 33480
(561) 655–6611, (888) BREAKERS
Web site: www.thebreakers.com

In the 1880s Henry Flagler, a railroad magnate and cofounder of Standard Oil, was advised to spend time in Florida for his health. From this happenstance evolved a world-class luxury resort. Flagler discovered the warm climate of the Atlantic Coast, was captivated by the scenery, expanded railroad lines down the Eastern seaboard, and set into motion the development of Palm Beach as a winter playground of the wealthy.

The original Palm Beach Inn, built in 1896, was destroyed by fire in 1903. A second hotel, The Breakers, also succumbed to fire in 1925. Efforts to rebuild were begun immediately, and the new facility was opened at the end of 1926. The project was inspired by buildings of the Italian Renaissance; the era's artistic influence is evident in the loggias, courtyards, and hand-painted vaulted ceilings that adorn The Breakers. Open year-round, the hotel has completed a $100 million renovation and maintains its status as a Mobil five-star and AAA five-diamond resort. The grand beauty of this sparkling structure is perhaps met only by its natural setting on 140 acres of lush semitropical landscape bordering the blue-green waters of the Atlantic Ocean.

Photo courtesy of The Breakers

Accommodations: The 569 well-appointed and recently renovated guest rooms, including 45 suites, have views of the ocean, the well-tended formal gardens, or the golf course. During the summer (low season), from May 21 to October 31, rates for a single/double room are $260 to $460 per day; there is no charge for children under seventeen sharing a room with parents. Cribs and rollaways are provided at no charge. During the high season, from November to the end of May, rates range from $420 to $715 per day. Extraordinary holiday and vacation packages are also available.

For those who enjoy more privacy, there is the Flagler Club, The Breakers' concierge level located on the top two floors, with restricted access and additional guest services and amenities. Rates here are $460 to $715 (varies by season).

Dining: Dining at The Breakers can be as formal or as casual as one desires. An array of hot and cold breakfast items, as well as an a la carte menu, is available in the Circle Dining Room. Lunch is available at The Reef Bar, Palm Beach's only bar on the beach, offering refreshing libations and light snacks, and at the new Beach Club Restaurant, the heart of The Breakers' new spa, featuring classic luncheon fare and selections of spa cuisine. Lunch and dinner are served in The Seafood Bar, an upscale oceanfront raw bar reminiscent of the plantation homes of old Florida; or The Flagler Steakhouse, featuring oversize steaks and chops. For dinner only, try L'Escalier, with its French ambience; jackets are required and reservations are recommended. To say L'Escalier's wine list is exceptional is an understatement; it has earned *Wine Spectator*'s "Grand Award" for the past nineteen years. More than 500 vintages are represented in the display wine cellar.

At The Breakers restaurants, the under-elevens have their own menus. Children under three eat free, and everyone gets a special coloring book.

Children's World: With its broad spectrum of amenities, creative recreational programs and activities, and pervasive family-friendly mindset, The Breakers was deemed worthy of the "Premier Property Award" by the Resort and Commercial Recreation Association (RCRA). The resort has formed a Kids' Advisory Board, composed of eight young people, ages five to twelve, who meet quarterly to advise the resort on children's wants and needs. In response to this advice, there is a year-round children's program called Coconut Crew Camp.

Children ages three through twelve enjoy Coconut Crew Camp's year-round supervised activities, including active sports, contests, pool and beach games, arts and crafts, indoor games, seashell hunts, nature walks, lawn games, swimming, croquet, and more. Offered from 9:00 A.M. to 12:30 P.M. ($40 per child, lunch included); or 12:30 to 3:00 P.M. ($25 per child).

Coconut Crew Summer Camp for children ages six through twelve offers an exciting list of events. Summer Camp takes place June through August, 9:00 A.M. to 3:00 P.M. Monday through Friday. The camp focuses on a new theme each week, incorporating field trips, afternoon swimming, professional instruction in golf and tennis, and more. The cost of the camp is $65 per day for hotel guests and includes lunch (some field trips may require an additional charge).

The agenda for all programs is relaxed and flexible, so your child has the freedom to choose only specific events or to stay with the group for longer periods. Baby-sitting is available around the clock.

Recreation: Allow yourself to be pampered; a staff of 2,000 people is dedicated to making a stay here memorable. Stroll through the beautiful gardens or the half mile of private beach, linger under the palm trees, relax on a patio surrounding a fountain, or indulge at the new Oceanfront Spa and Beach Club.

The award-winning Breakers Palm Beach now features a vintage golf experience, resulting from the recent renovation of its historic Ocean Course and the creation of a golf and tennis clubhouse designed in the grand "Old Florida" style. These elements have repositioned the resort in a new light among avid golfers and those travelers who simply enjoy golfing on vacation.

On par with the revitalized golf facilities are ten newly constructed tennis courts, all of which are lighted at night. Tennis fans will enjoy the spaciousness of the easily accessible clubhouse.

The Beach Club offers four pools, including a lap pool and children's pool, a Jacuzzi, and ten cabanas. The Spa at The Breakers features seventeen private treatment rooms, steam and sauna rooms, men's and ladies' lounges, a beauty salon, and an ocean-view fitness center.

Sunbathe beside the majestic Atlantic, or sip a tall, cool cocktail on the patio or at the Reef Bar. Bicycle or jog on the paths through the gardens, join a deep-sea fishing or fly-fishing excursion for an offshore adventure, go snorkeling, or sign up for scuba instruction. For periods when you are not feeling so energetic, play a game of shuffleboard, croquet, horseshoes, boccie ball, bridge, or backgammon. Other events throughout the week include exercise classes such as water aerobics, yoga, and Tai Chi, family movies, shopping at any of the resort's twelve boutiques, and historical tours. Add lectures, crafts, garden tours, concerts, shopping on the famous Worth Avenue, and cooking demonstrations and you'll have to stretch your vacation to fit it all in. ≈≈

Callaway Gardens

Pine Mountain, Georgia 31822
(706) 663–2281, (800) 225–5292
E-mail: info@callawaygardens.com
Web site: www.callawaygardens.com

C ason Callaway was a textile industrialist in Georgia. In the 1930s he became so enamored of the countryside around Pine Mountain that his life began to change. He turned from industry first to farming and then to gardening. He learned that the plumleaf azalea was peculiar to this area of Georgia, and he was determined to nurture it and share its beauty with others. He established the Ida Cason Callaway Foundation, in honor of his mother, and opened his gardens to the public in 1952. While the gardens remain the focal point of the setting, the resort has grown to include gracious lodging, pleasant restaurants, and sports activities ranging from golf and tennis to swimming and fishing. This naturally wooded and carefully cultivated land—14,000 acres of lakes, woodlands, and gardens—is located 70 miles south of Atlanta, in the Appalachian Mountain foothills of west Georgia.

Accommodations: The Callaway Gardens Inn, near the entrance to the gardens, is a 349-room hotel, which also houses restaurants, lounges, and the Fitness Center. From mid-March through December a double room starts at $119 a night. During the winter months rates start at $99; suites are $200 to $312 a night.

Next door to the inn is the Tennis and Racquetball Club; next to that are the Mountain Creek Villas: one- to four-bedroom units with fireplace, screened porch or patio, and fully equipped kitchen. Nightly rates for a two-bedroom villa are $288 to $352, depending on the season. The weekly rate during the summer is approximately $2,692.

Photo courtesy of Callaway Gardens

Many families opt for one of the Country Cottages, which are arranged in small clusters amid tall trees near Robin Lake. All have well-equipped kitchens; some have fireplace, screened porch, deck, or outdoor grill. Daily rates for a two-bedroom cottage range from $286 to $345. During the summer the weekly rate for a two-bedroom cottage is $2,161. The weekly rate includes admissions to the gardens and to the beach at Robin Lake and participation in the summer recreation program for families. Modified and full American meal plans are offered, and golf and tennis packages are featured. Cribs are provided at no charge; rollaway beds are $15 per day in the inn only.

Dining: In the inn are the Plantation Room, known for its buffets—particularly the Friday-night seafood buffet and the Sunday brunch—and the Georgia Room, featuring fine Southern cuisine enhanced by candlelight and flowers. While the former is open for breakfast, lunch, and dinner, the latter serves dinner only (dress code).

With red-checked tablecloths supporting the atmosphere that its name connotes, the Country Kitchen, located in the Country Store, serves breakfast, lunch, and dinner in a friendly, family-style setting. It's famous for its muscadine bread and country bacon. The Gardens Restaurant, where lunch and dinner are available, and the Veranda, for dinner only, are at the edge of Mountain Creek Lake; both are open seasonally. Sandwiches and snacks are available in the Champions Restaurant at the golf pro shop and the Flower Mill Restaurant near the cottages (open seasonally). The latest addition to Callaway dining is the Mountain Creek Cafe.

The Vineyard Green Lounge is a great spot for an evening cocktail, with live entertainment nightly.

Children's World: For forty-one summers Florida State University's Flying High Circus has performed at Callaway Gardens. With the big top pitched at Robin Lake Beach, this area becomes the focus of the Summer Family Adventure Program, June through mid-August. If daily (except Wednesday) circus performances are not enough to charm youngsters, the performers also act as counselors, directing kids in games and sports and teaching them a few juggling tricks and circus acts too. In addition, kids go sailing, swimming, waterskiing, rollerskating, and biking. They attend golf and tennis instruction and grow imaginative in crafts classes. Kids ages three to eighteen can participate. The Summer Discovery Program provides an informal look at the animals, plants, and ecology at Callaway Gardens. Family events, such as barbecues, square dances, and movies, are also planned.

These are one-week programs (Saturday to Saturday) with special introduction and orientation for which there is no charge when renting a cottage on a weekly basis. If you cannot schedule a full week in a family cottage and are staying a couple of days at the inn, you can enroll your child on a daily basis, for $50 a day. Besides the program, there are children's playgrounds at the inn and at the cottage area.

Recreation: The gardens are a continuous source of beauty, pleasure, peace, and serenity. This is a place to enjoy, to reflect, and to learn. The colorful, changing displays of begonias, snapdragons, geraniums, zinnias, pansies, tulips, marigolds, chrysanthemums—the list seems endless—are presented in the outdoor garden of the John A. Sibley Horticultural Center. Depending on the season, visitors who explore the walking trails are treated to mountain laurel, hydrangeas, narcissus, magnolias, dogwoods, crabapples, hollies, wildflowers, and 700 varieties of azaleas (the famous plumleaf blooms during the summer). At Mr. Cason's Vegetable Garden, you can wander through row after row of more than 400 different types of fruits and vegetables. Workshops on topics like flower arranging and bonsai techniques are available year-round. The John A. Sibley Horticultural Center, a five-acre, innovative greenhouse design, is an architectural as well as a horticultural feat. The Cecil B. Day Butterfly Center houses up to 1,000 butterflies (representing more than fifty species) in a lush tropical setting.

In 1999 Callaway Gardens added the world's largest azalea garden. The Callaway Brothers Azalea Bowl features more than 5,000 specimens of both hybrid and native azaleas in a forty-acre landscape.

Besides its magnificent gardens, the resort also offers more traditional diversions. Four golf courses (three eighteen-hole courses and one nine-hole course) unroll past forests and lakes. The names of the courses are descriptive of their surroundings—Mountain View (the most challenging and home to the PGA tour's Burch Challenge), Gardens View, Lake View (the most picturesque), and Sky View. A driving range, two pro shops, and a year-round instructional program complete the golfing facilities.

The Pete Sampras in your party has ten lighted tennis courts from which to choose. Eight clay and two Plexipave courts are at the Tennis and Racquetball Club, which also houses two racquetball courts and the pro shop. The instructional program includes private or group lessons, or you can practice on your own with a ball machine.

Robin Lake is the center of lots of summer fun, from paddleboat rides and circus performances to swimming and sunbathing along the mile-long sandy beach. Besides the lake, overnight guests can enjoy the pools at the inn, at the Mountain Creek Villas, and at the cottage area.

On the shores of Mountain Creek Lake is a boathouse where you can rent a motorboat and fishing tackle—the lake is stocked with bass and bream—or a Sunfish sailboat, paddleboat, or canoe. You can also discover the lakes from their shores as you bicycle along the trails and paths.

You may want to spend an afternoon at an organ concert (daily during the summer) in the chapel on Falls Creek Lake. For indoor exercise the Fitness Center offers equipment for unwinding. For an afternoon of history, you can take the 15-mile trip to Warm Springs and Franklin Roosevelt's Little White House. ≈≈≈

Cheeca Lodge

Islamorada, Florida 33036
(305) 664–4651, (800) 327–2888
Web site: www.cheeca.com

Stretching more than 150 miles south from Miami, the Florida Keys enjoy a subtropical climate and a friendly, laid-back philosophy. Just getting there is an adventure. As you travel along U.S. Highway 1, you get the feeling that you're the string connecting a necklace of islands. And sometimes there are no islands—just a narrow ribbon of concrete in the middle of a very wide ocean—or two! The Atlantic Ocean and the Gulf of Mexico both border this strip of islands. Islamorada is just 75 miles from Miami, but really it is another world.

Accommodations: Cheeca Lodge is a twenty-seven-acre luxury oceanfront resort (AAA four diamond), with more than 1,000 feet of palm-lined beach, not often found in the Keys. A variety of accommodations—154 villa rooms or

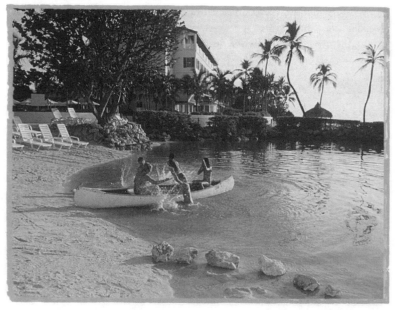

Photo courtesy of Cheeca Lodge

suites and 49 rooms in the main lodge—are spread throughout the landscaped grounds. Generous in size, all guest rooms are air-conditioned and also have ceiling fans, and most have a private balcony. Sixty-four villa suites feature kitchen, screened-in porch, living room, and one or two bedrooms. Mid-December to April rates are the highest, when standard rooms range from $295 to $650 and one-bedroom suites are $400 to $2,100. In summer the rates drop to $210 to $445 for rooms, $310 to $1,700 for one-bedroom suites. Children under sixteen stay free in their parents' room. Specials and packages are offered year-round.

Dining: Savor fine dinners at The Atlantic's Edge, a plantation-style restaurant with lovely panoramic views of the ocean. Dine inside or outside next to the free-form swimming pool at the Ocean Terrace Grill, sampling the local specialty, stone-crab claws, or soups and sandwiches; there is a special children's menu. Another indoor/outdoor dining option is the Curt Gowdy Lounge, great for snacks, cocktails, and piano entertainment in the evenings.

Children's World: Award-winning Camp Cheeca has a purpose: learning about the environment while having fun. Children ages six to twelve are busy from 9:00 A.M. to 4:00 P.M., Tuesday through Saturday in the summer, weekends year-round, and for special holiday weeks. There is a morning session on Sunday. A full day costs $26; a half day is $15. Learning to snorkel and fish, doing nature art or sand sculpture, feeding the fish or exploring the beach—everything has an ecological approach that kids really respond to. There's a good mix of activities, with field trips, scavenger hunts, arts and crafts, and Saturday Sundae (everyone's favorite). "Kids Night Out," Saturday from 7:00 to 9:00 P.M., costs $6.00, and includes entertainment, snacks, and games. When three children or fewer are present, camp will be open only for the morning session. Families with three or more children receive a reduced rate of $24 full day, $14 half day. Box lunches are available for $5.75. Baby-sitting rates vary according to season.

Recreation: You can be on the go from dawn to dusk, or make the most strenuous activity of the day deciding between a hammock, chaise longue, or tiki hut on the beach. Consider renting a paddleboat, catamaran, kayak, or beach cruiser bicycle, or try parasailing. Maybe just a pool float is more your speed. The three pools are all very different; a free-form swimming pool, a lap pool, and a saltwater lagoon keep boredom at bay. Play tennis on one of the six courts, or try the executive golf course. Take a self-guided walk along Cheeca's Nature Trail, or watch the sunrise from the pier—or maybe the sunset.

The Avanyu Spa is Cheeca's newest amenity. This newly constructed, state-of-the-art health spa and fitness center offers the latest in massage therapy, facials, aromatherapy, body wraps, spacious fitness room, men's and women's steamrooms, and a spa boutique.

It's a fisherman's paradise here, with more than 600 species of marine life and a calendar of what's running each month that fills a page. No wonder Islamorada is known as the sportfishing capital of the world. A nice touch is that the chef will, on request, prepare your hard-won catch. Cheeca has its own Dive Center, with equipment and instruction. The *Cheeca View* doubles as a dive boat twice a day, then does sunset and moonlight cruises. The biggest problem is trying to fit all the options in.

Theater of the Sea, the world's second-oldest marine park, is a natural lagoon where humans and marine animals interact (kids love getting kissed by a sea lion!). They've gone beyond a glass-bottom boat—here they have a bottomless boat. Hmm, neat trick. If you want to range farther afield, the concierge can help arrange a swim with the dolphins, or a trip to either Key West, the southernmost U.S. city, or Pennekamp State Park, the first underwater state park. Combine a visit to Miccosukee Indian Reservation with an airboat ride through the Everglades. ≋

The Cloister

Sea Island, Georgia 31561
(912) 638–3611, (800) SEA–ISLAND
Web site: www.seaisland.com

C harming, gracious, and so civilized—The Cloister brings all this to mind. Family holidays at this fine old resort are fun-filled, but the elegance of a bygone era prevails. The Cloister boasts that here children learn manners as well as golf, tennis, and swimming. The dress-for-dinner standard and the children's weekly dances (seasonally) reinforce this philosophy.

Sea Island's rich history dates back to the antebellum days of the Old South, when a large cotton plantation was active on what is now the Sea Island Golf Club. The ruins of a slave hospital standing near the Clubhouse recall this period. Early in this century the property was acquired by Howard Coffin, an automobile engineer who had visions of creating a resort on this lovely 900-acre island, with its temperate climate and ocean breezes. His dreams were realized in the construction of The Cloister. Designed by Addison Mizner, who is known primarily for his work in Palm Beach, this "friendly little hotel" (as Coffin described it) opened its doors in October 1928. It successfully weathered the Depression and over the years has warmly greeted guests from the rich and famous to the mere plebeian with good taste. Ivy-covered walls, gently swaying palm trees, impeccable gardens, and wide verandas set the stage for a memorable vacation. The resort is open year-round.

Accommodations: Accommodations are provided in the main building (the original hotel), set back a couple of hundred yards from the beach, and in guest and beach houses. The original structure has a Mediterranean style with red-tiled roofs and courtyards. The architecture of the newer buildings and the gardens complement this style and maintain the flavor of a gracious island retreat. Rooms range from standard, tastefully decorated bedrooms and baths to superior rooms and oceanfront suites.

Based on a full American plan, rates per night (double) are $314 to $1,000, depending on the type of room and time of year. In addition to three full meals a day, these rates include most recreational activities except golf, tennis, spa, shooting school, and horseback riding.

Children sharing a room with their parents are charged for meals only, determined by the age of the child. In addition, the eighteen-and-under group is exempt from golf and tennis fees (playing times may be restricted) when sharing a room with parents. Cribs are provided at no charge.

Dining: Dining is elegant as well as very appetizing and sumptuous. In the main dining room of The Cloister; gentlemen wear coats and ties for evening

Photo courtesy of The Cloister

dinners. On Wednesday and Saturday evenings, ladies frequently choose to wear cocktail dresses, while men wear dinner jackets. More casual attire is appropriate at the Beach Club (open for breakfast, lunch, and seafood dinner buffets) and at the golf clubhouses for luncheon and dinner.

American and Continental cuisines are featured. Given the oceanside location of the resort, it's no surprise that fresh seafood specialties are prominent on the menus. Whether you choose the gracious setting of the dining rooms, with fresh flowers on the tables and lovely views of the gardens, or the casual atmosphere of the clubhouses, you'll find that the careful attention to preparation makes meals a visual delight as well as a culinary treat.

For light refreshments during spring and summer, there's a snack bar near the swimming pools at the Beach Club, and high tea is served afternoons during cooler months in the Spanish Lounge. Special evenings are frequently scheduled, such as a supper at Rainbow Island.

Children's World: The junior staff will charm your child with active days. During the summer, from June through Labor Day, and during Thanksgiving and Christmas holidays, energetic, friendly counselors provide daily supervised play for youngsters ages three (no pull-ups or diapers, please) through twelve, from 9:30 A.M. to 3:00 P.M. (9:00 A.M. to 1:00 P.M. for three- and four-year-olds) at no charge. Activities include swimming, fishing, crabbing, art sessions, games, and nature walks, just to mention a few.

During the summer months children ages four through eleven can even join their counselors for dinner from 6:00 to 9:00 P.M. (Sunday and Family Beach Supper nights excluded), allowing parents to dine at their leisure. For younger children baby-sitters are available.

It's essential to check the weekly calendar for additional events, because the junior staff also plans various activities for different age groups. Teen dances and pool parties, table tennis tournaments, swimming and hamburger parties, and crabbing parties frequently appear on the agenda.

Recreation: Whether you choose a leisurely stroll along the 5 miles of private beach, a rigorous game of tennis, a round of golf, or a refreshing dip in the pool, your vacation stay can be as relaxing or active as you wish.

The Cloister offers twenty-five well-maintained clay courts, an automated practice court, and instruction by a professional teaching staff. Even a little criticism of your backhand is easy to take in a setting graced by oak trees and azaleas. At the pro shop you can pick up equipment and new tennis togs and sign up for a tournament.

The Sea Island Golf Club, located on neighboring St. Simons Island, is just a short drive over the small bridge spanning the Black Banks River. Once you arrive you'll be charmed by the Avenue of Oaks—majestic moss-draped oak trees leading up to The Lodge at Sea Island Golf Club. There are thirty-six championship holes. The Seaside Course, redesigned in 1999 by Tom Fazio and listed on numerous top courses lists, is a par-70 links course. The Plantation Course, redesigned by Rees Jones in 1998, is a par-72 parkland-style course. A third course, Retreat, was redesigned by Davis Love III and reopened in August 2001. The Golf Learning Center, a joint venture of Sea Island and *Golf Digest*, offers state-of-the-art practice and learning facilities. There's a driving range at each club, and back on Sea Island you'll find a putting green and a chip 'n' putt area for some extra practice time. And if you're a real devotee, rest assured that golfing interests do not fade with the setting sun; join the discussions with the pros at golf seminars two evenings a week.

The Beach Club overlooks the Atlantic, so you can choose an ocean swim or a few laps in one of the two pools. Besides a dining room and a snack bar, the Beach Club offers table tennis, volleyball, shuffleboard, and a terrific soak-up-the-sun atmosphere. Other water sports include sailboarding and sailing in the ocean, snorkeling and scuba diving, and boating and fishing in the river. After excursions through the waterways, you might try exploring the grounds as you jog, bike, or ride horseback. Many folks enjoy a horseback ride along the beach, or you may contact the stables about moonlight supper rides. At the Shooting School you'll find instruction in sporting clays, trap, and skeet shooting as well as all the equipment necessary to learn these sports. And after golf, tennis, swimming, sailing, and skeet-shooting lessons, if you're still dying to try something new or to brush up on dusty skills, sign up for dance instruction. After a couple of sessions, you'll no doubt be a hit dancing nightly to the hotel's Sea Island Orchestra.

The Sea Island Spa offers a full range of services. You can join an exercise class, develop an individualized program, consult a nutritionist, have a massage, or relax with a facial.

Special programs are planned throughout the year; they may be just the thing to schedule a family vacation around. Food and wine seminars, bridge festivals, and a personal financial-planning seminar are standard events at The Cloister.

At any time of the year, be sure to check the weekly calendar. You might want to see a movie, play bingo, listen to a classical piano concert, head to an exercise workout, join a nature walk, or take in a lecture on the local wildlife. But don't crowd your schedule too much, for one of the nicest pleasures at The Cloister is simply strolling through the gardens and discovering the camellias, gardenias, wisteria, geraniums, and petunias. ≋≋

Club Med/Sandpiper

3500 SE Morningside Boulevard
Port St. Lucie, Florida 34952
(561) 398–5100
Web site: www.clubmed.com

C lub Med is practically synonymous with a carefree, fun-in-the-sun holiday, a tradition going back more than forty years. The only warm-weather village that Club Med operates in the United States is Sandpiper, and it has not only a Mini-Club but a Baby Club as well. Located in Port St. Lucie, Florida, about an hour's drive north of Palm Beach, the Club Med village covers more than 400 beautifully landscaped acres along the St. Lucie River. The verdant green landscape and the clear blue waters make an attractive setting for a fun-filled, sun-filled vacation.

Accommodations: Sandpiper is one of the most luxurious Club Med properties, termed the "Finest." It seems more like a deluxe hotel, boasting brick-colored tile floors covered with kilim carpet, original artwork by local artists, and a separate dressing area, with large closets. Unlike most Club Med villages, the rooms here have telephone, TV, and minifridge. Each room has a private balcony or terrace and is located in one of several three-story buildings near the river.

Weekly rates for adults range from $1,036 (summer/fall) to $1,134 (winter/spring); Christmas, Presidents' Week, and Easter are higher. Children's rates are from $700 to $800; children younger than two years of age stay free. Sandpiper is one of the few Club Meds with daily rates; these range from $148 to $166 for adults and $15 to $99 for children ages four months to eleven years.

A Club Med membership is required; this is a one-time fee of $30 per family plus an annual membership fee of $50 per adult, $20 per child. The rates include accommodations, all meals, the children's program, and most of the activities, with instruction.

Dining: The main dining room is informal, serving breakfast, lunch, and dinner buffets. Dining at Club Med is a bountiful experience, with selections of American, French, and Continental delicacies. (It's also a good chance to meet people and socialize.) The Club has its own baker and pastry maker—yum. No fewer than twelve different fresh-baked breads are served at every meal. But not to worry, there are enough activities daily to work off any calories from overindulging. A special kid-friendly menu is served to children early at lunch and dinner. Parents may join their children while they eat, and the G.O.s (*gentils organisateurs*—French for "gracious organizers") supervise as well. High chairs and booster seats make life easier for the little ones. After their early dinner kids return to the Mini-Club. Mom and Dad, meanwhile, savor a superb and blissfully quiet dinner, perhaps in one of the two specialty restaurants— beautifully decorated, smaller and more intimate, table service is the order of the day here. Choose La Fontana, with the freshest of fish, or The Riverside, which offers fine French dishes. Complimentary wine is served with lunch and dinner, thanks to the French heritage of the Club.

Children's World: Kids are thoroughly entertained at Club Med. In fact, you may almost have to make an appointment to see your little one. The Baby Club is available for infants ages four to twenty-three months. Strollers, baby monitors, bassinets—all the necessary equipment can be borrowed; and a pediatrician is either in the village or on call, plus one registered nurse. Each baby gets her own crib, and there's even a special Baby Chef, who prepares food using only natural ingredients. Lunch is handled by the G.O.s, but parents are on duty for dinner. Need juice or milk in the middle of the night? No problem; just go to the twenty-four-hour convenience room. Depending on their ages, babies are changed, fed, napped, and played with in the adjacent garden, with swings and toys. The more mobile go on walks or play on the beach. A new service available only at this Baby Club is "Twilight Care." Babies are brought back to the Baby Club at 7:00 P.M., in their pajamas, and can sleep there while parents take in a show or stroll along the river. The Siesta Service is provided from 8:00 P.M. to 1:00 A.M. at a cost of $20 per child per night.

The Petit Club is for two- to three-year-olds, the Mini-Club is for four- to ten-year-olds, and the Junior Club entertains eleven- to thirteen-year-olds. Each has its own area, its own G.O.s, and an unbelievable number of activities. In addition to all the usual activities of children's programs, Club Med also offers circus workshops, with real trampolines, trapeze and low-wire work, juggling, trick bikes, and clowns. At the end of the week, the entire group puts on a show under the Big Top for adoring parents. It's really terrific, and the kids are so proud of themselves. Children also rave about the scuba experience in the swimming pool, with kid-size masks, fins, and tanks. In one-on-one instruction, even four-year-olds get to breathe under water—what a thrill! There's intensive tennis for kids eight and older, and soccer, softball, in-line skating, sailing, waterskiing, and much more—all included in the one price.

Recreation: The sun is warm, the water inviting. You have five swimming pools to choose from and a little sandy beach where you can splash in the river. A shuttle leaves hourly for the twenty-minute ride to the Atlantic for ocean swimming. In the calm water of the river, you can glide along on a sailboat and later have a go at waterskiing. Tennis clinics are held daily on the eighteen courts; after intensive two-and-a-half-hour sessions, you will surely find improvement in your game. A normal program with one-hour daily lessons at all levels is another option. Aerobics classes, calisthenics, and volleyball games always pop up on the agenda. Perhaps you prefer a routine in the fitness center or biking and jogging along the paths through the property. Maybe you can sneak in a trial swing on the trapeze—it's scary, but very safe.

Speaking of swings, unique to Sandpiper is a concentrated golf program, including two eighteen-hole championship golf courses, Saints and Sinners, designed by Mark Mahannah; a driving range; a free nine-hole par-3; an enclosed driving range, with free lessons at all levels; two putting greens; a chipping green; and a practice sand trap. For serious golfers the Golf Academy provides two and a half hours daily of instruction and course play at an additional cost.

The Mini-Clubs run from 9:00 A.M. to 9:00 P.M. Afterward the whole family can enjoy the evening entertainment, usually a show or participatory fun. After the kids finally fall into bed, the nightclub continues into the night.

If you have time, which we doubt, Club Med offers a mind-boggling array of excursions. You may not want to mention it to the kids, but Disney World is only two hours away. Also nearby are the Kennedy Space Center, hot-air ballooning, and deep-sea fishing. Palm Beach shopping is also within close striking distance. ≋

Hawk's Cay Resort

Mile Marker 61
Duck Key, Florida 33050
(305) 743–7000, (800) 432–2242

L ocated in the heart of the Florida Keys is Hawk's Cay Resort, a tropical sixty-acre island. The resort was built in the late 1950s and has hosted numerous presidents and film stars. The rambling Caribbean-style hotel sets the tone for the relaxed, elegant atmosphere that you'll find here. Ceiling fans, indoor plants, wicker furniture, and French doors in the lobbies and lounges echo the easygoing pace. The temperatures are mild, averaging in the low eighties in summer and the low seventies in winter, and the water stays warm and comfortable year-round. Water sports, from deep-sea fishing, fly-fishing, sailing, diving, and snorkeling to swimming, sunset sails, ecotours, and waterskiing, are, naturally, the main focus of this island resort. The only living coral reef in the continental United States is just offshore.

Accommodations: This comfortable inn has the ambience and style of a Caribbean resort. Most of the 160 rooms and 16 suites have views of the Atlantic Ocean or the Gulf of Mexico. Each has a private balcony, separate dressing area, and a small refrigerator. During the high season, December through April, room rates range from $220 to $375; suite rates, including the presidential suite, range from $425 to $850. Low-season rates, May through mid-December, are $180 to $250 and $235 to $750, respectively. The resort has added 240 new two- and three-bedroom villas that offer water settings and a full kitchen with four different styles. They are the perfect home away from home for families.

Dining: If you like fresh seafood, you'll find dining here a treat. There are four tempting restaurants to choose from, each with its own distinctive style and menu selections.

Start the day with a fabulous breakfast buffet presented in the Palm Terrace. Breakfast hours begin as early as 7:00 A.M. and continue until 11:00 A.M. For casual lunches and dinners, the Cantina at poolside offers a variety of Mexican fare, as well as rum concoctions that recall the island's history as a stopover for Prohibition rumrunners.

Photo courtesy of Hawk's Cay Resort and Marina

The WatersEdge, dockside at the marina, is open for dinner, specializing in steak and fresh-off-the-boat seafood. Porto Cayo features Italian specialties, accompanied by the sounds of live entertainment nightly.

Children's World: Children's programs at the resort feature a variety of opportunities for children of all ages (baby-sitting services also can be arranged). Daily activities include tiki boat races, field trips, scavenger hunts, fishing, ecology tours, and a kids' night out.

The clubhouse features a children's theme swimming pool and fitness center, an area designed especially for teens, and an additional location for indoor games and activities.

Located just off the main lobby, your child will find a room filled with the latest electronic games.

Recreation: The water tempts, entices, and captures the heart of visitors. It establishes the mood and is the setting for most of the recreation. Swim in one of the many pools or the saltwater lagoon, or stretch out beneath the tropical sun.

Discover the mysteries and wonder of undersea life. The coral reef offshore is home to a colorful array of tropical fish and is one of the best spots in the country for snorkeling and scuba diving.

Fishing here puts you in the big league, and it's exciting. Just offshore you'll find red snapper and mackerel; farther out in Gulf Stream waters are marlin, dolphin, and tuna; and tarpon ply the waters in Florida Bay. Charter a vessel at the marina for an excursion. The Marina at Hawk's Cay offers eighty-five slips and can dock yachts more than 100 feet long.

Explore the island by bicycle or take a self-guided walking tour to learn about the indigenous vegetation and tropical birds such as the brown pelican and the blue heron.

Unique to Hawk's Cay is the Dolphin Connection, a program designed to study, protect, and increase public interest in dolphin biology and ecosystems. Training sessions and interactive programs are offered daily. Sign up for a once in a lifetime memory-making experience with the dolphins. ≋

Hutchinson Island Marriott Beach Resort and Marina

555 Northeast Ocean Boulevard
Hutchinson Island
Stuart, Florida 34996
(561) 225–3700, (800) 444–3389
Web site: www.hutchinsonislmarriott.com

Hutchinson Island Marriott Beach Resort and Marina is tucked away on Hutchinson Island, a 16-mile lush barrier isle in a surprisingly subtle spot in the Atlantic. This natural island playground enchants guests with its serene nature and intimate island hospitality. Edged on one side by aquamarine ocean waves and complemented by the shimmering Indian River on the other, the resort stretches across 200 acres of plantation landscape and hosts a range of sun-splashed options, from miles of shell-colored shores and a seventy-seven-slip marina to aquatic adventures.

Accommodations: The retreat offers 295 riverside-to-oceanfront guest rooms and suites, with daily rates ranging from $79 to $99 June through September, to $209 to $269 January 16 through April 17 (depending on room type and days of stay). One- and two-bedroom villas overlook the water or the golf course; each has a fully equipped kitchen and private balcony. Rates range from $129 to $159 a night June through September, $249 to $279 January 16 to April 17 and December 19–31. Special rates apply for golf, honeymoon, holiday, and seasonal packages; complimentary cribs are provided.

Dining: Dining options tempt any appetite, offering enticing seafood delights and casual, bistro-style fare. Panoramic views from Scalawags, a seafood restaurant overlooking the Indian River, surround guests in perfect pastel sunsets while savory dishes are served. Combining a kaleidoscope of colors and a market-style ambience, Gratzi offers a selection of light Italian fare with sit-down service, an expansive deli, and gourmet take-out options. Bunkers, a newly remodeled restaurant catering to famished golfers seeking a quick bite, features a pub menu for post-play fare and cheer. The Emporium Cafe treats families to an all-American selection, from burgers and conch fritters to delectable ice-cream sundaes. Poolside tiki bars offer light bites and snacks for lunch and dinner.

Children's World: Children on Hutchinson Island will thoroughly enjoy Castaway Summer. In addition to capturing the imagination of younger guests with their "mini-matey" adventures, Don Pedro and his crew will keep everyone at the resort entertained during the summer months with dive-in movies, pirate appearances, and fancy feasts. Parents can capture their swashbuckling children in action with fabulous photos that will provide memories for years to come. Teens enjoy shared activities as well, with movie nights, teen shoreline fishing, and teen in-line skating parties scheduled monthly. The resort is transformed into a pirate's lair with "Pirate Island," a fun, family-oriented summer program.

Recreation: Stuart is the "Sailfish Capital of the World," where first-time mates to seasoned fishermen pursue the coveted game fish. Hutchinson Island's full-service seventy-seven-slip marina offers deep-sea and river charter fishing and backwater trolling excursions. If you prefer cruising to catching, relax aboard the *Island Princess,* the resort's own luxury vessel, and scout out the lifestyles of the rich and famous along the Indian River. Year-round guided ecotours take guests through mangrove-woven waterways to explore the area's flourishing natural surroundings, seeking dolphins, manatees, sea turtles, and native birds. Aquatic adventures abound from the Atlantic Ocean to the Intracoastal Waterway, where seafarers frolic by sailboat, Wave Runner, windsurfer, and kayak. For more relaxing recreation take a dip in one of the resort's four pools.

Golfers of all skill levels enjoy the challenging fairways and greens of twelve courses in the area, as the resort is the gateway to an array of championship and executive courses, including Nicklaus, Fazio, and Player designs.

Guests preferring their backhand to the back nine can indulge in thirteen NovaGrass tennis courts at the heart of the island. With a quick-drying surface, the courts bounce back from a good soaking in about an hour. Health enthusiasts will find a newly installed fitness facility with a complete line of workout equipment and an all-glass wall providing a panoramic view of the tennis courts. ≈≈

Marco Island Marriott Resort and Golf Club

400 South Collier Boulevard
Marco Island, Florida 34145
(941) 394–2511, (800) 438–4373
Web site: www.marcomarriottresort.com

An island oasis drifting off the southernmost tip of the Florida Gulf and nearly lost in the Ten Thousand Islands, Marco Island Marriott Resort and Golf Club blends a tempting twist of tropical passions and sun-splashed excitement into an enchanting, unforgettable island escape. The resort's privileged travelers get lost in the intriguing contrasts: Waves of sun-drenched beaches, always-warm Gulf waters, and passionate sunsets present a tame, pampered complement to the tangled wildness and sweeping sawgrass prairies of Florida's famous Everglades nearby.

Accommodations: All of Marco Island Marriott Resort and Golf Club's 735 guest rooms and suites have private balconies. Poolside or beachfront lanais—each with a private balcony entrance—and a secluded cluster of seaside villas complete the resort's accommodations. Daily rates, depending on size, are $129 to $219 in the low season (May through November) and start at $275 in the high season (December through April). Packages are available.

Dining: Shimmering turquoise-flecked waters, sweeping pearlescent sands, and lush, cascading gardens create an enchanting tropical backdrop and alluring ambience for five distinct restaurants and four lounges at the resort. Here you'll find everything from a seabound beach hut and classic pizzeria to the finest Northern Italian cuisine. Quinn's on the Beach cooks up a treasure trove of savory seafaring delights from dawn until after dusk. At the Voyager Restaurant, open for dinner and a superb Sunday champagne brunch, a range of tasty treasures begins with appetizers such as succulent escargots and Maryland-style crab cakes. For anytime eating, Café del Sol creates popular family fare. Aromas of just-baked bread and bubbling tomato sauce entice sun-seeking crowds to the Pizzeria for huge slices of homemade pizza, subs, barbecue, hot dogs, spaghetti, ice cream, and frozen yogurt. The resort also has a Tiki Bar and Grill, specializing in chilled concoctions.

Photo courtesy of Marco Island Marriott Resort and Golf Club

Children's World: The Kids Klub at Marco Island Marriott Resort and Golf Club—the first resort in North America to be awarded The National Parenting Center Seal of Approval—is a pinnacle of pint-size fun, occupying youngsters ages five through twelve with cool pool dips, sand-castle creations, coconut bowling, arts and crafts, and zany relay races. Special Saturday evening programs allow parents a slice of solitude under the South Florida stars. The unique Rainy Day program offers hours of indoor entertainment for the whole family.

Recreation: Choreographed by a team of fun-in-the-sun experts, daily activities include aquaslimnastics, tennis aerobics, island bike and trolley tours, beach volleyball, table tennis, and step aerobics. Sun worshippers and soul searchers relax under thatch-topped tiki huts, play beach volleyball, or scour the shore for seashells. Endless Gulf activities include sailing, kayaking, windsurfing, water-skiing, bumper tubing, and parasailing. Three sparkling pools and a children's wading pool are available. Golfers can enjoy a 6,925-yard, eighteen-hole executive golf course. The extensive clubhouse facility includes an elaborate pro shop, complete locker room facilities, Clubhouse Grill for breakfast or lunch, and John Jacobs' School of Golf. For tennis enthusiasts there are thirteen Har-Tru and three hard-surface courts (four lighted for night play), a tennis shop, daily clinics, private lessons, round-robins, match mate services, and special instruction for young learners. Fabulous fishing is accessible, or you can work out with Florida-style aerobics and fitness programs. Be sure, though, to save time for island shelling adventures or some on-site shopping. ≋

Marriott's Grand Hotel Resort and Golf Club

1 Grand Boulevard
Point Clear, Alabama 36564
(334) 928–9201, (800) 544–9933
Web site: www.marriott.com/marriott/PTLAL

The charm and graciousness of the Old South has not faded in southern Alabama. Marriott's Grand Hotel has preserved its rich tradition of elegant service as a premier resort for more than 150 years. Known as the Queen of Southern Resorts, the hotel is set on 550 acres in Point Clear, on a peninsula in Mobile Bay. In this secluded location the quiet lagoons, majestic oak trees draped in Spanish moss, and beautiful gardens can make you forget the worries and concerns of the workaday world. Leave your troubles and anxieties on the doorstep and enter this vacation retreat, where your biggest dilemma will be whether to play a round of golf, ride horseback in the peaceful landscape, stroll along the sandy beach, or sip a mint julep while watching the sun set over the bay.

The fascinating legacy of the Grand Hotel captures the heart of many a history buff. First discovered as an ideal location for a resort retreat in 1847, the hotel was the site of lively antebellum social events in its early years. Then, during the days of the Civil War (or as some folks down here still call it, the War of Northern Aggression), it served as a hospital for Confederate soldiers. After the war the hotel resumed its original function and once again became the center for leisure activities. A fire in 1869 and a hurricane in 1893 destroyed some of the old facilities, but rebuilding efforts and expansion were frequently undertaken in order to maintain accommodations for guests. Today's main hotel building was constructed in 1941. In 1967 the Bay House was added, and 1983 witnessed a restoration of the existing rooms and the addition of two buildings—the North Bay House and the Marina House.

Accommodations: The main building has been described as rustic, but don't be deceived; this is rustic in a grand old manner. The lobby here is a charming octagonal structure that focuses on a massive fireplace. From its wide planks of pine flooring to its cypress-beamed ceiling, visitors immediately sense a warm, hospitable atmosphere. There are a total of 306 guest rooms in the different buildings and the cottages. Many rooms are decorated with white cypress paneling and ceiling fans (maintained primarily for ambience, but also to capture the bay breezes; air-conditioning relieves the sultriness of summer days). Open year-round, the hotel has several rate structures. In the winter season, daily room-only rates range from $94 to $124 midweek, $104 to $164 weekends. Special rates that include breakfast for two are just $10 more, and

Photo courtesy of Marriott's Grand Hotel Resort and Golf Club

children under five can dine from the special children's buffet. Summer rates are higher: For example, the breakfast-for-two plan is $159 to $179 weekdays or $219 to $239 weekends. There is no charge for cribs and rollaways.

Dining: The Grand Dining Room offers an elegant atmosphere for breakfast, lunch, and dinner. An orchestra performs nightly here during dinner and afterward for dancing. Since the hotel is located on Mobile Bay and so close to the Gulf, many of the house specialties rely on the fresh local seafood. Oysters, red snapper stuffed with crabmeat, and seafood gumbo are a few of the selections. The hearty-meat-and-potatoes fan will find excellent prime rib of beef. The gourmet will be enticed by the elegant Bayview Room, for intimate and scenic dining.

For a sumptuous buffet breakfast, try the Grand Buffet in the Grand Dining Room, where you may sit in a gazebo area with beautiful bay views. Lunch is served not only in the Grand Dining Room but also at the Lakewood Golf Club, which is set in a wooded landscape. While soaking up the sunshine, you may choose the Poolside Grill and Snack Bar for a light lunch (seasonal). The Birdcage Lounge also provides light snacks and delightful cocktails with spectacular views.

Children's World: The Grand Fun Camp is in operation from Memorial Day to Labor Day and on all major holidays. Every day but Sunday a group of friendly hostesses coordinates fun-filled activities. Five- to twelve-year-olds frolic from 10:00 A.M. to 4:00 P.M. and from 6:00 P.M. until 10:00 P.M. Swimming, shuffleboard, putt-putt golf, arts and crafts, video games, fishing, and sand-castle building entertain children, who will no doubt entertain their parents as they recount a day's adventures. Special events include movies and puppet shows. Individual baby-sitters are also available on an hourly basis ($5.50 and up per hour).

Recreation: In the old days of the resort, two favorite spots were the wharves—one for men and one for women, because sunbathing and swimming in mixed company were unacceptable. Having come a long way since then, the Grand now offers innumerable popular activities for its guests. Given this prime location and mild climate, water sports attract many visitors. After a little warm-up fishing in the bay, you might take on the challenges of deep-sea fishing. Your catch may be your evening's dinner, prepared especially for you by the hotel chefs. Reserve a sailboat or paddleboat for an afternoon's outing, or bring your own boat to the forty-slip marina. Splash in the waters of the bay along the sandy beach, or take a dip in the beautiful pool, the largest pool on the Gulf Coast.

If you're more of a landlubber, the championship thirty-six holes of golf are a suitable diversion. Regardless of their level of play, all golfers appreciate the rolling, wooded setting of oak and pine. The facilities of the club abound—instructors, carts, putting greens, and locker room. The eight rubico tennis courts lure many ace players, and novices can enroll for lessons with one of the pros. And no day of golf or tennis is complete without the requisite stop at the pro shops; there's always that extra bit of new equipment to pick up. Head to the stables for horseback riding around the picturesque lakes and lagoons, or jog or bicycle (rentals available) through the gardens and along the boardwalk.

Slower-paced activities include croquet, putting green, and video games, or you may want to wind up the day in the hot tub. In the 1930s The Grand Hotel advertised itself as the place of "Every Creature Comfort." Many visitors today feel that reputation has withstood the test of time. ≋

The Resort at Longboat Key Club
301 Gulf of Mexico Drive
P.O. Box 15000
Longboat Key, Florida 34228
(941) 383–8821, (800) 237–8821
Web site: www.longboatkeyclub.com

An island retreat, The Resort at Longboat Key Club specializes in relaxation and recreation for golfers and tennis players. Located on a barrier island in the Gulf of Mexico just west of Sarasota, it doesn't shortchange swimmers and sun worshippers either. The resort enjoys a lush, tropical setting between the Gulf and Sarasota Bay that seems worlds away from your regular routine, yet it is only fifteen minutes away from the Sarasota Airport.

Accommodations: Seven modern buildings, four to ten stories high, are arranged throughout the property to afford guests magnificent views of the Gulf, the bay, and the golf course fairways. Of the 232 accommodations, each with its own balcony, the majority (220) are suites, each with a king-size bed, a sleeper sofa, and a fully equipped kitchen. Summer is the low season, when guest rooms range from $145 to $275 a night and suites start at $160 a night; the deluxe two-bedroom suites command $445 to $525 a night. During the high season (Christmas and February through late April), a guest room is $325 to $410 a night, while suites cost $400 to $1,075 a night. During the rest of the year, prices fall between these parameters. Up to two children (seventeen and younger) can stay in a suite with their parents at no additional charge.

Dining: Dining can be as elegant or as casual as you choose. On the sophisticated side is Sands Pointe. Tempting fresh seafood dishes are frequently featured on its menus. For more casual dining drop by Spike 'n' Tees, and for truly relaxed mealtimes, saunter over to Barefoots, at poolside.

Children's World: The Kids' Klub operates year-round, Monday through Saturday. Experienced counselors direct youngsters ages five to twelve in a full 9:30 A.M. to 3:00 P.M. program. Swimming, beach fun, volleyball, basketball, field trips, and arts and crafts are all part of the schedule. The program is $25 per child, per day. The average cost of individual baby-sitting is $15.00 an hour, with a three-hour minimum.

Recreation: The Islandside Golf Course has eighteen holes, and the Harborside Course has twenty-seven holes. With palm trees and quiet lagoons throughout these courses, who can have a bad game? Two complete pro shops, a golf school, and professionals to guide players in private lessons and tournaments round out the picture for golfers.

Thirty-eight Har-Tru tennis courts await your ace serves and graceful lobs. Six of these are lighted for night play. Tennis play is complimentary. Two tennis shops, ball machines, a videotaped game analysis, and a professional staff will urge you on to better play.

Swimming in the outdoor pool or the gentle waters of the Gulf may top off your day. Bicycle along the nature trails, stroll on the snow-white beach, or spend an afternoon snorkeling or sailing. You can even organize a deep-sea fishing expedition through the concierge.

The resort's newest recreational amenity is a 4,000-square-foot Fitness Center, which features weight-training and cardiovascular equipment as well as instructor-led aerobics classes. Fitness Center equipment is available to guests on a complimentary basis. For soothing life's daily stress and the ultimate in personal pampering, neuromuscular, sports, and Swedish massage are also available. ≋

South Seas Resort

P.O. Box 194
Captiva Island, Florida 33924
(800) CAPTIVA
Web sites: www.southsearesort.com; www.ssrc.com

Located at the northern tip of Captiva Island on the Gulf of Mexico, 3 miles off Florida's southwest coast, Captiva Island is connected to the mainland via Sanibel Island and the Sanibel Causeway. South Seas Resort is approximately 30 miles from the Southwest Florida International Airport in Fort Myers.

Dubbed "Florida's Tahiti" for its subtropical climate and lush foliage indigenous to the Southern Hemisphere, Captiva Island—famous for its shell-covered beaches—was recently rated one of America's most romantic beaches. South Seas Resort is a 330-acre island resort with 2½ miles of beach, a full-service yacht harbor and marina, recreational options from golf and tennis to island excursion cruises and water sports, fine restaurants, shopping, children's programs, and a complimentary open-air trolley transportation system.

Accommodations: The South Seas Resort boasts more than 600 luxurious units, ranging from deluxe hotel rooms and villa suites to three-bedroom beach homes and cottages. Contact South Seas Resort for additional accommodation information and costs.

Dining: The resort's legendary King's Crown Restaurant features exquisite architecture and an award-winning culinary team. Discover fine dining in an elegant waterfront setting where New American cuisine is graciously served, traditions of yesterday are preserved, and new traditions are created. *Florida Living* magazine readers have honored King's Crown with the distinction of "Best Restaurant with a View." Chadwick's Restaurant features casual dining in a tropical setting. It is open for breakfast seasonally, and lunch and dinner menus feature daily breakfast and lunch buffets, a Sunday champagne brunch, and evening theme buffets, including Caribbean Celebration Buffet, Bourbon Street Bash, Key West Clambake, and Seafood Extravaganza.

Dine indoors or in the open air at Cap'n Al's Dockside Grille overlooking the Yacht Harbour. Cap'n Al's serves breakfast, lunch, and dinner daily. Enjoy Mama Rosa's Pizzeria, offering eat-in or take-out dining; the convenience of delivery is provided after 5:00 P.M. Choose from mouthwatering pizza, garden-fresh salads, and delicious subs. Fresh dough is made daily on the premises. Uncle Bob's Ice Cream Emporium serves delicious, old-fashioned soda fountain and ice-cream treats and tempting candies, and sells educational toys and kites. Pelican Pete's Pool Bar is a full-service bar specializing in tropical libations; poolside dining at the north end features grilled sandwiches, snacks, and more.

For dining entertainment the King's Crown Lounge, located in the King's Crown Restaurant, offers cocktails and live, easy-listening entertainment. Chadwick's Lounge has a full bar and live entertainment nightly. A steel drum band is featured Tuesday evening and a jazz quartet during dinner on Thursday evening.

Children's World: Activities for all ages are available. A professional staff organizes daily itineraries of recreational and educational activities. Fun Factory™, for children ages four to eleven, includes activities such as Nature Camp, Pirate Mania, Circus at South Seas, and Dinner Theatre. Supervised social events for teens, such as parasailing, waterskiing, volleyball tournaments, pool parties, canoeing, kayaking, and golf are sure to provide hours of enjoyment.

Recreation: Dozens of recreational activities are available to guests of South Seas Plantation, including a par-36, regulation nine-hole golf course; tennis on eighteen courts; biking; and water sports, including game fishing, sailboarding, snorkeling, sailing, and excursion cruises to nearby islands.

Family activities and workshops also feature yoga, professional fitness training, aerobic exercise classes, canoe excursions, sailing clinics, guided shelling excursions, family fishing, shell art, and more. A variety of nature activities for the whole family include Dolphin and Manatee Awareness, Shells of Captiva, Wildlife Refuge Trips, and Birds of Captiva. *The Explorer Bulletin,* a current schedule of activities, is given to guests upon check-in. Preregistration is required for all activities.

Shopping at South Seas includes quality boutiques, gift shops, pro shops, grocery store and gourmet deli, ship's store, and full-service beauty salon. ≋

TradeWinds Island Resorts

5500 Gulf Boulevard
St. Pete Beach, Florida 33706
(800) 237–0707
E-mail: reservations@twresort.com
Web site: www.tradewindsresort.com

Hugging the sugary white sands of the Gulf of Mexico, three stellar beach resorts are making history as the largest resort complex on Florida's Gulf Coast. Known collectively as the TradeWinds Island Resorts, these properties occupy thirty-five of the most desirable acres on St. Pete Beach. With limitless beachfront recreation, flexible meeting space, sumptuous dining, and exclusive golf privileges at one of the area's private country clubs, the TradeWinds Island Resorts offer guests access to three spectacular resorts in one.

Building on a rich tradition of outstanding accommodations and exceptional service, the TradeWinds Island Resorts offer a truly unique opportunity for guests to discover the best of St. Pete Beach.

Accommodations: TradeWinds Island Resorts include three distinct resorts located just steps away from one another. While staying at one of the resorts, you can enjoy the amenities of all three! An eighteen-acre island hideaway, TradeWinds Island Grand offers endless diversions, award-winning service, and classic Florida charm.

Everything about the TradeWinds Sandpiper Hotel & Suites whispers of hospitality and relaxation. Lush landscaping and tropical courtyards highlight the five acres of pristine beach, and you'll find an uncommon level of personal service in a cozy setting with a friendly, casual ambience.

Be one of the first to experience the TradeWinds Sirata Beach Resort, the newest addition to the TradeWinds collection. Set on twelve acres of natural beachfront, this sun-drenched resort provides a relaxing resort experience with a Mediterranean flair and warm, personable service.

Choose from one-, two-, and three-bedroom suites; soaring penthouses; and convenient parlor and hotel rooms. Special comforts may include a wet bar area with coffeemaker, toaster, and refrigerator; suites feature a kitchenette, living area with sofabed, and private bedroom. Contact the resort for information on the many packages offered with a price range that is sure to fit your family quite nicely. The concierge will be pleased to help with reservations or arrangements for a variety of excursions and area attractions.

Dining: Feast on the specialties of the house: island medleys of Gulf Coast cuisine, tall tropical coolers, and barefoot beach bars. Enjoy breakfast buffets, poolside lunches, and sunset dinners. Savor aged steaks and fresh native seafood, or experience the intimate elegance and excellent fare at Palm Court. Indulge in room service, deli specialties, an ice-cream shop, and even a Pizza Hut. Unwind at the waterside piano bar or enjoy evening entertainment at the lounge. At TradeWinds Island Resorts, seventeen dining and entertainment venues, with charging options to your room account, await your pleasure.

Children's World: It just doesn't get any better than the TradeWinds for kids . . . and their parents. All day, every day, the enthusiastic recreation counselors (known as T.A.Z. Team members) of TradeWinds Action Zone offer activities from A to Z, with recreational options for every member of the family. T.A.Z. Team members supervise tons of planned fun stuff from aerobics to zany, wacky wordies, family swim meets, sun catcher creations, or a hunt for sharks' teeth.

The KONK Club, short for "Kids Only, No Kidding!" is specially designed for children three to eleven years old. Each program is themed a little differently, lasts from two to four hours, and usually includes a meal or snack. KONK Club activities are scheduled at each resort, or kids can go "exploring" and discover the wide variety of activities at the other resorts. Kids even have their own special night out, providing a great way to make friends with other kids, and it gives mom and dad a little time alone.

Be sure to look for Beaker, the TradeWinds huggable purple toucan mascot. You're likely to spot Beaker at KONK Club activities or making rounds at each of the resorts. Or call Activities to schedule a tuck-in: Beaker will come to your room to make sure all kids are tucked in toucan-style.

Teens will enjoy the variety of activities and attractions at the three resorts and in the surrounding area. With tennis, golf, swimming, snorkeling, Wave Runners, Shell Island and Dolphin Watch Cruises, minigolf, parasailing, and numerous other activities teens can be as active as they choose. Scheduled teen programs are for ages twelve to eighteen. What a great opportunity to meet young people from all three resorts. Preregistration is required for off-site trips.

Recreation: Escape to the magic of the TradeWinds Island Resorts and discover a place where you can do "everything under the sun"—or absolutely nothing at all. The swirl of whirlpools, the heat of sauna, the refreshing depths of ten pools entice. Dip into the shimmering surface of the sea. Comb miles of sandy beach for shells. Curl up with a book in a tropical courtyard. Toast the sunset. Explore the resorts' meandering waterway, complete with swans, ducks, and egrets. Pamper yourself at Body Works salon with massage, aromatherapy, and body wraps. Relax. You're a million miles away . . . from everything. You're now on island time. ≈≈

The Westin Innisbrook Resort

36750 U.S. Highway 19 North
Palm Harbor, Florida 34684
(727) 942–2000, (800) 456–2000
E-mail: westin-innisbrook.com
Web site: www.westin-innisbrook.com

Just 25 miles from Tampa International Airport on Florida's sparkling west coast lies the pride of the Florida resort market, The Westin Innisbrook Resort. This beautiful property includes more than 1,000 acres tucked away from the mainstream of city life and traffic, in a picturesque setting that is beautifully landscaped and heavily wooded with mature oaks and pines. The resort is open year-round, which is very good news for the golf enthusiast, as here you will find ninety holes of championship golf on five pristine courses. Innisbrook became a member of the honored Westin Hotel and Resort family in July 1997, and has since enjoyed the addition of several new services and facility enhancements that are sure to keep guests returning year after year. The resort has planned a $50 million renovation over the next few years to include refurbishment of their spacious guest suites, as well as the addition of several new recreation facilities and dining establishments. Convenient to all of central Florida's attractions including Walt Disney World, SeaWorld, and Busch Gardens, this is a setting that the whole family will adore.

Accommodations: Twenty-eight lodges containing 1,000 guest suites are located throughout the resort. Starting at 800 square feet for the popular Club Suite, to more than 2,000 square feet in a two-bedroom deluxe unit, a stay at Innisbrook affords all the comfort and conveniences of home. Each suite offers a fully stocked kitchen, daily newspaper and complimentary Starbucks coffee, a beautiful line of personal soaps and shampoos, complete in-suite bar, and private patio or balcony overlooking the golf courses and lush landscape.

Depending on the season, the rates for accommodations range from $115 to $485 per night. Children under eighteen stay free in the same room as their parents or guardians.

Dining: Dining at the resort offers a variety of cuisine, from a casual, family-style restaurant to the newly opened DY's Steak House. DY's was fashioned by the owners of the famous Shula's Steak House, offering the finest steak, seafood, and signature martinis in the state. Try Turnberry Pub for a casual, all-American menu that is sure to please the whole family, as well as light Mexican fare at the new Iguana Cantina. If dining poolside sounds enticing, you'll savor the aroma coming from the open-pit grill at The Grill at Loch Ness. Breakfast and lunch are also served at each golf clubhouse, and for those who seek the

Photo courtesy of The Westin Innisbrook Resort

privacy and comfort of dining in their suite, Cafe Express offers gourmet food, promptly delivered. A spectacular Sunday brunch is also offered seasonally.

Children's World: At The Westin Innisbrook Resort there is plenty of fun in store for kids of all ages. Offered year-round, the resort's Camp Innisbrook children's program (a Westin Kids Club program) offers a fun-filled day for ages four through twelve. Every day of the week brings a different theme curriculum, which includes swimming, crafts, movies, games, playground time, miniature golf, and group sports, as well as golf and tennis clinics geared to each age. Evening programs are also offered seasonally, allowing mom and dad to enjoy a late round of golf or dinner for two, all the while knowing the children are having their own special fun. Be sure to check with the resort for various summer programs offered each year for toddlers, small children, and teens.

Recreation: Best known for outstanding golf, Innisbrook is considered a true golfer's paradise with ninety holes of championship golf on five well-groomed courses. The resort's Copperhead and Island courses have been ranked in *Golf Digest*'s Top 50 Resort Courses in America. And if you're looking to improve your game, look no farther than the Innisbrook Troon Golf Schools, operated at a private instruction facility at the resort. Three- to five-day programs are offered, as well as specialty schools focusing on a specific aspect of the game or for ladies only. There are daily clinic and instruction programs with the resort's award-winning instructional staff. Three complete practice facilities are also available for practice on any part of your game, day or night.

For the tennis enthusiast, eleven clay courts are available for open play, as well as a complete instructional program for all levels. There are also six swimming pools, basketball, miniature golf, jogging and nature trails, fishing, biking, and a complete fitness center. Of special interest is the new $3.4 million Loch Ness Pool and Spa. This unique recreation park offers a 15-foot cascading waterfall, two winding water slides, a plunge pool, two sand beach areas, and zero-based gradual entry—great for smaller children who are just learning to swim. Already a family favorite, Loch Ness also offers a monster-size spa that seats thirty-six! Fabulous white-sand beaches are also nearby, as well as a variety of water parks and specialty shopping.

A centrally located clubhouse was added in 1999, with guest registration, a lobby bar, a new restaurant, a golf shop, specialty shopping, and a grocery/deli. Upcoming plans at the resort include the addition of a new full-service spa with eighteen treatment rooms and the latest in massage and spa offerings. ≋

MIDWEST

Illinois

Indiana

Michigan

Minnesota

Missouri

Wisconsin

Eagle Ridge Inn and Resort

U.S. Route 20
Box 777
Galena, Illinois 61036
(815) 777–2444, (800) 892–2269
Web site: www.eagleridge.com

With 6,800 acres of rolling, wooded terrain and sixty-three challenging holes of golf, Eagle Ridge is a major Midwest resort. When you're not on the links, you'll find that 220-acre Lake Galena is a focus of resort activity. Located in northwest Illinois just minutes from historic Galena, with its well-preserved nineteenth-century architecture, Eagle Ridge is only 150 miles from Chicago.

Accommodations: The Eagle Ridge Inn, with its eighty rooms, sits at the edge of the lake. In addition, resort homes are scattered throughout the hills and consist of one- to five-bedroom accommodations. During peak season, from May 14 to late October, inn rooms are $199 to $279 a night (children sharing a room with parents are free); the resort homes are $199 to $940 a night. The resort homes are also available for weekly rental, and many different packages are offered.

Dining: An elegant dining spot in the inn is the Woodlands Restaurant, where you'll enjoy steaks, pastas, and seafood along with beautiful views of the lake. Next door is the Woodlands Lounge, for cocktails and more casual dining. Each golf course has its own snack bar and nineteenth hole! The Clubhouse Bar and Grill offers great views of Eagle Ridge's newest golf course, The General, and a casual dining menu of appetizers, soups, salads, sandwiches, and wonderful entrees. When stocking up on provisions, stop by the General Store for delicious deli selections and freshly baked pastries.

Children's World: The Kids Klub is in operation from Memorial Day through Labor Day as well as weekends and holiday times throughout the year; it is designed for four- to twelve-year-olds. The 9:00 A.M. to 4:00 P.M. day is filled with swimming, hiking, boating, games, and arts and crafts; the fee of $28 a day includes lunch. A half day with lunch is $23; a half day without lunch is $20. On three nights a week, dinner, movies, and games entertain children from 7:00 to 10:00 P.M. ($23 an evening). Teens enjoy a Saturday-evening excursion (to $25) that might include a volleyball game, bowling, movie outing, or Alpine slide—all with dinner at a local pizza parlor. Individual baby-sitting is available at $10 an hour.

Recreation: The North and South Courses provide eighteen holes of championship golf set in rolling hills and wooded countryside. The nine-hole East Course, characterized by elevated tees, is an excellent test of accuracy. The latest addition, The General, is a challenging layout. For serious instruction the professionals of the Troon Golf Institute at Eagle Ridge can guide you in everything from the basics to business golf. One-, two-, and three-day programs are offered.

On Lake Galena, fishermen go in search of bass, walleye, and crappie, and boaters head out in paddleboats, canoes, and pontoons. Swimmers can take a dip at the indoor pool adjacent to the fitness center in the inn. Horseback riding along 40 miles of trails begins at the Shenandoah Riding Center. Rent a mountain bike, or hike the trails to seek out native plants and wildlife. For a solitary excursion the fitness trail has twenty-one exercise stations, or round up the whole family for a volleyball game (two courts) or a tennis match (four courts). From the end of July to mid-August, you can combine an Eagle Ridge holiday with watching the Chicago Bears in summer practice at nearby Platteville.

In the winter, sports lovers turn to tobogganing, sledding, and ice skating. Forty miles of cross-country ski trails are carefully groomed. Nearby Chestnut Mountain offers downhill skiing on seventeen runs. ≋

French Lick Springs Resort

8670 West State Road 56
French Lick, Indiana 47432
(812) 936–9300, (800) 457–4042
Web site: www.frenchlick.com

French Lick Springs is a curious name with an interesting history behind it. This area of southwest Indiana was settled by French traders more than 200 years ago. Subsequently, mineral springs were discovered, and, because animals lapped the waters from the wet rocks, locals dubbed it "The Lick." The British moved in during the early nineteenth century; by the 1830s the first hotel was built on this site because visitors were attracted to the healing powers of the mineral waters.

At the end of the century, fire destroyed the original buildings, but the property was purchased and the facilities reconstructed and expanded by Thomas Taggert, then mayor of Indianapolis. Under Taggert's guidance French Lick Springs developed into a first-class resort, with restaurants, golf courses, and a spa. The early-twentieth-century elegance and the devotion to health and recreation were maintained for the next thirty years. Popularity waxed and waned through the Depression, World War II, and the postwar years. For the last nearly four decades restoration has been emphasized; today French Lick Springs encompasses 2,600 acres of the rolling foothills of the Cumberland Mountain range and is dedicated to making the "Golden Days" of the Taggert era an ongoing reality. It is open year-round.

Photo courtesy of French Lick Springs Resort

Accommodations: The rambling main building and its adjacent wings house almost 500 rooms and suites. The large and gracious front porch hints at the relaxed pace that prevails here. Rates for accommodations vary depending on the size, location, and view of a room and range from $79 to $99 per day, based on double occupancy. Children under age seventeen are free; cribs are $10 a day. Package plans are available for golf, tennis, holiday weekends, and the spa's health and fitness programs.

A modified American plan is available (breakfast and dinner). The cost is $30 per day per adult, $20 per day for ages six to twelve years, and free for children five and younger.

Dining: Dining possibilities are many and varied. Chez James is the right choice for an intimate, gourmet dinner, while Le Bistro is a casual steak-and-sandwich restaurant open for lunch and dinner. Combine pizza and bowling at the family-oriented Pizzeria in the Recreation Center, and don't forget to stop at Double Scoops for ice cream. The Country Club Restaurant overlooks the golf course, and the Hoosier Dining Room serves Sunday brunch and international buffet dinners. Sip cocktails in the Derby Bar, the Country Club Lounge, or Le Bistro Bar.

Children's World: The Pluto Club, for five- to twelve-year-olds, starts Memorial Day weekend and runs through Labor Day. Counselors guide kids in arts and crafts, swimming, hiking, and games. The fee is $1.00 an hour. Younger children (three to five years old) have a less rigorous program, for which the fee is $2.00 an hour. Lunch is available for $3.50.

From September to May children's activities are offered Saturday afternoons. At the Christmas and Easter holidays, more elaborate programs are planned.

The unsupervised outdoor playground—filled with swings, slides, monkey bars, teeter-totters, a merry-go-round, and a sandbox—is also a big hit with youngsters.

Children's Tennis Clinics and "Horse Sense" programs are also available for a fee. These supervised activities last about an hour and include instruction. Teen events such as mini-golf tournaments, horseback rides, and scavenger hunts are organized by the Social Staff but are not supervised.

Daily family and social activities are open to children accompanied by an adult; these include hayrides, cookouts, bingo, treasure hunts, lawn sports, and card games.

Recreation: You may not be able to shine in sports quite like Boston Celtic whiz Larry Bird, a native son of French Lick, but at least you have the facilities here where you can focus on improvement. On the gentle, wooded hills, through stands of butternut and oak trees, you can play golf from mid-March to mid-November on two eighteen-hole courses, one of which was designed by Donald Ross. The golf clinics offered April through September put you through the paces in improving your swing, grip, and stance and provide guidance in scrutinizing a course with a bit of strategy.

The tennis complex includes eight indoor courts and ten outdoor lighted courts. Tennis players, too, can have workouts in clinics that cover analyzing a stroke and planning a strategic performance in doubles.

Choose a mount from among thirty horses (lessons available) and head for the trails through the hills; take to the hilly terrain on foot, hiking along the many paths; or hop a surrey to see the scenery. Try out the skeet and trap range, or go for a warm lazy swim in the indoor or outdoor pool. Stroll through the gardens and challenge other guests to lawn games like shuffleboard, volleyball, croquet, badminton, and horseshoes. Rent a bicycle, go bowling (six lanes), play pool, or hit the video games in the Recreation Center. During the winter, cross-country skiing, horse-drawn sleigh rides, and ice skating draw attention.

Don't forget the tradition of the magical quality of the mineral waters. At the Spa you can have mineral baths and massages. Work out in the exercise room, soak in the whirlpool, and block out the rest of the world while sitting in the sauna; a total fitness program can be designed for you.

Nearby activities include the restored Pioneer Village at Spring Mill Park, Marengo Caves, skating at the Roller Dome, and a train ride at the Railway Museum. ≋

Grand Geneva Resort and Spa

Highway 50 East at Route 12
7036 Grand Geneva Way
Lake Geneva, Wisconsin 53147
(414) 248–8811, (800) 558–3417
E-mail: info@grandgeneva.com
Web site: www.grandgeneva.com

T
ucked into the southeastern corner of Wisconsin, between Milwaukee and Chicago, are Lake Geneva and the Grand Geneva Resort & Spa. Less than a day's drive from nine states and sixty million people, the resort sits in the midst of 1,300 acres of pristine Wisconsin countryside and has as its stated goal "to be a destination for relaxation and pleasure." Built in the 1960s as a Playboy Club, it has undergone extensive renovations and reopened in 1994 with a brand-new image. The town of Lake Geneva has been called "the Newport of the Midwest," and that flavor is cultivated here.

Accommodations: A total of 355 guest rooms and suites overlook the rolling green hills and clear blue lake (some also overlook a courtyard parking area, so specify view desired when you book). Decor is that of an elegant and comfortable vacation home. In summer, rooms are $219 to $259 and in winter $119 to $159. Suites range from $189 to $259 in winter and from $279 to $389 in summer. One- to three-bedroom villas are available on-site; summer rates are $269 to $419 and winter rates are $189 to $309.

Dining: Almost everyone likes Italian food, so the bistro-style Ristorante Brissago is sure to please. Open for dinner only, the restaurant features homemade pastas, and the atmosphere is special without being stuffy. Another restaurant choice, The Newport Grill, puts the kitchen right on display, so you get the full effect of sight and aroma as well as the taste of typical Midwestern dishes such as grilled steak, chops, and fresh seafood. The Grill is open for lunch and dinner and serves a bountiful Sunday brunch. The Grand Cafe offers American cuisine, with a children's menu; it's open for breakfast, lunch, dinner, and a special Sunday buffet. Snacks and sandwiches are available in the Links clubhouse at the golf pro shop. For evening cocktails or live entertainment, stop by the Newport Lounge or the Lobby Lounge.

Children's World: The Grand Adventure Kids Club operates year-round on weekends and holidays, daily from Memorial Day through Labor Day, for ages four to twelve years. The morning session is from 10:00 A.M. to noon ($15); the afternoon session is from 1:00 to 5:00 P.M. ($30); the full-day session from 10:00 A.M. to 5:00 P.M. includes lunch ($40). The evening session is from 6:00 to 9:30 P.M. ($20).

Activities include arts and crafts, pony rides, swimming, paddleboating, hiking, and evening movies.

Recreation: All the amenities for a resort vacation are here. Two PGA tour-quality golf courses lure golfers. The Highlands, one of the first Scottish-design courses in the United States, was designed by Jack Nicklaus and Pete Dye. The other course, The Brute, is one of the longest courses in the Midwest, measuring 6,997 yards. Putting greens, driving ranges, and scrupulous attention to grooming keep golfers coming back. Pick up a tennis game on one of the four indoor or five outdoor courts, or work out at the Sport Center, which features a variety of cardio and weight-resistance equipment. A private lake provides paddleboating or hydrobiking opportunities. Exercise your arms with a rowboat or your legs with a paddleboat, or just relax and cruise beautiful Lake Geneva on one of the excursion boats, like the *Lady of the Lake,* a modern reproduction of a Mississippi paddle-wheel steamer. More water opportunities present themselves at the indoor and outdoor pools or with some serious swimming in the lap pool. Jogging, biking, and fitness trails wind through the property, taking advantage of the natural beauty.

You may want to spend the entire day in the Spa. Day membership is $10 for guests and includes use of the whirlpool, sauna, steam, and robes. Fitness classes, therapeutic baths, herbal wraps, antistress facials and massages, and a variety of body masks are just a few of the treatments guaranteed to make you feel like a new person. Enjoy them a la carte or preplanned—for example, an antistress day ($114) or custom spa day ($133).

In the wintertime Grand Geneva has its own mountain for skiing. Even if there is no snow elsewhere in Wisconsin, with snowmaking there will be snow at the resort. Twelve slopes descend from the top elevation of 1,086 feet, with a 211-foot vertical drop. Night skiing, 10 kilometers of cross-country skiing, and a special area for snowboards ensure winter fun for everyone. The Ski School uses Station Teaching to allow individuals to progress at their own rate, mastering each "station," then moving on. ≋

Grand Traverse Resort and Spa

Acme, Michigan 49610
(800) 748–0303
E-mail: info@gtresort.com
Web site: www.grandtraverseresort.com

Long known as the Cherry Capital, this area of northwest lower Michigan has a lot more to offer visitors than just its beautiful orchards and fine fruit. Besides providing memories of Ernest Hemingway, who spent many summers here and used this area as the setting for several short stories, Grand Traverse Resort and Spa offers guests golf, swimming, sailing, cross-country skiing, and a complete sports complex and spa. Set on 950 acres of forests and orchards with ½ mile of shoreline on East Grand Traverse Bay, the year-round resort boasts fine golf courses designed by Jack Nicklaus and Gary Player.

Accommodations: The resort hotel and tower, which house 424 rooms, are adjacent to the Traverse Pavilion, the site of summertime barbecues and wintertime ice skating. The 236 condominium units are spread throughout eight clusters of buildings. Some overlook the bay, and some skirt the golf courses; many have a fireplace. A shuttle service connects the condominiums with the other resort facilities. Rates range from $109 a night (hotel room, low season) to $409 a night (three-bedroom condo, summer). The deluxe Tower encompasses 186 suites, two lounges, a restaurant, and twenty boutiques. This is consummate luxury, with a private two-person whirlpool in each bathroom. Children under eighteen sleep free when sharing a room with their parents. Be sure to inquire about the many package plans. Cribs are available at no charge; rollaway beds are provided at a daily charge of $15.

Dining: Sweetwater Cafe features an open kitchen in the center of the restaurant and serves American fare plus select pasta dishes; it is open seven days a week for breakfast, lunch, and dinner. The Trillium Restaurant, located in the Tower, serves regional American dishes. A children's menu is available in most restaurants. The Grille, in the resort's clubhouse, also provides an informal setting for dining and cocktails. Other choices include Jack's Lounge, the Trillium Lounge, and the Shores Beach Club, on the bay.

Children's World: For six- to twelve-year-olds, a day camp is scheduled half days and full days, Monday through Sunday in the summer and weekends the rest of the year. Activities include arts and crafts, games, swimming, exercise classes, and hiking; fees may be charged for some events. For younger children day care is available in the Cub House, a 2,000-square-foot children's center. Each event through the day is geared to a specific age group; you must register in advance. An adventure playground near the Spa Complex also keeps youngsters well entertained, and the electronic game room may keep them mesmerized. Individual nannies can be scheduled with the assistance of the spa staff.

Recreation: The pride of Grand Traverse Resort and Spa is The Bear. Designed by Jack Nicklaus, this golf course meanders through cherry and apple orchards, with plenty of hardwood forest areas for contrast; it is quite scenic as well as challenging. The older course, Spruce Run, also offers championship play. The resort's third course is a championship course designed by Gary Player, complete with a state-of-the-art clubhouse. Located within walking distance of the

Photo courtesy of Grand Traverse Resort

main resort, the clubhouse serves all three courses. The Jim McLean Golf School program provides sessions from May through September.

The Spa Complex is a championship setup, too. With four outdoor and five indoor tennis courts (instruction available), indoor and outdoor swimming pools, and an exercise/weight room, you'll get quite a workout. Afterward you'll probably head straight to the saunas. A full-service spa provides all the pampering you need. Mountain bikes are available for rent.

If water sports capture your interest, try swimming, sailing, or sailboarding, or take an evening cruise or a charter fishing trip on the bay. Fishermen seek out the many lakes and streams for trout and salmon. Hike or jog through the hills and past the orchards; the scenery is so good for the soul that you may not notice you're also helping your body.

But don't be deceived; Grand Traverse is not just a summertime resort. In the fall trees burst into autumn colors and make a beautiful backdrop for horse-drawn hayrides and trips to nearby wineries for sampling and festivals. In the winter cross-country skiing takes over; Nordic trails weave through the forests and gently rolling hills. Private lessons and group clinics are offered at the Village Nordic Center. Take a sleigh ride through the woods, or go ice skating in the Traverse Pavilion. And remember, while working out at the Spa Complex, you'll never know how low the temperature dips outside. In the spring, when the weather is warm enough for you to want to pick up a golf club, the cherry orchards come to life. The white blossoms of the trees blanket the hillsides for more than half the month of May. ≈≈

Grand View Lodge

23521 Nokomis Avenue
Nisswa, Minnesota 56468
(800) 432–3788
E-mail: vacation@grandviewlodge.com
Web site: www.grandviewlodge.com

Nestled among the Norway pines on the north shore of Gull Lake is Grand View Lodge, the focal point of this 900-acre resort. Built in 1918 of native cedar logs and now a National Historic Site, the lodge welcomes guests year-round. In addition to the lodge, sixty-five cottages border the lake. Deluxe suites and town homes are also nearby. Located 142 miles northwest of Minneapolis, the lodge is within a fifteen-minute drive of seven golf courses, Paul Bunyan Center, and animal parks.

Accommodations: The twelve rooms in the lodge are comfortable for couples, while a cottage is the right choice for a family. Since these range in size from one to eight bedrooms, owner Fred Boos explains that they "try to fit the cabin to the family." Some cabins feature a kitchenette and living room; all have decks as well as large picture windows and views of the lake. Suites and town houses overlooking The Pines golf course also are available. Daily maid service is provided for both the lodge and the cabins. Reservations are accepted on a daily as well as weekly basis. Rates from $325 (double occupancy, per day) include two meals a day, golf at the Garden Course, discounted golf rates at The Pines, The Preserve, and Deacon's Lodge championship courses, tennis, and the children's program. For children the charge is $10 to $55 a night, American plan, depending on the age of the child.

Dining: There are several restaurants: the main dining room in the historic lodge, Freddy's in the Pines Clubhouse, The Preserve Steak House in the Preserve Clubhouse, Sherwood Forest (also a historic building), and Italian Gardens. Dress is casual. Barbecues on the beach are often planned. Children may dine with their parents or their counselors. A special menu for children features fresh fish, steaks, chicken, and ribs. Cocktails are served on the large, three-level redwood deck or in the North Woods Lounge, where you'll hear live music nightly. The smorgasbord is a traditional Sunday event—great fun and all you can eat.

Children's World: From Memorial Day weekend to Labor Day weekend, Grand View has two well-organized programs, for children ages three to six and seven to twelve. There is a wonderful wooden playhouse in the woods with slides and climbing equipment, a well-stocked play area, and the beach along Gull Lake. The programs run from 9:00 A.M. to 3:00 P.M. and from 6:00 to 8:00 P.M., Monday through Saturday. The schedule includes arts, games, storytime, movement activities, exercise, and swimming.

The staff is college age and generally has past experience with children. The program is free except for special tours and trips. For those under age three, the front desk can arrange baby-sitting with either an off-duty staff member or selected local persons.

Recreation: The lake attracts swimmers, fishermen, sailors, and sunbathers. Here you can also venture out in a pontoon or kayak or practice some waterskiing. A twenty-seven-hole championship golf course is aptly named, given its setting: The Pines. The nine-hole Garden Course is perfect for the entire family. The Preserve, an eighteen-hole championship course, is located just 10 miles north of Grand View Lodge. Arnold Palmer's Deacon's Lodge, rated one of the "Top ten new public courses in the nation" by *Golf Magazine,* is the newest addition to Grand View's golf family.

A tennis complex with seven Laykold courts is set among tall trees. Court time is free. The tennis pro teaches private lessons, organizes tournaments, and conducts free group lessons for children eight to nineteen years old. Two hitting walls and an automatic ball machine allow for extra practice before a good match. ≋

Harbour View Inn

P.O. Box 1207
Mackinac Island, Michigan 49757
(906) 847–0101
Web site: www.harbourviewinn.com

For a truly unique vacation experience, take your family to Mackinac Island where the main modes of transportation are by bike or horse-drawn carriage. Mackinac Island is accessible by auto, plane, or boat. When arriving by automobile, you will find passenger ferry services to the Island conveniently located in the downtown areas of Mackinaw City and St. Ignace. Secure overnight parking and luggage handling services are available from both ports. If you choose to arrive by boat or yacht, complete marina services are available.

When you visit the Harbour View Inn you are visiting a great place for families who love history. This stately manor was built in 1820 by Madame La Framboise, a Great Lakes fur trader and granddaughter of Returning Cloud, Chief of the Ottawa Indian Nation. The inn, featured in *The Detroit Free Press, Victoria Magazine, Colonial Homes,* and *Traverse,* has also been awarded three-diamond status by AAA.

Accommodations: Charming Victorian detail has been preserved for your stay at the Harbour View Inn. Elegant accommodations offer views of the historic harbor or the landscaped gardens. In-room whirlpools and balconies are also available and a complimentary deluxe continental breakfast is served each morning. Chateau LaFramboise rooms are decorated in a blend of French and Victorian styles, while a Mackinac Island Summer Cottage theme defines the Carriage House and Guest House rooms. Spacious studio-style suites are also available. Daily rates range from $85 to $295 depending on room/suite type, the season, and occupancy.

Dining: A variety of dining opportunities are within close proximity of the Harbour View and include Three Brothers Sarducci Pizza, Zach's Deli, the Pilot House, Martha's Ice Cream and Sweet Shop, Astor Street Cafe, and many more. The contrast in offerings is sure to please the whole family.

Children's World: Mackinac Island will provide hours of adventure for your child. You can rent bicycles, in-line skates, boats, horses, or even carriages for family fun. Make sure you visit Fort Mackinac and the Butterfly House. Take a carriage tour or visit the Haunted House. If you get tired of what you can find to do on land, try one of the cruise or fishing charters, or you can always relax at the beach. Child care is available.

Recreation: For the golf enthusiast try the Grand Hotel Golf Course. For a rigorous workout, explore the parks and hiking trails that help make Mackinac so unique. During the winter months the island offers skiing and sleigh rides. ≈≈≈

The Homestead

Wood Ridge Road
Glen Arbor, Michigan 49636
(231) 334–5000
Web site: www.thehomestead.com

The Great Lakes are truly great—and not just in size. While Lake Michigan's 22,400-square-mile area is indeed impressive, imagine the possibilities it affords in recreation and relaxation: swimming, boating, and fishing in the water, and on land, hiking and biking the wooded trails beyond the lake's sandy beach. At The Homestead all this great potential is realized, combined with tennis facilities, variety in dining, and comfortable, attractive lodging. When the weather cools the swimmers give way to skiers, who discover nature's wintertime beauty.

The Homestead is located on the northwest shore of lower Michigan. Its 500 acres embrace gently rolling land covered with pine trees, aspens, and oaks; 1 mile of sandy beach on Lake Michigan; and 6 miles of shoreline along the banks of Crystal River. Surrounding the resort is the Sleeping Bear Dunes National Lakeshore; besides ensuring The Homestead's secluded position, this national preserve opens up additional opportunities for nature explorers. The resort is closed in April and November.

Accommodations: The Village is the center of most activities; accommodations, restaurants, shops, and a heated swimming pool are located here. Fiddler's Pond and Little Belle in the Village offer guest rooms and suites overlooking the pond. One- to four-bedroom condominiums, each with a full kitchen, are located on the beach, along Crystal River, on a ridge overlooking the shoreline, and in the Village. Crystal River cuts through the hills and runs more or less parallel to the lakeshore a short way before emptying into the lake. Where the river and the lake merge is another center of activity, the Beach Club.

Photo courtesy of The Homestead

Fiddler's Pond rooms are $69 to $159 a night; Little Belle's rates are $89 to $209 a night. A one-bedroom condominium unit ranges between $126 and $311 a night, depending on the location you choose; lakefront and lake-view units are the most expensive. The rates for larger units graduate to $633 a night for a four-bedroom home/condominium. These rates are applied during the summer and on weekends through the year; package plans are also available. Cribs are provided at no charge; children are free when staying in their parents' room.

Dining: At the Beach Club the Cafe Manitou draws diners to its ideal location on the beach; open daily in the summer only, its setting and attire are casual.

Around the bend in the Village, Nonna's boasts a bountiful breakfast and Northern Italian dinners, and Whiskers attracts pizza and burger fans. Also in the Village, at Cavanaugh's you can pick up groceries or deli sandwiches for lunch and snacks all day long. In the winter skiers gather in CQ's Cabin for its cozy atmosphere and friendly conversation.

Children's World: The children's summer program runs from late June through late August and entertains guests from toddlers to teenagers.

Daily, half and full days keep five- to twelve-year-olds busy with soccer and volleyball games, hiking, fishing, exercising to music, and arts and crafts. The Kids Kamp cost is $25 for half days and $40 for full days. Activities for this group and for teens are published in a weekly calendar. Kids can also join junior golf or tennis programs.

Teenagers enjoy a loose schedule that focuses on meeting other teens during canoe races, volleyball games, tennis matches, and pizza parties. Like the events for the younger group, some are free, while others require a fee. Private swimming lessons can be arranged, and tennis clinics are offered for young adults ages twelve to seventeen and juniors ages six to eleven.

In the winter the children's program teaches five- to twelve-year-olds fun-in-the-snow activities with ski lessons. It is offered for two and a half hours twice a day, Friday through Sunday, and on holidays from mid-December through March. The fee is $25 for a half day or $65 for a full day with lunch.

Any time of year, individual baby-sitters can be hired, at approximately $5.00 per hour. The resort staff assists in making the arrangements.

Recreation: The clear waters of Lake Michigan are fine for sailing, boating (rentals available), fishing, and swimming. Maybe still a little nippy in June, the lake's temperature averages 65 to 70 degrees by July and August, and its sandy bottom is particularly attractive to young swimmers. The river waters tend to be warmer, and both the Beach Club and the Village have a heated pool and a hot tub, so guests have their pick of swimming conditions. You can also enjoy the spa at the Beach Club. Fishing is good sport in the river as well as in the lake, and canoeing up the river allows you to investigate the local wildlife.

Hike, jog, and bicycle (children's bikes and bikes with children's seats are available for rent) on the 24 miles of wooded trails; a self-guided nature tour can introduce you to the area's flora and fauna.

Visit the nearby Sleeping Bear Dunes National Park, take a ferryboat ride to the islands in Lake Michigan, sample the wines of local vineyards, or just take a relaxing stroll along the beach at sunset.

For tennis players the Beach Club, with its five clay courts, is the site of many exciting matches. Here you can join a clinic, take private lessons, and watch real talent during professional exhibitions. If you're still looking for things to do, drop by the aerobics exercise class; work out on the fitness trail, with twenty exercise stations; head to the playground at River Park; or throw your hat into a volleyball tournament. Now here's ingenuity in utilizing space: In 1995 a nine-hole par-3 golf course opened—built in part on the downhill ski slopes!

In the winter 36 kilometers of trails attract cross-country skiers to The Homestead's wooded hills, and the frozen ponds are ideal for ice skating. Downhill skiing is modest, with thirteen runs and 350 vertical feet, but the view down a snowy slope to whitecaps on the lake is an uncommon juxtaposition you'll long remember. All runs benefit from artificial snowmaking, and those lighted for nighttime skiing add another dimension to a winter holiday. ≋≋

The Lodge of Four Seasons
Championship Golf Resort and Spa

Horseshoe Bend Parkway
Lake Ozark, Missouri 65049
(573) 365–3000, (800) THE–LAKE
Web site: www.4seasonsresort.com

Lake of the Ozarks, a man-made lake developed in the 1930s, has provided scenic and recreational diversions for the residents of central Missouri for more than sixty years. Overlooking the lake, in the wooded gentle hills of the Ozarks, is The Lodge of Four Seasons. Opened in 1964, The Lodge has grown over the years into a major year-round resort with extensive recreational facilities and award-winning restaurants. Today it is a convenient escape from city cares for the residents of St. Louis and Kansas City and is sought as a vacation spot for visitors from farther afield as well.

Accommodations: Guests choose from 303 newly renovated guest rooms or 86 two- and three-bedroom condominiums—frequently more suitable for families. Charleston is The Lodge's newest condo development, built around a secluded cove with a breathtaking view of the lake. Some units have private boat slips. Condominium prices range from $185 to $385 a night, March to November; the rates are $89 to $149 in the lodge itself. Rates are lower during the rest of the year. Children under eighteen share their parents' room at no extra charge; complimentary cribs are available.

Dining: Toledo's offers a unique combination of great dining and live entertainment. Toledo's moderately priced menu features a variety of fresh selections incorporating specialties indigenous to the area. A children's menu is available, as well as an extensive wine selection, winner of the *Wine Spectator* award since 1997. Enjoy the finest cuts of certified Angus beef (or turkey steak if you prefer) at HK's Steak House, located on the golf course; it features a custom-designed, elevated grill. Have breakfast or lunch at Roseberry's Cafe in a casual, family-style setting. Soleil's is the place for baked goods hot from the oven, or for tasty panini sandwiches.

Children's World: The Adventure Club provides a fun-filled day of activities for children age three to twelve. The Adventure Club is open every day (seasonally) from 9:00 A.M. to 5:00 P.M., and offers a weekend Kids Night Out from 6:00 to 9:00 P.M. Half- and full-day adventures are available; there is a daily charge for each child. Lunch is provided in the full-day program. Enjoy swimming, nature walks, fishing, games, movies, arts and crafts, theme days, and cookouts. The Adventure Club's staff is certified in Red Cross first aid and water safety training.

Photo courtesy of The Lodge of Four Seasons Championship Golf Resort and Spa

Recreation: The sports enthusiast will be well satisfied at The Lodge of Four Seasons, named one of the "Top 50 Golf Resorts" by *Condé Nast Traveler.* One championship eighteen-hole golf course was designed by Robert Trent Jones Sr., and interests players with its narrow, undulating fairways and glimpses of the lake's blue waters. A second eighteen-hole championship golf course, Seasons Ridge, is carved into the rolling Ozark terrain, where multiple tee boxes accommodate golfers of all skill levels. Golf instruction is offered at both of these courses. In addition, golfers can turn to the nine-hole course to sharpen their skills. Equipment and attire can be purchased at the pro shop, if you've forgotten anything. If water sports are your life's love, you certainly won't feel slighted with both indoor and outdoor pools to enjoy. Swimmers can also venture out into the lake or sunbathe on the private beach. The lake is a favorite of boaters; the full-service marina can handle more than 200 boats and is the base for lake activities, from boat rentals and waterskiing to fishing guide services and parasailing. The Lodge of Four Seasons also offers a scenic excursion boat that takes guests on a smooth journey around the lake.

Guests can unwind at Spa Shiki. Try a full body massage or other services at the full-service spa. Browse through on-site shops, catch a movie in the lodge's cinema, or simply take a stroll through beautifully landscaped Japanese gardens. If you have any energy left, hike along wooded paths or try your hand at trapshooting. Volleyball, basketball, and tennis are even more options to fit into a busy schedule. At the end of a very full day, you may choose to stop and have a drink at the Lobby Bar, dance at Studios Entertainment and Dance Club, or retire early for a well-deserved repose. ≈≈≈

Ludlow's Island Lodge

P.O. Box 1146
Cook, Minnesota 55723
(218) 666–5407, (877) 583–5697
Web site: www.ludlowsresort.com

Minnesota has a reputation as the land of 10,000 lakes (ever wonder who counted them all?), and Ludlow's Island Lodge is well situated on one of these—picturesque Lake Vermilion. The resort facilities are located on Ludlow's Island and on the north and south shores of the lake. A boat shuttle connects the three areas. Water-related activities are the primary recreation at this wooded resort. Fishing, swimming, sailing, and exploring any of the 365 islands provide wonderful experiences. The seclusion among the pines and birches, with the lake practically at your front door, makes this retreat a real back-to-nature experience. The resort is open May through September.

Accommodations: Twenty cabins with enchanting names like Stardust, Evergreen, and Twilite are located on the island and the shores. Designed with knotty pine or cedar interiors, all have a fireplace and outdoor deck; most have a screened porch. They range from one to five bedrooms, with a fully equipped kitchen (yes, even a dishwasher and microwave). Daily rates start at $200 for two adults and $30 for each child. Summer weekly rates start at $1,950 for two people.

Dining: Ludlow's offers full menu choices for evening meals delivered to your cabin. Each cabin has a menu with items ranging from $9.50 to $17.50. Pizza and burgers are also available. The order is placed with the lodge by 5:00 P.M. and delivered to your cabin by 7:00 P.M., to be served on cabin dishes.

Children's World: Planned activities just for children are scheduled only an hour or two each day, Monday through Friday. Boat rides, nature hikes, and fishing derbies introduce kids to the surrounding woods and waters. Movies are shown in the afternoons. The two-story tree house and a small camping island for overnight trips are probably the biggest attractions for the younger set, but the swings, the lake (with a section roped off for children's safety), and the sandy beach are good play areas, too. Kids also enjoy the video-game room and exploring the trails in the forest, just like Paul Bunyan of Minnesota lore. The recreation complex on the south shore has a children's play area. The management can help arrange baby-sitters.

Photo © Jack Rendulich, courtesy of Ludlow's Island Lodge

Recreation: Fishing buffs relish this bit of paradise on the south shores of Lake Vermilion. Walleye, bass, and crappie lure fishermen to these waters. There's no excuse for not landing the big one; a fishing clinic is held every week, and a guide is available for private excursions. The staff at the lodge will fillet and freeze your catch. Besides fishing boats, the lodge has canoes, kayaks, paddleboats, and a sailboat for guests' use.

The recreation center houses an indoor racquetball court, two Tru-Flex tennis courts, and a fitness center. After a good workout there, you may enjoy a leisurely swim or a relaxing sauna. Along the north shore you can take a stroll down the 1½-mile hiking trail. There are many additional miles of hiking and biking trails in the area. ≋

Marriott's Tan-Tar-A Resort and Golf Club

State Road KK
Osage Beach, Missouri 65065
(573) 348–3131
Web site: www.tan-tar-a.com

Located in central Missouri, Marriott's Tan-Tar-A Resort rests comfortably in the foothills of the Ozark Mountains. The resort complex covers 420 acres and sprawls along the shores of the scenic Lake of the Ozarks. The hilly terrain and lakeside exposure provide a lovely backdrop for the many recreational activities. Tan-Tar-A is only a three-hour drive from either St. Louis or Kansas City.

Accommodations: The 930 guest rooms and suites are in the main resort buildings and in smaller two-story accommodations bordering the lake and the golf course. Some have a fireplace and a deck or patio. The high season is mid-May to mid-September, when rates are $99 to $165 a night. During the low season (November to mid-March) prices drop to $65 to $110 a night. In the remaining months the rates are $89 to $145 a night.

Dining: The casual family-style restaurant, the Cliff Room, has a large deck for outdoor dining. Between 5:00 and 7:00 P.M. children eight years old and younger eat free. For a fancier evening try Windrose on the Water, where you'll enjoy luscious steaks and fresh seafood. If all you want is a quick bite, there are fast-food facilities nearby. At the golf course The Oaks serves breakfast and lunch, overlooking the course.

For liquid refreshment The Landing is a daytime pub, The Jetty Bar is adjacent to the Arrowhead Pool, and Tradewinds is near the Tradewinds Pool. Mr. D's also serves cocktails, and The Nightwinds Lounge offers live music for dancing in the evening.

Children's World: Camp Tan-Tar-A, for children ages five to ten years, is in session Monday through Friday, from early June through mid-August and at holiday times the rest of the year. The fee for the 9:30 A.M. to 4:00 P.M. schedule is $25 for the first day and $20 for each additional day. Activities include swimming, beach games, races, treasure hunts, and crafts. Kids ages seven to ten can join a guided fishing tour for two hours ($25 per child).

A less structured routine is found at the Children's Playhouse, which is open to four- to ten-year-olds, Saturday from 9:00 A.M. to 5:00 P.M. and Monday through Saturday evenings from 6:30 to 11:00 P.M. Here counselors supervise children as they play with an array of toys, board games, puzzles, and books. During the spring, fall, and winter, the schedule at the Playhouse is limited to all day Saturday and Friday and Saturday evenings. The fee is $4.00 an hour for the first child and only 50 cents an hour for each additional child. These same rates apply for individual baby-sitters.

Recreation: The lake is the venue for boating fun for everyone. You can rent ski boats (waterskiing instruction available), sailboats, paddleboats, kayaks, fishing boats, and Wave Runners. You can even try parasailing. Though there's a small sandy beach nice for sunbathing, the lake is primarily the domain of boaters and fishermen. Swimmers usually opt for time at one of the five pools (four outdoors, one indoors).

Golfers can take on the challenges of The Oaks (an eighteen-hole course) or Hidden Lakes (nine holes). The Racquet Club houses tennis and racquetball courts as well as billiards. Outdoors and adjacent to the club are basketball and volleyball courts. Tennis buffs can also try the indoor or outdoor tennis courts near the Racquet Club.

At the fitness center you can use the exercise room as well as the indoor pool, and you can indulge in the many programs at the Windjammer Spa. Facials, massages, aromatherapy, and detoxification treatments are just some of the pleasures from which to choose.

Back in the great outdoors, find a good horse at the stables for a nice trail ride, rent a mountain bike, jog along the paths around the property, test your skill at the trap range, or challenge the kids to a round of miniature golf. If you still have time and energy, try bowling, shuffleboard, horseshoes, and table tennis. Even the shoppers in your family will have plenty of fun in the dozen shops, featuring jewelry, toys, fashions, and country crafts. And be sure to take an evening cruise on the lake; the *Ozark Princess* sails four nights a week during the summer season.

In the winter ice skating is available for both adults and children. ≋

Mission Point Resort

One Lakeshore Drive
Mackinac Island, Michigan 49757
(800) 833–7711
E-mail: missionpoint@missionpoint.com
Web site: www.missionpoint.com

Mission Point Resort is privately owned property encompassing eighteen acres of Mackinac Island lakefront. The resort is situated along the southeast coast of the island and is just minutes from downtown. The island's early-twentieth-century ambience is enhanced by the noticeable absence of cars, since the only access to the island is by ferry or plane. This all-American lakeshore retreat is complemented by the natural adventures and historic discoveries of Mackinac Island. The island boasts the nation's second oldest park, and pine forests are threaded with hiking and biking paths as well as unusual limestone foundations and caves.

Taking advantage of existing architecture, Mission Point has renovated The Observation Tower, offering island visitors extraordinary views of Lake Huron and the Straits of Mackinac. This all-glass structure on the resort's property serves as the perfect spot to watch sailboats approach the southeast coast during the island's annual yacht races.

Accommodations: Mission Point has 242 guest rooms and suites, including family suites. The resort has a health club, art gallery, and much more. All the resort's guest rooms and suites, including the new outdoor Hot Tub Suites, celebrate the beauty of Northern Michigan. The heated swimming pool, therapeutic massage, saunas, and hot tubs are great ways to relax. You may want to spend some of your time on The Greens on Mackinac on the water's edge or on The Courts enjoying tennis, lawn bowling, or croquet.

Dining: The resort has four restaurants. At The Great Straits Seafood Company, world-renowned Chef Ernst Ackermann adds his flair to a culinary palette of fresh fish and steaks. For the casual side of island dining, try The Round Island Bar and Grill, where guests can watch passing freighters while enjoying appetizers, sandwiches, and spirits in a warm setting. Freighters Deli and Outdoor Cafe offers sandwiches and salads for guests on the go as well as indoor and outdoor dining with spectacular views of Lake Huron and the Straits of Mackinac. The Euro Garden Cafe, an open-air dining experience, serves a tempting array of European dishes from the chef's own personal recipes. It's worth noting that the resort has gourmet picnic baskets to go, a great addition to a day of island exploration. Children twelve and younger dine free of charge.

Children's World: Mission Point Resort's children's program Discovery Club is staffed with dedicated, trained counselors. Discovery Club offers island field trips and exciting activities, such as Wild Kingdom Day and Space Day, for children ages four through ten. The fee for the program is $12.00 for a full day or $7.00 for a half day. Families with more than one child receive a 50 percent discount for each additional child registered in the program.

With a 3,000-square-foot area in which kids spark their imagination with a variety of interesting activities, Discovery Club includes a Parent and Toddler Room, Gross Motor Skills Rooms, and a Kreative Korner Room, as well as some of the kids' traditional favorites like the 12-foot tepee. The active atmosphere of the resort is complemented by Mackinac Island itself, a natural adventure park offering outdoor explorations and historic sites.

At Discovery Club kids enjoy a variety of supervised opportunities including arts and crafts, learning ancient Indian lore, plus field trips to the Island's Butterfly House, the 150-year-old British Fort, or along the Island's bluff for bald eagle spotting. Discovery Club is not only fun, it is also a safe place for young guests to stay while parents enjoy the resort's art gallery, island boutiques, or the nearby championship golf courses. Parents are encouraged to sign up children one day in advance, allowing the counselors to plan appropriate activities and guarantee its one-to-six counselor/child ratio. As an added convenience, pagers are available for parents of young guests.

Recreation: Experience the island by guided tours or independent exploration. Attractions include miles of forest trails for hiking, horseback riding, and carriage tours. Sites you won't want to miss are Fort Mackinac (circa 1780), the restored British and American military outpost where you can see Colonial reenactments, period characters, and cannon firings; Mackinac Island State Park, which encompasses two-thirds of the entire island and preserves natural forests;

Benjamin Blacksmith Shop, where you see, smell, and even feel the heat from the nineteenth-century forge as craftsmen still practice their skill; Astor Warehouse (circa 1820), where mink, muskrat, otter, and beaver pelts were graded for Indians and fur traders; Biddle House (circa 1820), a restored home of a prominent fur trader that brings to life the domestic side of island history; McGulpin House (circa 1780), the oldest structure on the island; and Skull Cave—to name just a few.

If you still want more to do, the Activities Desk can arrange for Mission Point guests to tee off at one of six championship golf courses. Sailing cruises are an invigorating experience and fishing charters yield catches of perch, whitefish, and chinook salmon. Whatever you choose to do, you can be sure that a brand new experience is waiting for you and your family at Mission Point Resort. ≋

Ruttger's Bay Lake Lodge

Box 400
Deerwood, Minnesota 56444
(218) 678–2885, (800) 450–4545
E-mail: reservations@ruttgers.com
Web site: www.ruttgers.com

If you have ever entertained thoughts of owning your own lakefront cottage in the land of 10,000 lakes, Ruttger's Bay Lake Lodge may satisfy your yearning. Set on 400 acres directly on Bay Lake, in north-central Minnesota, the Lodge emphasizes relaxed outdoor recreation in surroundings of clear lake waters, tall trees, and pine-scented air. Open May through September, it is family run and family oriented. With its tradition of old-fashioned hospitality, the lodge allows you a well-deserved escape to the peace and serenity of the North Woods.

Accommodations: For years the lakefront cottages and the lodge rooms have been favorites among vacationers. To these have been added condominiums and villas. Many have views of the lake, and all include a refrigerator and are air-conditioned. Rates are $98 to $183 per person per day, modified American plan. Children three and under are free; the rate for four- to eight-year-olds is one-third the adult rate and for nine- to fifteen-year-olds, one-half the adult rate. Cribs are provided at no additional charge with a weekly package plan.

Dining: The modified American plan is mandatory for cottage guests, and the homemade pastries are practically a requirement. The main dining room is an inviting setting, with natural logs, an open-beamed ceiling, and a stone fireplace. For casual dining and drinks, lunch and dinner are also served at Zig's, which overlooks Bass Lake and the eighteenth hole of The Lakes golf course.

Auntie M's Kaffeehaus offers specialty coffees, panini sandwiches, pastry, and ice cream. You may cook lunch for yourself in the condos. The main lodge and Zig's both have picture windows that are great for viewing the North Woods while you're sipping a cool drink.

Children's World: Kids' Kamp is a supervised and complimentary program for children, in operation from mid-June until Labor Day, Monday through Saturday, on the modified American plan. Beginning at age four, kids join their counselors from 9:00 A.M. to 3:00 P.M. A certified teacher and counselors organize the day for fishing, swimming, crafts, treasure hunts, nature programs, and talent shows. A playground is located near the aesthetic Kids' Kamp building. Two times a week the children can join a dinner and activities evening from 5:00 to 8:00 P.M. Baby-sitting can be arranged by the staff for approximately $5.00 per hour.

Recreation: With such a beautiful lake, you might find yourself drawn to the water almost continuously through the day—for sunning, swimming, waterskiing, fishing, and boating, and for building sand castles along the beach. Swimmers also enjoy the indoor and outdoor pools, and tennis fans turn to the two Omni-turf and three Laykold courts. Round up a game of volleyball, basketball, or horseshoes; play table tennis and shuffleboard; or go walking through the woods. Practice on the putting green, and plan a round of golf on the eighteen-hole championship course or Alec's Nine. And treat yourself to relaxation in the lounge or TV lobby, the whirlpool, or the sauna. The staff naturalist directs programs introducing visitors to the loon, osprey, and bald eagle. Waterskiing, sailboats, motorboats, pontoon boats, and fishing boats are available. ≋

Shanty Creek

1 Shanty Creek Road
Bellaire, Michigan 49615
(800) 678–4111
E-mail: info@shantycreek.com
Web site: www.shantycreek.com

Shanty Creek, located in northern Michigan, is actually two resorts in one, which translates into a bit of variety for guests. Summit Village is elegant and contemporary, while Schuss Village is modeled on an Alpine village. Together they encompass 4,500 acres of rolling woodlands on the shores of Lake Bellaire. In the summertime golfing is the favorite activity; in winter skiing is the preferred sport.

The summer of 1999 witnessed the grand opening of The Lodge at Summit–Schuss–Cedar River. This eighty-five-room, all-suite luxury hotel offers outstanding views of the new Tom Weiskopf–designed Cedar River Golf Club and the newest ski runs on the Schuss slopes.

Accommodations: Lodging choices are innumerable: guest rooms, studios, condominiums, and chalets. Some are equipped with a fireplace or whirlpool; others have a deck. You might have a view of the lake, the forests, a fairway, or the Alpine village. Rates start at $86 a night for a guest room and rise to $390 a night for a deluxe two-bedroom condominium. Children ages seventeen and under stay free when occupying a room with their parents. Cribs can be added to your accommodation for a fee of $10.00 a day. The many package plans offer good savings.

Dining: The Lakeview Dining Room is an elegant restaurant at Summit Village. At Schuss Village a down-home, fun, family atmosphere prevails at the more casual Weiskopf Grill. For light meals and easy dining, try Arnie's at The Legend Pro Shop. Whispers, at Cedar Lodge, provides fine gourmet dining. The Beach Club, right on the shores of Lake Bellaire, also offers refreshments.

Children's World: When the weather warms up, just as the golf season begins, infants to ten-year-olds can be accommodated in a daily child-care program. From 9:00 A.M. to 5:00 P.M., children join together in storytime, movies, arts and crafts, and music. The fee is $30.00 full day, $21.00 half day. Lunch is $6.00 extra.

From early June through Labor Day, Camp Gandy explodes with summertime fun: nature hikes, basketball, volleyball, scavenger hunts, shuffleboard, and swimming. This program is designed for children ages six and older. The fees and hours are the same as above.

When the ski season starts in November, the daily child-care program applies to infants to six-year-olds. In addition to stories, movies, and indoor play, the older children discover the excitement of outdoor play in a winter wonderland. The same fees as above are charged for this program.

Young skiers, ages three to five, combine indoor play with sledding and ski instruction in their 10:00 A.M. to 4:00 P.M. schedule. The fee is $55 a day and includes ski rental and lunch.

Kid's Academy, for older children (ages five to eleven), runs from 10:00 A.M. to 4:00 P.M. daily. This is more serious instruction but still doesn't lose sight of the fun of skiing. The fee is $40 full day, $30 half day with lunch. Ski rentals are not included in these fees.

At any time of the year, baby-sitting can be booked through the concierge for $6.00 an hour.

Recreation: Golfers experience a bit of a dream come true here. The resort's original course is the eighteen-hole Summit Golf Course. Another championship eighteen holes make up the beautiful Schuss Mountain Course. And the crowning gem is The Legend, an exciting eighteen-hole course designed by Arnold Palmer. With the carefully maintained courses complemented by an experienced teaching staff, all golfers will surely improve their games here. The new Cedar River Golf Club, designed by Tom Weiskopf, is sure to win accolades from all players.

Other summertime activities include tennis, with eight courts; biking on the mountain trails; and boating. At the Fitness Center work out on the Nautilus equipment, head to the racquetball courts, hit the steam room or sauna, and wind up the day with a massage. With indoor swimming pools and a heated pool outdoors, swimmers are satisfied whatever the season.

The ski season starts in November and continues through late March or early April, depending on how generous Mother Nature has been. There are forty-six runs for downhill skiers, almost 20 miles of groomed trails for cross-country skiers, and two terrain parks for snowboarders. When you're not on skis, pile the whole family into a horse-drawn sleigh for an old-fashioned ride in the woods. ≋≋

SOUTHWEST

Arizona

New Mexico

Oklahoma

Texas

Angel Fire Resort

P.O. Drawer B
Angel Fire, New Mexico 87710
(505) 377–6401, (800) 633–7463
E-mail: reserve@angelfireresort.com
Web site: www.angelfireresort.com

I mpressed by the pink glow on the mountains, Indians named this area "the land of Angel Fire." This year-round resort in the ancient Sangre de Cristo Mountain range of northern New Mexico allows for escape, renewal, and rejuvenation. Angel Fire encompasses 20,000 acres of mountain scenery and beauty and extends its Southwestern ambience with a warm, neighborly feeling in spite of its size.

Accommodations: Angel Fire can accommodate approximately 4,000 guests in a variety of lodges and condominiums scattered through the village area. At first glance, so many guests conjures up images of crowds, but remember that this still leaves five acres of land per person! In addition, the Starfire Lodge and Angel Fire Resort Hotel offer rooms and suites, so you may take your choice of accommodation styles. Prices range from $75 to $160 for a room up to $125 to $345 for a three-bedroom unit. Cribs are provided at a nominal nightly fee. Prices vary depending on season.

Dining: Hungry? The village has eleven dining areas. Choose from a variety of foods including Italian, Mexican, and steak house specialties. Dress is casual, and selected restaurants cater to children with special menus. For relaxing with drinks, most of the restaurants and clubs have lounges, many with inviting fireplaces. The Angel Fire Country Club matches up spectacular mountain views with tasty breakfasts, lunches, and dinners. Live entertainment enlivens weekends at Angel Fire.

Children's World: The Angel Fire Resort offers children's programs in both summer and winter.

During winter, from Thanksgiving to the end of March, the focus is on skiing and snowboarding. Young skiers ages three to twelve can join the Children's Ski and Snowboard Center, which runs from 8:30 A.M. to 4:00 P.M.; a $65 to $75 daily fee covers lessons, lift tickets, rentals, and lunch. And in case you do not believe your eyes, a Disneylike "Snow Bear" does indeed ski with the children.

Very young or nonskiing children can participate in daily activities at the Angel Fire Resort Day Care. Children six weeks to twelve years old can join the fun on an hourly basis from 8:00 A.M. to 5:00 P.M. daily. These sessions are a combination of indoor play—such as games, treasure hunts, and crafts—and

Photo courtesy of Ben Blakenburg and Angel Fire Resort

outdoor play that emphasizes fun in the snow, such as "snowercise" and snow sculpture. The fee is $6.00 per hour, $45 for a full day, or $30 for a half day. Parents must provide diapers, bottles, formula, and other supplies.

Recreation: The primary diversion in winter is skiing or snowboarding. Angel Fire has hosted the World Cup Freestyle Competition, but don't be intimidated. More than two-thirds of the trails are for beginners and intermediates. The vertical drop is 2,077 feet, and the longest trail is a cruising 3½ miles long. Six chairlifts cover 30 miles of trails, two ski shops are ready to rent or sell equipment and accessories, and lessons are available. The Nordic skier can enjoy unlimited trails at the Angel Fire Resort Golf Course. In varying levels of difficulty, these trek through aspen, spruce, and ponderosa pine groves. Sleigh rides and snowmobiles round out the wintertime fun.

Once the snow melts, these same trails offer fantastic opportunities for mountain biking, hiking, backpacking, and horseback riding. Catching a trout from the annually stocked lake can be an exhilarating experience, but if fishing is not your sport, you can canoe and sail in these waters. Have a swim in the pool, play tennis, or bicycle on the paths around the village. At an elevation of 8,600 feet, the eighteen-hole golf course weaves through a wooded terrain. Practice on the driving range and putting green, or enlist the expert advice of the golf pro. Summer Adventures offers such things as white-water rafting or gold panning for a fee. Whatever your activity, the crisp mountain air enhances it. ≋

The Arizona Biltmore

2400 East Missouri Street
Phoenix, Arizona 85016
(602) 955–6600, (800) 950–0086

The Arizona Biltmore is often referred to as the "jewel of the desert." At the entrance to the grounds, Main Drive is lined with lovely private homes and landscaped with citrus trees and flowering oleander, petunias, and pansies. The main structure at the end of this drive is an architectural masterpiece. Inspired by Frank Lloyd Wright and constructed of Biltmore block-tile, the buildings reflect the gracious charm and innovative spirit of the 1920s. Exploring the thirty-nine acres of this fine establishment is an adventure in architectural history and a delightful experience in imaginative landscaping. Stroll along the beautifully manicured lawns and gardens for visual delights in carefully tended beds of yellow pansies or pink petunias or multicolored snapdragons. In dining, shopping, and recreational activities, The Biltmore has consistently maintained its reputation as a world-class resort. It is open year-round.

Accommodations: There are 750 well-appointed rooms and suites, approximately 100 of which are located in the main building. The others are arranged in several buildings and cottages bordering flower beds. Many rooms have mountain or garden views, and all rooms have been recently remodeled. Rooms begin at $170 in the summer, $300 September to December, and $340 January 1 to April 30. Children under eighteen can stay free in the same room with their parents. Cribs are provided at no extra charge.

Dining: Enjoy regional and American cuisine for breakfast, lunch, and dinner in the casual atmosphere of the Biltmore Grill and Patio or The Café. A children's menu is available. Or you can experience the award-winning New American specialties at Wright's, where the striking architecture enhances the enjoyment of the food. Wright's serves lunch and dinner. Private wine tastings can be arranged—the Biltmore has one of the most extensive wine lists in the region. If you're near the water slide and new pool, try the Cabana Club Restaurant and Bar for sandwiches and cool drinks during the day and cocktails and entertainment in the evening. The grand atmosphere of the lobby also provides several grand options for the tummy. Traditional tea is served from 2:30 to 5:30 P.M. The Squaw Peak Lounge allows you to sit either indoors or outdoors, listen to music, and savor the view of the mountain along with your drinks and hors d'oeuvres. For the morning hours, The Café serves a bountiful breakfast buffet, including espresso, cappuccino, imported coffees, and delicious pastries. The Gift Shop is a nostalgic soda fountain for small gifts, breakfast, lunch, snacks, and, of course, ice-cream sodas.

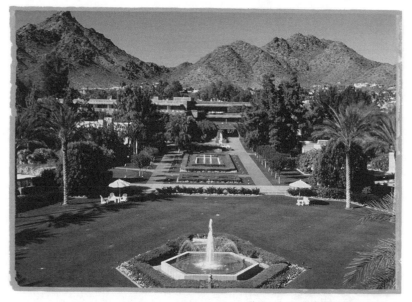

Photo courtesy of The Arizona Biltmore

Children's World: "Kids Kabana—A Learning Center" is a well-planned activity center where children ages four to twelve can enjoy a variety of activities—crafts and computers as well as outdoor activities such as swimming, croquet, putting, or cycling. It is open daily year-round from 9:00 A.M. to 5:00 P.M. The cost is $10 per hour (two-hour minimum), $35 for a half day ($45 half day with lunch), and $60 for a full day. Children under four may visit the center at the same rates if accompanied by a responsible adult.

Recreation: The setting alone of The Biltmore could charm you for days on end, but once the inner spirit is renewed, try your hand at some of the many recreational activities. Eight lighted tennis courts attract tennis enthusiasts; schedule yourself for a tennis clinic or private lessons.

The avid golfer can take on one of the two eighteen-hole PGA courses or refine a technique on the putting greens and driving ranges. At the pro shop you can seek out the guidance of the teaching staff, pick up some vital accessories, or rent equipment.

The eight swimming pools can mean either invigorating laps or a relaxing dip. One of the twenty-three cabanas will protect you from the desert sun, and the 92-foot water slide is guaranteed to get a "wow!" To check out the scenery and still test your athletic abilities, rent a bicycle or jog along the trails flanking the Salt River Canal. Indulge at the Biltmore Spa, which offers more than eighty European body and skin treatments, fitness center, steam room, saunas, and whirlpool. Or perhaps you will alternate rigorous athletics with less demanding games of croquet, lawn chess, and volleyball.

If shopping is your interest, discover a varied and extensive line of merchandise in the hotel shops: jewelry, silver, regionally crafted products, both Southwest and Native American artists; and tennis, golf, and swimming clothes and accessories. Adjacent to the grounds is the Biltmore Fashion Park, filled with more shops and restaurants and reached by a shuttle bus. ≋

The Bishop's Lodge
P.O. Box 2367
Santa Fe, New Mexico 87504-2367
(505) 983–6377
E-mail: bishopslodge@nets.com
Web site: www.bishopslodge.com

Just a five-minute drive north of Santa Fe, 1,000 acres of the foothills of the Sangre de Cristo Mountains comprise the range of The Bishop's Lodge. At an elevation of 7,200 feet, this area of north-central New Mexico shares its warm sunny days with cool crisp nights. The clean mountain air, the setting, and the atmosphere of the lodge combine to emit the flavor and tradition of the old Southwest. The adobe architecture reminiscent of a Spanish and Native American heritage and the friendly spirit of the resident wranglers give The Bishop's Lodge its true Western flair.

In the nineteenth century, the ranch was the home of Archbishop Jean Baptiste l'Amy, a pioneering French cleric who became the Southwest's first Catholic bishop. His life was the inspiration for Willa Cather's novel *Death Comes for the Archbishop* (good background reading for an introduction to the history and topography of the region). The property was bought by the newspaper publisher Joseph Pulitzer and then acquired in 1918 by James Thorpe. The Thorpe family operated the lodge as a vacation resort until 1998, when it was bought by The Coastal Hotel Group, a management company that operates boutique family resorts and properties. The facilities have undergone expansion and renovation during the years, but the private chapel built by the archbishop still stands, a sentinel to the lodge's history. The lodge has been open year-round since 1994.

Accommodations: The lodge's eighty-eight rooms and suites are grouped in several adobe buildings nestled among fruit trees and flower beds. The North and South lodges are the oldest, both having been grand summer homes before World War I; the newest one, "Chamisa," contains fourteen deluxe accommo-

Photo courtesy of The Bishop's Lodge

dations above the banks of Tesuque Creek. Many of the rooms are decorated in warm earth colors with a Southwestern flair; deluxe rooms include fireplaces and many have outdoor sitting areas. European plan is available year-round; based on two adults, daily historic rooms are $110 in winter, $195 spring and fall, and $230 to $271 from late May to early September. Deluxe room rates for the same periods are $185, $295, and $345 to $408. Children under four stay at no charge; others pay $15 per day. Cribs and rollaways are available on request. In summer, modified American plan rates are offered for $328 to $369 standard, and $443 to $469 deluxe; each additional person in the room is either $10 (under three) or $64. Besides lodging and two meals, these rates include the supervised children's program. Special packages are offered throughout the year.

Dining: New American and Southwestern cuisine are featured in the main dining room; jackets for gentlemen are suggested at the evening meal. The decor is classic Santa Fe: beamed ceilings, Navajo rugs, Spanish chandeliers, and four life-size murals done in the 1920s by W. E. Rollins. You can also have a box lunch prepared and enjoy your own picnic. For cocktails and snacks there's El Rincon, a delightful corner bar opening onto the Firelight Terrace, which offers sunsets, stars, and firelight as accompaniments to Mexican margaritas.

Children's World: During the summer months, kids four to twelve years old can participate in full-day programs (8:00 A.M. to 4:00 P.M. and 6:00 to 9:00 P.M.) of supervised activities, such as swimming, tennis lessons, pony rides, picnics, games, and fishing. Children can even have meals with their counselors in their own dining room or at picnics, pool parties, and cookouts. In addition, a pond stocked with trout and an outdoor play area of swings, a slide, and a sandbox translate into active fun for kids. Included with the modified American plan, the program is also available to European plan guests in day ($40 per child, meals included) and evening ($30) sessions.

Recreation: Recreation at The Bishop's Lodge starts with horseback riding in the wide open country. Experienced cowboys match you and your ability with the appropriate steed from a stable of more than seventy horses and then guide you on trail rides throughout the lodge's 1,000 acres. The cost is $35, children must be over eight years and 4 feet tall, and the maximum weight is 225 pounds. Free pony rides are offered for the little ones at 11:30 A.M. daily. A memorable experience is the Sunrise Ride through the canyons and foothills of the Sangre de Cristo Mountains followed by a hearty "cooked on the range" breakfast of eggs, pancakes, and biscuits. The Santa Fe National Forest is adjacent to the grounds of the lodge and provides more opportunities to explore the scenery on horseback.

If you're a little skittish about mounting a horse, you can fill your days with lots of other recreational fun: Hike on the trails through the foothills, fish the mountain streams for trout, swim in the pool, and bask in the sunshine. At the Tennis Center, you can play on one of four courts, have a lesson with the resident pro, and purchase some new accessories at the pro shop. On the skeet- and trapshooting ranges, experts offer instruction, and rental equipment is provided. Play a game of table tennis or treat your sore muscles to a relaxing hour in the whirlpool and sauna. The nearby country clubs of Santa Fe, Cochiti Lake, and Los Alamos grant lodge guests golfing privileges on their eighteen-hole courses. Be sure to take at least a day to discover the narrow streets, interesting adobe architecture, quaint shops, and art galleries of old Santa Fe. Open-air performances of the Santa Fe Summer Opera Festival are a special attraction for summertime visitors. Pueblo Indians show their jewelry and pottery on blankets around the Palace of the Governors or the famous Indian Market, and visitors are welcome to attend the colorful ceremonies at nearby pueblos. ≋

Flying L Guest Ranch

P.O. Box 1959
Bandera, Texas 78003
(830) 460–3001, (800) 292–5134
E-mail: sales@flyingl.com
Web site: www.flyingl.com

B andera, 40 miles northwest of San Antonio, claims to have invented dude ranching during the Depression when an enterprising rancher decided to take in "dudes" for extra money. So now, with true Texan style, they have laid claim to being the "Cowboy Capital of the World." Seven rodeo world champions have hailed from here, however, so there may be something to it. Set in the midst of the beautiful Texas Hill Country, this is not the dry, barren Texas of the movies. Here there are verdant green hills, oak and maple trees, wildflowers and flowing rivers, not sagebrush and sand.

The Flying L Ranch was first settled in 1874. It became a dude ranch in 1946 when Jack Lapham, a retired Air Corps colonel, started to realize his dream of a place where "a modern person can go and find himself in the midst of yesterday." (OK, who can figure out the name of the ranch based on this story? You already did? Good!) The ranch became a favorite "watering hole" for celebrities, including John Wayne, Tex Ritter, Buck Owens, Chill Wills, Slim Pickens, and Willie Nelson; the television program *The Cisco Kid* was filmed here.

Accommodations: You can bunk in style here—all forty-four suites offer real Texas-style lodging with room to spread out. The villas are geared toward comfort; all include a refrigerator, microwave, coffeepot, and cable TV. Daily rates in low season are $80 to $99 per adult; high season (summer and holidays) rates are $98 to $118 per adult. Children twelve to seventeen are two-thirds of the adult rate, and ages three to eleven are half the adult rate. Children under three stay free. Discount rates are given for five nights or more.

Dining: Two full meals are included in the rate and are hearty samples of fine Texas Hill Country cuisine. Seven days a week, from 7:30 to 9:30 A.M., start your day with a delicious breakfast buffet in the Main House dining room. Lunch is

Photo courtesy of Flying L Guest Ranch

on your own, with burgers and fries at the pro shop or an afternoon picnic from your refrigerator. Dinner is from 5:30 to 7:30 P.M., either in the Main House dining room or creekside. At 5:00 P.M. the Branding Iron Saloon opens, and there's family entertainment every night—cowboy music, dancing, gun slinging, or a rodeo, usually topped off with a marshmallow roast and s'more making. Do the kids love that!

Children's World: Children are divided into two groups, ages three to five and six to twelve. Programs run from 8:30 A.M. to noon and from 1:00 to 4:30 P.M. Activities include feeding animals, nature walks, scavenger hunts, sports, fishing, and crafts, such as making leather bracelets and vests. Golf and tennis clinics are included for the older children along with trail rides with the grown-ups, while the little ones can take pony rides at the Kids Korral every day. The program runs Monday through Saturday during summer, spring break (March through April), and holidays. The supervised children's activities program is included in the package.

Recreation: The only activity not included in your price is golf. Drive, chip, and putt on the par-72, fully irrigated course. A driving range lets you perfect your skills if you don't get distracted by the beautiful view; private lessons are also available. Try the outdoor heated swimming pool or venture off the "Ranch" to the Medina River for a little inner tubing or canoeing. Tennis, bikes, sand volleyball, horseshoes, hayrides, rodeo events, a playground, and a seasonal petting corral add to the fun. Golf packages are available.

In the Bandera area, fish in the crystal waters of Medina Lake, tour a working Longhorn ranch, visit the Cowboy Artists Museum in Kerrville, tour the World War II Nimitz Museum, or enjoy antiquing in the German town of Fredericksburg. On Bandera's Main Street there's a working blacksmith shop. Nearby excursions include San Antonio (the Alamo, Market Square, and the River Walk) and various theme parks such as SeaWorld, Fiesta Texas, and Splashtown. Visit natural wonders such as the caverns or tour the Lone Star Brewing Company to see how beer is made. All in all, the ranch promises "a rootin', tootin' time." ≋

Hyatt Regency Hill Country Resort

9800 Resort Drive
San Antonio, Texas 78251
(210) 647–1234, (800) 233–1234

The Texas Hill Country is as much a state of mind as it is a region. It certainly doesn't look like Texas—its green rolling hills, abundance of water, and variety of trees surprise the first-time visitor. San Antonio calls itself "a big city with small town charm," and, as the #1 tourist destination in Texas, has a multitude of attractions for families to enjoy—including the famous Alamo, centerpiece of Texas history, and the River Walk, lined with shops and restaurants along the tree-shaded banks of the San Antonio River.

Twenty minutes from downtown, a scenic drive meanders through the landscape, culminating at the lobby entrance, reminiscent of a Texas ranch house and complete with fireplaces and overstuffed furniture—even a shady back porch. In fact, the resort's 200 acres are a part of the Rogers–Wiseman Ranch, honored for being in continuous agricultural production at the hands of one family for one hundred years or more. Hyatt has successfully adapted a full-scale destination resort into this casual, laid-back lifestyle; the results are downright pleasurable. Enjoy a championship golf course, nature trails, a health club, and a wonderful four-acre water park featuring the 950-foot-long Ramblin' River— the centerpiece of the property and the greatest place to get into an inner tube, kick back, and just relax.

Accommodations: Traditional German-style Hill Country architecture with native limestone and decorative wood exterior, the two- and four-story hotel has nine guest-room wings, housing 500 rooms. A stand-alone two-story luxurious guest house styled after a ranch house is in the courtyard—there's even an authentic windmill! As usual with Hyatt, the rooms are large and well decorated, ranging from standard to Regency Club level, with no-smoking rooms and suites available. Room rates are from $190 to $315; suites from $295 to

Photo courtesy of Hyatt Regency Hill Country Resort

$2,250. Children under eighteen are free in the same room as parents. Packages are a good value and may include golf, the children's program, or other family excursions. Be sure to ask.

Dining: The flavor is definitely Tex-Mex, so expect tortillas even for breakfast, but you have lots of options here. The Springhouse Cafe features regional specialties, a large buffet and salad bar, and Sunday brunch. A wood-burning oven makes great pizzas. In the clubhouse, The Antlers Lodge has the ambience of a country lodge and puts the accent on regional Southwestern cuisine of steak, chicken, and seafood. Many entrees are mesquite-grilled and accompanied by a spicy Tex-Mex sauce. Golfers will find sandwiches and light snacks in the Cactus Oak Tavern at the halfway point on the golf course. The General Store offers hamburgers, deli sandwiches, and home-baked cookies as well as licorice sticks, wine, sodas, fresh coffee, and muffins. In the evening, relax at Aunt Mary's Porch, an open-air bar just off the lobby, or kick up your heels at Charlie's Long Bar, an old-fashioned Texas saloon complete with tin ceiling and a 56-foot copper-top bar. Yes, they have the tequila with the worm. Pool, shuffleboard, backgammon, and chess enhance the bar area.

Children's World: Camp Hyatt, developed in 1989, offers not only supervised programs but also children's menus and an opportunity to buy a second room for the kids at half-price. Custom tailored for ages three to twelve, Camp Hyatt operates during holidays, weekends, and daily throughout the summer. The program runs from 9:00 A.M. to noon and from 1:00 to 4:00 P.M. and keeps the kids busy with games and activities. There is a special Camp Hyatt room with a different schedule for every day of the week. The cost is $18 for a half day; $30 for a full day (lunch included for $5.00 additional), or $26 for the Friday and Saturday evening sessions from 5:00 to 9:00 P.M.

Recreation: Golfers enjoy the Arthur Hills–designed course with its 170 acres of rolling, scenic terrain. It truly blends into the countryside and has been recognized as one of the premier courses in the United States. Tennis is available on three courts, with a pro on hand. Walking, jogging, and biking paths crisscross the property, and the health club features aerobics classes and all the latest equipment—and, of course, a massage to help you recover from your workout.

By far the most popular spot, though, is the Ramblin' River, modeled after all those Hill Country river experiences. Pick up an inner tube, drop your cares, and let the lazy current carry you away. The journey varies from brisk to slow and allows riders to swim, walk, or take detours into two swimming pools, a cascading waterfall, or even a little sand beach.

Day excursions to SeaWorld, Six Flags, Fiesta Texas, Splashtown water park, or many of the nearby Hill towns, each with its own personality and charm, can pleasurably fill your days or evenings. Visit the Natural Bridge Caverns, with active formations more than 140 million years old, or stroll through Bandera, the self-proclaimed "cowboy capital." The Alamo is a must, and the IMAX production, *Alamo—the Price of Freedom,* does help in understanding the role of the Alamo and in bringing it to life (although it's pretty violent at times). Missions, museums, and Market Square, which feels like shopping in Mexico, are all nearby. ≋

Hyatt Regency Scottsdale at Gainey Ranch

7500 East Doubletree Ranch Road
Scottsdale, Arizona 85258
(602) 991–3388, (800) 233–1234
Web site: www.hyatt.com

Entering the private road that leads to this resort does not prepare you for the beauty of this lush and luxurious oasis in the midst of the Arizona desert. Water surrounds, cascades, falls, bubbles, flows, even sprays from the air; water and flowers are everywhere. You feel as though you are part of the landscape, not separated from it. Twenty-eight fountains, forty-seven waterfalls, and hundreds of palms, fir trees, and flowers create a 27-acre garden, part of the 560-acre Gainey Ranch, a planned residential complex that includes golf, parks and lakes, private homes, and businesses.

Accommodations: The double "H" shape of the four-story resort provides five courtyards and four glass-enclosed atriums, with a movable 820-square-foot glass wall at the center of the lobby that allows a panoramic view of the McDowell Mountains and Sonoran Desert. The main building, inspired by the desert work of Frank Lloyd Wright, houses 493 rooms and suites; on either side are seven two- and four-bedroom freestanding casitas with fireplaces and terraced balconies overlooking the lake. The decor blends with the desert setting, using natural textures and artifacts. Children under eighteen stay free in existing bed space of parents' rooms, and every room has the Disney channel. Rates vary according to season: High season (February to May), rooms are $395; $505 in the Regency Club, which offers VIP service, complimentary breakfast, beverages, and evening hors d'oeuvres. January and fall season is approximately $20 lower, and June to early September is the lowest-priced season, with rates from $175 to $215. Casitas range from $1,250 to $3,045 per night.

Dining: The Golden Swan is the hotel's specialty restaurant, named one of the best in the world by *Travel/Holiday* magazine and one of the top five in the Southwest by *Condé Nast Traveler.* One can dine indoors or out, in a charming gazebo nestled inside a lagoon. A special Sunday buffet, the "Chef's Brunch," is served right in the kitchen, where you can watch and talk with the chefs, making sure your food is hot and fresh. The Squash Blossom restaurant is open for breakfast, lunch, and dinner, with a warm Southwestern ambience and regional specialties (try the Arizona toast or a wide variety of salads and sandwiches or fajitas). Ristorante Sandolo is a casual Italian bistro, overlooking the pool, where the servers serenade you. After you dine, enjoy a Venice-style gondola ride on the resort's waterways. Again, a *sandolier* will sing to you. (You can enjoy the gondola ride for $5.00 even if you don't eat.) Both restaurants have

Photo courtesy of Hyatt Regency Scottsdale at Gainey Ranch

indoor/outdoor seating with very clever "air-conditioning." A very fine, invisible mist cools and moisturizes the air above you, making it comfortable year-round. Poolside, the Waterfall Juice Bar and the Water Garden Cafe serve snacks, lunch, yogurt, and fruit drinks. The new Coffee Bar features gourmet blends complemented by homemade Italian biscotti. In the evening, watch the cascading fountains and listen to classical flamenco guitar or perhaps a marimba band as you relax in the Lobby Bar.

Children's World: Camp Hyatt Kachina, designed in 1989, is the prototype children's program for all Hyatt resorts. It operates daily year-round and offers three- to twelve-year-olds a well-balanced program of activities focusing on the flora, fauna, culture, and geography of the area. A specially appointed Camp room has all the crafts and games children like best, and the playground, Fort Kachina, has lots of climbing and "imagination areas." And don't forget the ten swimming pools, one complete with a white sand beach and a three-story water slide. Each day has a different theme, such as Rootin' Tootin' Reptiles, It's a Powwow, South of the Border, or Feathered Friends. Age groups are three to five and six to twelve. The morning session, from 9:00 A.M. to noon, is $25, and the afternoon session, from 1:00 to 5:00 P.M., is $35. Lunch, from noon to 1:00 P.M., can be added to either session for $10. The full-day costs $60, including lunch, and $35 per evening session from 5:00 to 9:00 P.M., including dinner. If you have an active child who loves the program, the best deal is all day (9:00

A.M. to 9:00 P.M.) and all meals for $85. During holidays the resort offers family camp "destination specific" activities designed for the entire family, from cowboy roping, cowboy guitarists, and Native American storytelling to family fun sing-alongs round the campfire.

Recreation: Where do we start? With the twenty-seven-hole championship golf course at Gainey Ranch Golf Club? Actually, it's composed of three separate, individually designed courses—the Dunes; the Lakes, with five lakes and lots of water hazards; and the Arroyo, the most difficult. Or with the eight tennis courts or 3 miles of jogging and cycling trails? Or the Sonwai Spa, with state-of-the-art equipment, classes, sauna, and massage? Let's start with the two-and-a-half-acre water playground—most impressive in this dry, desert area. The design is a combination of Roman, Greek, and Art Deco and is truly spectacular. Zip down the 30-foot water slide, stroll over an aqueduct connecting six of the ten pools, swim around (or through!) the "Big Gun," a 5-foot-wide waterfall, or "thunderfall" as the hotel terms it, at the end of the aqueduct. Relax in the Grecian temple with 16-foot hot tub and four "cold plunges" in each corner. Water comes from all directions—from fountains, trailing down tall glass columns, and from waterspouts along the roof. Build sand castles on the beach at one end or play volleyball at the other. Kids never want to leave this watery fantasyland.

Phoenix attractions include a zoo, a desert botanical garden, and stately old homes; in Scottsdale, find an IMAX theater, the world's highest fountain, and shopping on Fifth Avenue. View large cats in the wild at Out of Africa; experience a re-creation of the Old West at WestWorld or Rawhide, Arizona's largest Western-themed attraction. Pick up a copy of *GUEST* for lots more ideas. If you have time to venture farther, the concierge will help you plan excursions to the Grand Canyon (five hours away) or Montezuma Castle, a 600-year-old Pueblo Indian cliff dwelling only ninety minutes away. Who knew the desert could be like this? ≋

Inn of the Mountain Gods

P.O. Box 269
Mescalero, New Mexico 88340
(505) 257–5141, (800) 545–9011
Web site: www.innofthemountaingods.com

Not many families can boast a vacation on an Indian reservation. At the Inn of the Mountain Gods, your family can enjoy all the amenities of a full resort while learning some of the history and customs of the Mescalero Apache tribe. They are a proud people with infinite respect for the land and an eagerness to introduce you to the natural beauties of a setting believed to have been home to the Apache gods. Whether horseback riding or big-game hunting, Indian guides navigate excursions over the rugged terrain of this 460,000-acre reservation. The reservation, established over a hundred years ago, sprawls through the Sacramento Mountains of south-central New Mexico. Open year-round, the inn sits on the shores of the 140-acre Lake Mescalero. The clear blue waters of the lake provide the setting for anglers and the picturesque backdrop for golfers. Views of nearby Sierra Blanca (12,000 feet) complete the scenic ambience.

Accommodations: The 253 guest rooms (including twenty suites) are located in lakeside buildings adjacent to the main lodge. Each has a private balcony, which allows impressive views of the lake and the mountains. Prices range from $95 to $135 a night for a double room depending on the time of the year; May through September is the high season. Slightly higher rates are applied for suite accommodations. There is no charge for children twelve years and younger sharing a room with adults (each room has two double beds), but a rollaway carries a $14-per-night fee. Package plans are arranged for golf, skiing, and hunting.

Dining: The lobby of the main building greets guests with a massive, copper-sheathed fireplace; this is a popular gathering spot for afternoon and evening cocktails. The GoKan Lounge also serves refreshments in the piano bar, which provides evening entertainment, and on the sundeck, which affords views over the lake.

The Dan Li Ka Restaurant in the main building serves a buffet breakfast, casual lunches, and more formal dinners. Specializing in American and Continental cuisine, the menu offers steak, veal, seafood, and chicken dishes and many tempting desserts. The Apache Tee Bar and Grill is adjacent to the golf pro shop; it is open for breakfast, lunch, and dinner. A snack bar is located at the swimming pool.

Children's World: Children's events are low-key. The Tipi Arcade is open for children eight years of age and older. There is no supervised play; for younger children an adult is a must. Children twelve and older can meet guides for horseback riding without parental supervision.

In the wintertime kids six years and older can learn how to ski in the ski school of nearby Ski Apache resort.

Recreation: The most unusual sport offered at the inn is big-game hunting on the reservation. Because of a conscientious wildlife preservation program, elk, deer, antelope, bear, wild turkey, and quail are plentiful. Apache guides lead expeditions into the heavily wooded mountain terrain. Package plans are available for hunters during the season from mid-September through December; these

Photo by The Amador Studio, courtesy of Inn of the Mountain Gods

include facilities for processing and packaging game. You can also enlist the services of a taxidermist for trophy preparation.

More traditional sports include golfing on an eighteen-hole championship course designed by Ted Robinson. This well-maintained course on rolling terrain skirts the lake and winds through tall pines and aspen. A resident pro is on hand for lessons, and there's a well-stocked pro shop.

Water sports are popular on Lake Mescalero. Rowboats and paddleboats can be rented at the boat dock. The lake's good stock of rainbow and cutthroat trout adds up to fine fishing. Swimmers and sunbathers are found at the heated outdoor pool and adjacent whirlpool overlooking the lake. There's a wading pool, too.

The stables, a couple of miles from the inn, maintain twenty to twenty-five horses. You can take half- or full-day trail rides with a guide. Combining exercise and solitary scenic enjoyment, some visitors take to the jogging and hiking trail by the lake. Casino Apache provides lively indoor gaming entertainment. After a full day of activities, you might enjoy wandering through the gift shop, where you'll find lovely Indian jewelry, weaving, and pottery.

Wintertime brings skiing at the nearby Ski Apache Resort. Snowmaking equipment aiding Mother Nature translates into a ski season from Thanksgiving to Easter. Owned and operated by the Mescalero Apache Tribe, the ski area includes in its services lessons for all levels of skiers, restaurants, a lounge, and a ski rental and repair shop. Guests at the inn are shuttled daily to the mountain, where they find thirty-two designated groomed trails and a vertical drop of 1,700 feet.

There are recreational fees for many of the activities. Package plans for golfing and skiing, for example, eliminate the need for additional assessment. ≋

Los Abrigados Resort and Spa

160 Portal Lane
Sedona, Arizona 86336
(602) 282–1777, (800) 521–3131
Web site: ilxresorts.com

Close to the Grand Canyon and just two hours from Phoenix, Sedona is noted for its spectacular red rock formations and scenic canyons. For centuries, it has been a sacred place to The People, the earliest inhabitants, and legend holds that the Grandmother Spirit of the World still lives here. There is a magic quality in the air that many attribute to the energy points that converge here. At the least, the light, color, and awe-inspiring rocks combine with the many artisans living here to create something special.

Accommodations: Los Abrigados, Portuguese for "the shelters," is in the heart of the small town of Sedona but stands in the midst of twenty-two acres of private ranchland/park and feels secluded. All 173 guest suites have oversize living rooms and separate bedrooms plus a balcony or private patio. Many feature a private whirlpool and fireplace. The plazas, walkways, and bridges connect the suites and main hotel area. Suites range from $225 to $395; $240 reserves one with spectacular views of the red rocks. Children under fifteen are free in the same room with parents.

Dining: Steak and Sticks, for casually elegant dining with a Southwestern flavor, is the domain of award-winning chef Scott Uehlein (serving breakfast and dinner). Imaginative dishes with an accent on indigenous ingredients make dining an adventure. Also available here is the "spa cuisine," healthful and lighter versions of many favorites. On-The-Rocks Bar & Grill serves lunch, snacks, and dinner in a casual atmosphere and features a large-screen television—the area's largest. Steak and Sticks and On-The-Rocks both feature children's menus. More restaurants are right next door at Tlaquepaque Village, a re-created Mexican village/plaza with tiled courtyards, fountains, and many craft shops.

Children's World: Children are always welcome at Los Abrigados and various activities are planned during the summer months. Available at the resort are a pool, playground, and basketball and tennis courts. More fun abounds in the surrounding area with jeep rides, horseback riding, and other events that can be arranged by the concierge.

Photo courtesy of Los Abrigados Resort and Spa

Recreation: After a game of tennis or volleyball, relax at the heated outdoor pool and chat with other guests. Enjoy the jogging and walking trails or just sit by the creek and dream. The centerpiece of activities here is the Sedona Spa— 10,000 square feet of state-of-the-art equipment and professional services providing a combination of fitness and relaxation. Massage, full body treatments and masks, facials and fitness classes/personal training contribute to physical and mental well-being. Nearby are two championship golf courses, designed by Robert Trent Jones and Gary Panks. Hiking, fishing streams, horseback riding, and jeep tours can also be arranged. The Grand Canyon is a two-hour drive; and closer is Oak Creek Canyon, with Slide Rock State Park, aptly named for the stretch of slippery creek bottom that forms a natural slide. For Southwestern art at its best, Tlaquepaque demands a visit (see Dining).

Red Rock Fantasy is the West's largest holiday light display, with more than one million lights. From late November until mid-January it transforms Los Abrigados into a spectacular holiday light show. ≋

Shangri-La Resort and Country Club

57401 East Highway 125
Afton, Oklahoma 74331
(800) 331–4060, (918) 257–4204
Web site: www.shangrilagrandlake.com

Located along the shores of Grand Lake O' the Cherokees in north Oklahoma, Shangri-La Resort and Country Club invites you to experience incomparable service and amenities. Whether you are staying for a family get-together, romantic interlude, or golf outing, Shangri-La allows you to discover natural surroundings unlike anywhere else.

Accommodations: Choose from more than 350 guest rooms and suites. All accommodations are within easy walking distance of resort activities and offer beautiful panoramic views of the lakefront or golf courses.

Dining: Multiple restaurants and lounges offer variety, excitement, and style. Experience Grand Lake's finest, Waters Restaurant, featuring Southwestern cuisine and traditional entrees. Other options range from casual-elegant dining to burgers and pizza or hot entertainment and cool drinks.

Children's World: Ahoy mate! Pirates Crew is a program for kids ages four to seven and eight to twelve, with supervised fun and games of all kinds: arts and crafts, group indoor/outdoor games, and snacks. Pirates Crew is available daily 9:00 A.M. to 10:00 P.M. at a cost of $5.00 per hour. In-room baby-sitting service is available as well; price varies.

Recreation: Thirty-six holes of championship golf, indoor and outdoor tennis, and 1,300 miles of scenic shoreline are just some of the many reasons to visit Shangri-La. The resort features a complete recreation center and spa, with a marina that offers boat rentals, charters, and all the water-sport activities you can imagine. ≋

Sheraton El Conquistador Resort and Country Club

10000 North Oracle Road
Tucson, Arizona 85737
(520) 544–5000, (800) 325–7832
Web site: www.sheratonelconquistador.com

The Arizona desert climate is perfect sporting weather practically year-round. The sun shines warmly and the humidity is low, just the right combination for the world-famous saguaro cacti that seem to be everywhere. It's also the perfect combination for nudging that golf ball farther down the links or sending an ace across the tennis court. El Conquistador wraps up tennis, golf, horseback riding, and terrific sunshine together for a holiday present for you. It sits among imported palm trees and native cacti with stark mountains towering behind it. The golden tan stucco facades and the red-tiled roofs of the low-rise buildings blend well with the colors nature has given the surrounding landscape.

Accommodations: There are more than 400 rooms and suites, each decorated with contemporary-style furnishings. The use of Mexican tiles and brick in ornamental designs adds to the Southwestern ambience. All the rooms have balconies or patios that open up to the mountains, the golf course, or a flower-filled courtyard, and each room has a minibar. During the high season (from January through April), a double room is $230 to $310 a night and in the low season (June through Labor Day), $89 to $125 a night; autumn and spring rates are $169 to $240 a night. No charge is applied for children (seventeen and younger) staying in their parents' room. Golf, tennis, and equestrian packages are offered.

Dining: For a fun evening of Western fare, head to the Last Territory for thick, juicy steaks broiled over a mesquite fire, barbecued ribs, and chicken. The Sundance Cafe is a casual restaurant for breakfast and lunch. Around the pool, sip a bit of cool refreshment from the Desert Spring; indoors, have your favorite cocktail at the Lobby Lounge. Dos Locos serves Latin American specialties; the country club, La Vista, offers American cuisine for lunch and happy hour on Friday.

Children's World: Camp Conquistador offers daily summer activities for kids six to twelve years old. From 8:00 A.M. to 3:00 P.M. youngsters play tennis, volleyball, and basketball; show off artistic talents in crafts classes; and swim. Four two-week sessions are offered June 11 through August 3; lunch is included.

Children's movies are shown at the country club and individual baby-sitting arrangements can be made through the concierge.

Recreation: Tee up for the nine-hole or either of the two eighteen-hole golf courses, and watch your shot soar a bit farther in the clean desert air. Even taking

Photo courtesy of Sheraton El Conquistador Resort and Country Club

lessons is no chore when the setting is so beautiful. Play tennis day or night on any of the thirty-one lighted courts. Lessons are available, too, for tennis and for racquetball (seven courts).

At the stables, choose a horse for a breakfast ride or a sunset champagne trail ride. Jog on one of the four designated trails ranging from $1\frac{1}{2}$ to 7 miles in length. Fitness centers are located at the main hotel and at the country club; join an exercise class, then wind down in the whirlpool or sauna and pamper yourself with a massage. Take a dip in one of the four swimming pools. Rent a bike or get the whole family into a game of horseshoes, badminton, or volleyball. Explore the exciting possibility of a balloon ride, or poke around the Arizona terrain during a four-wheel-drive desert ride. ≋

Tanque Verde Guest Ranch

14301 East Speedway Boulevard
Tucson, Arizona 85748
(520) 296–6275, (800) 234–3833
Web site: www.tanqueverderanch.com

In the Arizona desert, 2,800 feet high in the foothills of three mountain ranges, Tanque Verde Guest Ranch has been serving travelers for more than one hundred years. Once merely a stagecoach stop, today it is a year-round resort. The area is rich in the history of Native Americans and Spanish settlers who dubbed the area Tanque Verde—immortalizing the deep pools of artesian water found here. Located 12 miles outside Tucson, it borders Saguaro National Park. The saguaro cacti are immediately recognizable to anyone who has seen a western movie or a picture of the desert. They stand quite tall, with "arms" curving up toward the sky. From here visitors can take side trips to Tucson, to old Spanish missions, and to Mexico, which is about a ninety-minute drive away.

Accommodations: The seventy-one guest rooms and suites are located in the main ranch house and in individual cottages called "casitas"; most of the casitas have patios and corner fireplaces. The decorative motif is Native American, and antiques and original art are carefully arranged to lend a warmth to the inn. Cribs are available, and there are refrigerators in the rooms. Rates range from $260 to $735, depending on season and type of accommodations selected. Based on a full American plan, room, three meals a day, and all ranch activities (including the fully supervised children's program for ages four through eleven) are covered by the rate paid.

Dining: Everyone eats at long tables in the one main dining room, encouraging an informal, friendly atmosphere. Dress is casual and appetites are generally big due to the desert air and the exercise. American and Continental dishes are standard fare and, as expected, Spanish and Mexican specialties also appear on the menu. A separate children's dining room is reserved for youngsters and their counselors, who can take all meals together. Children are also welcome to dine with their parents. Many guests look forward to outdoor dining, enjoying hearty Western meals either on the range or at poolside.

Children's World: The ranch offers a year-round, seven-day-per-week, fully supervised program for four- to eleven-year-olds. Horseback riding forms the core of the program and is adjusted to fit the abilities and interests of the youngsters. Children under twelve must ride with the children's program; adults may join their children on these rides.

Besides riding, children are offered tennis lessons, nature programs, hikes, swimming, and some evening activities. Winter program hours are from 8:00 A.M. to 3:00 P.M. and 6:00 to 8:15 P.M.; summer hours are 7:00 A.M. to 3:00 P.M. (no evening program). The cost is included in the daily rates. For infants and toddlers, baby-sitters can be hired for $5.00 to $6.00 per hour.

Recreation: Active relaxation is the byword at Tanque Verde. The clear desert air and low humidity, coupled with abundant sunshine, make all the activities pleasant. Horseback riding is the major part of the program. Whether you're interested in a slow-moving trail ride or a spirited sprint, the right mount can be found from a string of one hundred horses.

Early morning and late afternoon are perfect times for strenuous outdoor activities such as tennis (five courts). In the middle of the day, seek out one of the two swimming pools for a cool dip. Numerous guided nature walks introducing visitors to the Arizona desert ecology are conducted along trails throughout the 25,000 acres. Some 200 species of birds have been identified in the area, making the ranch very popular with avid bird-watchers. The final touch to the active relaxation concept is the El Sonora Spa, well equipped with its swimming pool, sauna, whirlpool, exercise room, and lounge. In nearby Tucson, six championship golf courses grant playing privileges to ranch guests. ≈≈≈

Taos Ski Valley

P.O. Box 90
Taos Ski Valley, New Mexico 87525
(505) 776–2291, (800) 776–1111
E-mail: resvisitnewmexico.com
Web site: visitnewmexico.com

Nine hundred years ago the Pueblo Indians settled the area around Taos. They were followed in the sixteenth century by the Spanish and in the nineteenth century by fur traders. In the early 1950s, Ernie Blake searched carefully for just the right spot for a ski resort and rediscovered this bit of northern New Mexico. Since then, skiers have been coming to Taos Ski Valley for the incredible powder snow and the glorious sunshine. Several ski magazines are calling Taos one of the hottest places to ski, citing the steep, challenging terrain and trails for all abilities so all levels may ski together. Once again, Taos has the #1 ski school in North America, featuring the Ski-Better-Week. Grouped according to ability, each group remains with the same instructor, developing new, close friendships and improving skills.

A three-hour drive from Albuquerque, Taos Ski Valley combines lodging, restaurants, shops, and a beautiful mountain. The town of Taos is only 18 miles away and, with its Indian and Spanish heritage, is an interesting alternative for dining, shopping, and entertainment. The Ski Valley operates during the ski season only, which generally runs from Thanksgiving through mid-April.

Accommodations: Although there are inns and hotels in the town of Taos, every skier's dream is to be on the mountain. The Taos Valley Resort Association (800 number above) represents more than 95 percent of all lodging in and around Taos. For lodges right near the slopes—such as Hotel St. Bernard and the Thunderbird Lodge—rates for a one-week package run $1,490 per person double occupancy; besides your room, this package includes meals, lifts, and

Photo © Jeff Caven, courtesy of Taos Ski Valley

morning lessons. Condominiums right at the slopes charge $758 to $1,105 per person for a one-week package; based on four people in a two-bedroom unit, this fee covers lodging, lifts, and morning lessons. All facilities offer a nightly rate, but the week package, known as a Ski-Better-Week, is good value for your money.

Dining: Whatever your dining mood, you'll be satisfied in Taos with more than fifty restaurants to choose from. On the mountain there are quick and easy stops like the Phoenix Restaurant; the Whistlestop Cafe, serving hamburgers, sandwiches, and pizza; and the Bavarian. At the base, you can go really casual at the Snack Bar or delightfully international at the restaurant in the Thunderbird Lodge or very family-style at the nearby Amizette Inn. In the town of Taos, try Cajun and Creole at Carl's French Quarter, seafood at Casa Cordova, or Mexican at Casa De Valdez. And of course there's always your own fine cooking in your condominium!

Children's World: The Kinderkafig, Taos Ski Valley's 18,000-square-foot child-care facility, is designed for children between the ages of six weeks and twelve years. The Kinderkare (six weeks to two years old) full-day program includes two snacks, lunch, and nap time. The half-day program includes snack and either snow play or nap time. Reservations are required. Walk-ins are accepted on a space-available basis. The cost for this program is $68 for a full day, $32 for a half day, or $15 per hour. The Junior Elite program (three to twelve years old) includes all-day lesson, lift ticket, lunch, and rentals. Reservations are required for children kindergarten age and younger. Little ones must be potty-trained. Cost is $68 per day or $390 for six days.

Also for kids, there's ice skating or tubing on the bunny hill on Wednesday, Friday and Saturday nights between 4:00 and 7:00 P.M.

Recreation: Partially located in the Carson National Forest, the Taos ski area is in the Sangre de Cristo Mountains, the southernmost part of the Rockies. The base village sits at 9,207 feet, and the peak towers above at 11,819 feet, affording skiers more than 2,600 feet of vertical drop down seventy-two different slopes. This is a challenging mountain with just over 50 percent of its runs classified as expert; however, even the novice can feel that classic mountaintop high, since some beginners' runs descend directly from the peak. In a ski season that lasts from about Thanksgiving to Easter, the average annual snowfall is over 320 inches, plus snowmaking on more than 98 percent of beginner and intermediate terrain.

When you can pull yourself away from the open bowls, dramatic chutes, and lazy meandering-down trails lined with spruce and aspen, you might consider cross-country skiing, a sleigh ride, or an evening skier's seminar on such topics as avalanches and adjusting to the altitude. Skiers in January experience the added pleasures of Taos's jazz festival.

Late spring and summer bring great white-water rafting, trout fishing, mountain bikes and hikers, horseback riding, and golf. Six museums, art galleries, and music festivals entertain those less athletically inclined. The Taos Chamber of Commerce (800–732–8267) publishes a *Kid's Guide* with advice from local children. ≋

ROCKIES

Colorado

Montana

Utah

Big Sky of Montana

P.O. Box 160001
Big Sky, Montana 59716
(406) 995–5000, (800) 548–4486
E-mail: info@bigskyresort.com
Web site: www.bigskyresort.com

The sky isn't really bigger in Montana—not by scientific measurements, that is. But don't tell the folks around here that. These die-hard Westerners believe they've got the market cornered on the best, biggest, bluest sky ever; and if you don't watch out, by the end of a visit here, you'll be a believer too.

In the wintertime, skiing Lone Mountain (summit elevation 11,166 feet) can make you feel that it's almost possible to touch that beautiful, clear sky. Lone Mountain and adjacent Andesite and Flat Iron Mountains are carved with more than 135 runs that add up to fine skiing at Big Sky. During the summer, these mountains and their evergreens, the sunshine and clean mountain air, make the perfect setting for hiking, horseback riding, mountain biking, scenic gondola rides, white-water rafting, and fishing as well as golf and tennis.

Open late November through mid-April and early June through early October, Big Sky is located in southwestern Montana just north of Yellowstone and is surrounded by rivers and national forests.

Accommodations: The Huntley Lodge is at the base of Lone Mountain; the Explorer chairlift is right out the back door. The lodge has more than 200 rooms, some with views straight up the mountain, and an outdoor heated swimming pool, sauna, and Jacuzzi.

Attached to the Huntley is the Shoshone Condominium Hotel, with ninety-five suites. The resort's newest property, the Summit, houses ninety-eight condominiums that lock off into 213 one-, two-, and three-bedroom units slopeside to three lifts.

With dozens of choices for accommodations, and several seasons to pick from, you are sure to find amenities that meet both your expectations and your budget—from the Stillwater Studio (starting at $138 per night) to the four-bedroom Summit Penthouse (at $2,582 per night). Contact the resort for the rates and packages available during the time you are planning your stay. Children ten and younger stay free in their parents' room. Cribs and rollaways are $15.

At the area's condominiums, the studios and one- to four-bedroom units have kitchens and fireplaces. While all the complexes (Stillwater, Skycrest, Lake Big Horn, Powder Ridge, Saddle Ridge, Arrowhead, Beaverhead, Shoshone,

Photo courtesy of Big Sky of Montana

Snowcrest) are all in close proximity to the slopes, Snowcrest is closest to the lifts. Some complexes feature heated swimming pools, saunas, and Jacuzzis.

Dining: If you are staying in The Huntley Lodge or just cannot face cooking after a busy day, you can dine at The Huntley Dining Room. The Summit features the Peaks Restaurant and the Carabiner Lounge. In winter take the sleigh ride up into the mountains for dinner, and in summer join an outdoor Western barbecue. Next door to The Huntley Lodge is a collection of shops, restaurants, and bars in the Mountain Mall. Here you'll find casual spots for pizzas, deli sandwiches, and burgers. In the evening, Chet's Bar in the lodge is popular for its warm atmosphere, nightly entertainment, and regular game of poker.

Children's World: During the ski season, the Handprints Daycare Center in the Mountain Village Mall is open every day from 8:30 A.M. to 4:00 P.M. for children six months and older. Little ones enjoy a combination of indoor and outdoor play: sledding, stories, songs, and arts and crafts. The fee is $55 a day for two years and older and $65 for six- to twenty-three months old. The four- through six-year-olds at the center have ski lessons two hours a day in addition to their indoor activities. The daily rate for this group is $80. Older children six to fourteen years can enroll in the Ski Day Camp. The daily fee is $54 for an active 9:45 A.M. to 3:00 P.M. program. Kids ten and younger ski free (two per paying adult).

The game room in The Huntley Lodge, open from 10:00 A.M. to 10:00 P.M., offers video games and television. No special activities are organized for children during the summer, but baby-sitting arrangements can be made any time of the year through the activities desk at the lodge. The average rate is $8.00 per hour. There are free family activities organized daily throughout the winter. Daily après-ski children's activities include arts and crafts, rescue-dog demonstrations, and making s'mores out by the fire.

Recreation: The 4,350-foot vertical drop takes you through open bowls and tree-lined trails. The average annual snowfall is an amazing 400-plus inches. Skiing starts mid-November (an opening guaranteed by snowmaking if Mother Nature is skimpy with her supply) and continues into April. Whatever your level of skiing, you can join lessons at the ski school. Cross-country skiers enjoy treks over broad meadows and through stands of pine trees. Just 5 miles from the resort, the Lone Mountain Guest Ranch maintains 45 miles of cross-country trails. When you're not on skis, swim in one of the heated pools or take a trip to Yellowstone for snowmobiling and sight-seeing.

When the weather warms up, the mountains are terrific for hiking and backpacking. For horseback riding you can link up with Big Sky Stables through the resort concierge. You may prefer adventures in white-water rafting or the quiet solitude of fishing for prize-winning trout in the mountain streams.

The eighteen-hole golf course was designed by Arnold Palmer and is well situated in the mountain meadows. Play tennis (six courts, two of which are at the resort) and volleyball, or relax with a Swedish massage or a leisurely guided nature walk, learning the wildflowers of Big Sky. ≋≋≋

Breckenridge Ski Resort

Box 1058
Breckenridge, Colorado 80424
(970) 453–5000, (800) 789–SNOW
Web site: www.snow.com

The town of Breckenridge is 139 years old, and skiing at Breckenridge is more than 35 years old. Quite a good combination! An old gold and silver mining camp proud of its history, Breckenridge is a charming town with carefully restored buildings that attest to its Victorian-era heyday. And the years of skiing have resulted in the development of 2,043 acres of skiing territory on four beautiful mountain peaks. All this skiing in a historic setting is a one-and-a-half-hour drive west of Denver—not so close that it is inundated by locals, yet close enough that once you land at Denver International Airport, your ski holiday begins with a scenic tour through the Arapahoe National Forest on your way to Breckenridge.

Like every other western mining town turned ski resort, Breckenridge has numerous hotels, vacation homes, and condominiums that can be investigated through the Breckenridge Resort Chamber (800–221–1091). Best known as a winter recreation area, Breckenridge is in fact open year-round. Beaver Run Resort (800–525–2253) and the Village at Breckenridge (800–800–7829) warrant special attention because of their locations and amenities. With lifts just steps away from either one, these self-contained resorts make life just a little bit easier for families. Besides their own restaurants and shops, each resort houses a child-care center.

Accommodations: Beaver Run is an attractive complex of granite and wood buildings just skirted by the Country Boy trail and is home to the Beaver Run Superchair. The hotel rooms are spacious, and condominiums vary from suites with in-room spas to four-bedroom units. Fireplaces and private balconies are features of all the condominium units; the condominiums have fully equipped kitchens. Children are free when staying with their parents, and cribs for infants and toddlers are provided without charge.

During the high ski season, February 1 through the first week of April, a double hotel room is $210 and a one-bedroom/one-bath condominium that sleeps four is $280 a night. During the rest of the ski season, rates are lower, with the exception of the holiday period at the end of December when higher rates are in effect. In the summer season, from late April to mid-November, the rate for a double room is $90 a night and $125 a night for a one-bedroom/one-bath condominium.

The Village at Breckenridge is a Western-style resort with 332 units, ranging from hotel rooms to condos; the Liftside Inn building features studio apartments; and Plazas I, II, and III house one- to three-bedroom condominium units. Most of the accommodations have kitchens, fireplaces, and balconies with views of the mountains or Maggie Pond, the ice-skating center. Children twelve and younger sharing a room with their parents are free; crib rental is available upon request.

The Village defines the ski season as early November through late April; during this time a double hotel room is $120 to $195, studios are $125 to $210, and a one-bedroom/one-bath condominium is $160 to $290. Rates are lower during early and late weeks of the season and higher at holiday time. During the summer a double room is $85 to $120 a night, and a one-bedroom/one-bath condominium is $115 to $160 a night.

Dining: Elegant dining at Beaver Run takes place at Spencer's Steaks and Spirits Restaurant in a warm setting enhanced by oak and cane furnishings. Menu offerings include a selection of USDA choice beef entrees, seafood favorites, and other specialties like the "all you can eat" prime rib. The Copper Top Cafeteria and Bar is open winters only for skiers, but the deli is good for snacks year-round, and two bars provide evening and nighttime amusement.

For elegant dining in The Village at Breckenridge, try the Breckenridge Cattle and Fish Company, which features steak, game, and prime rib. The Maggie Restaurant and Cafe Breckenridge are casual spots open for breakfast, lunch, and snacks. Enjoy Italian food at The Village Pasta Company and casual pub fare at The Village Pub. Jake T. Pounders is ready to quench your thirst after that last, long run of the day.

In town more than five dozen restaurants and saloons (out West bars are called saloons—don't forget that!) offer atmospheres from quiet to lively and cuisines that run all over the globe—Mexican, Italian, Greek, and German. A popular spot for steak and seafood is the Whale's Tail on Main Street. The ice-cream shop, also on Main Street, makes for a nice break during an evening walk.

Children's World: Breckenridge's children's centers offer kids ages three to twelve a frolicking good time while they learn the joys of skiing in programs designed for specific age groups. Children's centers are located at both the Peak 8 and Village base areas. Parents must provide ski equipment, and lunch is provided for children enrolled in full-day programs. Reservations are recommended for children five and younger. Snowboarding instruction is also available.

For children too young to ski or who don't ski, Breckenridge provides fun and nurturing environments. Children's centers are conveniently located at base areas: The Peak 8 Children's Center accepts children two months through five years and the Village Children's Center cares for children three to five years of age. Both centers include facilities that have everything kids need to enjoy their day: cribs, toys, art supplies, lunch facilities, and loving trained personnel. These popular programs fill up quickly, so make a reservation (required) by calling (800) 789–7669.

Recreation: If you said to some skiers that you'd found 139 trails, an average annual snowfall of 300 inches, a ski season from late October to early May, and a vertical drop of more than 3,398 feet, they might think you'd died and gone to heaven. Breckenridge gives you all this on its four interconnected mountains—Peak 7 is the latest addition in skiable terrain, while Peak 10 boasts the highest elevation, at nearly 13,000 feet. It also gives outstanding views over Summit County, 60 percent expert runs, 26 percent intermediate runs, 14 percent beginner runs, bowl skiing, above-the-timberline skiing, and lots of famous Rocky Mountain powder. You can line up a free guided tour of the mountains or plunge right away into group or private instruction.

Cross-country enthusiasts head to the Breckenridge Nordic Center for more than 40 kilometers of groomed trails. Try snowmobiling at Tiger Run Tours; ice skating on Maggie Pond, at the base of Peak 9; and a horse-drawn sleigh ride to a steak-and-baked-potato supper in heated tents on the mountain.

At both the Village at Breckenridge and Beaver Run, you can jump into the indoor/outdoor pools, relax in one of the many outdoor hot tubs, or, if your muscles weren't tested enough on the slopes, finish up in the exercise rooms. An additional Beaver Run attraction is an indoor miniature golf course, where you can count on a fun family evening.

During warm-weather months venture out from the resorts and go biking through town, hiking in the woods, fishing in mountain streams, sailing on Lake Dillon, horseback riding on trails bordered by wildflowers, and white-water rafting on the Arkansas and Blue Rivers. Breckenridge's eighteen-hole championship golf course was designed by Jack Nicklaus. During July and August the mountains ring with classical and jazz music from the Breckenridge Music Institute. ≋

The Broadmoor

P.O. Box 1439
Colorado Springs, Colorado 80901
(719) 634–7711, (800) 634–7711
Web site: www.broadmoor.com

As majestic as the neighboring Rocky Mountains, The Broadmoor reigns over Cheyenne Lake and 3,000 surrounding acres. The original hotel, known today as Broadmoor Main, was built in 1918 by Spencer Penrose, an enterprising man who made his fortune in gold mining in Cripple Creek (less than 20 miles from Colorado Springs) and copper mining in Utah. He dreamed of fashioning a Colorado resort along the lines of the grand European hotels that he had seen. The Mediterranean-style structure, with its pink-stucco facade, almost glimmers in the sunshine. Inside the Italian Renaissance trappings include wood-beamed ceilings, crystal chandeliers, gilt-framed mirrors, and hand-painted wall and ceiling decoration. Penrose's dream was realized— The Broadmoor fared well indeed when compared with its European counterparts. And the guests who followed were as impressive as the hotel, from royalty and presidents to movie stars and millionaires.

Over the years, facilities and buildings were added to the original complex. Broadmoor South stands next to Broadmoor Main and is architecturally compatible with the original, because its design utilizes light-colored stucco for the exterior walls. Across the lake is Broadmoor West. A modern structure, it nonetheless blends well within the context of the resort as a whole. In 1995, an additional 150 guest rooms were completed, and Lakeside Suites was completed in 2001. This new twenty-one-room building hosts the most luxurious accommodations on the property. The architecture of the new wing is reminiscent of Broadmoor Main. The newer structures reveal precise attention to architectural design, aesthetic decoration, and fine art. The resort is open year-round.

Accommodations: Some 700 rooms and suites are divided among the five main buildings of The Broadmoor. All are handsomely decorated and look out at either the clear blue Cheyenne Lake or the dramatic Colorado mountains; it's a tough task to find a view that's less than terrific. Broadmoor West features rooms with private balconies. During the high season, from the first of May to mid-October, the European plan is $310 to $460 a night. Suites are higher. Cribs are provided at no additional charge. For an extra $15 a night, a rollaway bed can be added to your room. Rates are lower during the remaining six months of the year, and are based on one to four persons.

Dining: On the top floor of Broadmoor South, The Penrose Room is an elegantly formal restaurant, with traditional French menu, superb views, dinner music,

dancing, and an Edwardian decor, with emphasis on elaborate styling. Charles Court Game Grill, in the West building, offers fine dining without the formalities, yet still with wonderful lake views. One of the world's most extensive wine lists (more than 600 choices, with prices ranging from $12 to $1,300 a bottle!) complement such entrees as Colorado rack of lamb and Copper River salmon.

Also at Broadmoor Main are the Tavern, exquisitely adorned with Toulouse-Lautrec lithographs, and the Lake Terrace Dining Room, opening onto the Sun Lounge, with palms, ficus trees, and a tiered Italian fountain. Sunday brunches here are an extravaganza featuring more than seventy items. Café Julie, a sidewalk cafe in Broadmoor West, offers a relaxed shirtsleeves-and-shorts atmosphere for sandwiches, salads, and burgers. Espresso is a favorite stopping place for cappuccino, pastries, quiche, sandwiches, and eclairs in Broadmoor Main. One of the merriest dining spots is the Golden Bee, an authentic English pub located behind and below the International Center; it is open for lunch and dinner and until the wee hours, with live ragtime and sing-alongs. Stratta's Italian Restaurant, in the spa complex, is open for breakfast, lunch, and dinner with traditional American fare daytime and classic Italian favorites at night. Relax and find entertainment in any of six different lounges including the Stars' Club and Cigar Bar. From piano music to full orchestra dancing to sports on the big-screen TV, it's all there for your enjoyment.

Children's World: Children ages four to twelve are revved up for active pursuits Monday through Saturday, mid-June to mid-August, Christmas, and Easter, in the Bee Bunch Program. From 9:00 A.M. to 5:00 P.M., kids swim in one of the pools, explore the lake in a paddleboat, join games, and visit the zoo. And just wait until your child tells you about feeding the ducks! Golf, tennis, and cooking lessons or horseback riding provide more thrills, while games and crafts are quieter fun.

The youngsters meet again for dinner and games or a movie from 6:00 to 10:00 P.M. (summer only), granting their parents opportunities to sample the gourmet creations of the Broadmoor chefs. The children's meals are planned to ensure cleaned-up plates; the pizza, fried chicken, and hamburger dinners are favorites among the younger set and are included in the program cost of $45 (four to six years old) or $55 (seven to twelve years old) daytime and $45 evening (for those four to twelve years old). Baby-sitting is available for $9.00 per hour for one child and $3.00 for each additional sibling, with a three-hour minimum.

Recreation: Golfing at The Broadmoor began when the original hotel opened in 1918. Donald Ross designed that first course and was followed by Robert Trent Jones, who added nine holes in 1950 and another nine in 1965. The Ed Seay/Arnold Palmer course was completed in 1976. Once golfers discover the challenging variety of these forty-five holes, the incredibly scenic setting, the top-quality equipment and accessories of the golf shops, and instruction with the resident pro, they may never explore the rest of The Broadmoor—and that would be a pity.

Nine Plexipave tennis courts are located at the Golf Club; two of these are bubble-enclosed, allowing tennis play to continue through the winter. Both golf clubs include tennis shops, where you can purchase new equipment and attire or investigate classes and clinics.

An afternoon can be spent swimming at one of two heated swimming pools at Broadmoor Main and the Golf Club. Rent a paddleboat for a spin on the lake or a bicycle for a tour around the lake. Stroll along One Lake Avenue to enjoy a variety of specialty shops and an art gallery.

The Broadmoor Spa, Golf and Tennis Club is more than 90,000 square feet of luxury: state-of-the-art fitness facility, full-service spa, full-service salon, and private locker rooms with all amenities, including fireplaces!

A nonstop itinerary of off-property activities includes white-water rafting, hot-air ballooning, fly-fishing, mountain biking, and hunting expeditions. Or perhaps you'll opt to take the famous cogwheel up to Pikes Peak. A new addition is an 11,000-square-foot main pool with a water slide complex, children's pool, playground, and two adult whirlpools located on the north end of Cheyenne Lake. ≋

C Lazy U Ranch

P.O. Box 379
Granby, Colorado 80446
(970) 887–3344
E-mail: ranch@clazyu.com
Web site: www.clazyu.com

R ide 'em, cowboy! With a little time at C Lazy U Ranch, you could live up to this label. Experienced wranglers match you with just the right horse to call your own during a vacation stay, and they guide you through trail rides in the Colorado high country. Sitting at an elevation of 8,300 feet, less than a two-hour drive west of Denver, the ranch sprawls across more than 8,500 acres. A lot of territory to roam combines with warm sunny days that give way to cool nights—quite a setting for learning Western ways. For more than seventy years, C Lazy U has operated as a guest ranch. That adds up to a lot of experience, not only in riding and roping but also in welcoming and entertaining visitors. This working ranch is open for vacationers from mid-June to mid-October and mid-December through March.

Accommodations: About forty comfortable rooms and suites are in the lodge and the guest cottages that surround it. Seventy-five percent of these have a fireplace. During the summer and mid-December through New Year's, vacation stays are scheduled by the week, Sunday to Sunday. Guests can make reservations on a daily basis during the rest of the season.

Summer weekly rates per person are $1,200 to $1,650; Christmas weekly rates average $1,525 per person. Winter daily rates are $115 to $195 per person, and children receive a 20 to 40 percent discount. Children ages three to five are charged $200 a week less than the standard rate. These rates cover virtually everything you'll want or need during your visit: lodging, three meals a day, use of a horse, trail rides, use of the recreational facilities, and the supervised children's program.

Dining: At C Lazy U you'll get the hearty meals that you need to maintain an energy level consistent with the fresh air and outdoor fun. The warm, rustic dining room is in the lodge, the main building of the ranch. Here guests sit at tables set for ten—a good way to make friends—for relaxed family-style dining. But don't expect baked beans and coffee in a tin pot. More likely, you'll have Black Angus prime rib or jalapeño-stuffed mountain trout, for this five-star, five-diamond resort has outstanding menus. Children and teens eat earlier with their counselors, and after dinner families regroup for the evening activities. Buffet lunches are often served near the swimming pool, and evening cookouts are frequently planned. The lodge also houses a comfortable living room and bar, where drinks

Photo courtesy of C Lazy U Ranch

and hors d'oeuvres are served nightly at 6:30 P.M. Another bar is located in the Patio House, the recreation center adjacent to the swimming pool; enjoy an evening cocktail and swap tall tales with other guests about the day's adventures.

Children's World: The way they take to things so easily, the kids may turn into wranglers before you do. And with C Lazy U's special attention to youngsters, they've got a good shot at calling themselves cowpokes by the time they head home.

Starting at age three (the ranch does not provide care for younger children), kids get a good introduction to life out West. They learn how to ride (at age six they can go out on trail rides) and a little of how to care for and feed horses, and they go swimming and fishing—all under the watchful eye of trained counselors. Everyone is assigned a horse for the entire week, based on individual ability, and children are divided into three groups: three- to five-year-olds, six- to twelve-year-olds, and teenagers. The Kids Corral is a comfortable indoor children's place for reading, art projects, and napping. A Game Room offers billiards, table tennis, and Foosball. Teens, as they much prefer, have their own separate program of riding, hayrides, and cookouts. The children's program is available from early June to Labor Day and from mid-December through March. The last week of August is Baby Week, when children under three years are accepted.

Recreation: Naturally, the main attraction of a ranch is horseback riding. From a string of more than 160 horses, you'll be assigned a mount that suits your ability. With experienced wranglers you'll ride the high country across mountain meadows, through tall evergreens, along Willow Creek.

But there's a lot more to this ranch than just horses. Between trail rides sneak in a little fishing in the lake near the Lodge or at a secluded spot along Willow Creek, and have the trout for breakfast! Go hiking or spend an afternoon on the skeet range (the only activity not covered in the package rates), swim in the heated pool, or simply laze about nearby in the sunshine. Play tennis on two Laykold courts or try racquetball.

For less strenuous activities you may seek out The Patio House, the principal recreation center, which includes exercise equipment, locker rooms, complimentary laundry facilities, game room, bar, TV room (good news—there's no television or phone in the rooms!), and a large, all-purpose activity room with fireplace. And when you fear that saddle sores and tennis elbow may set in, retire to the whirlpool and saunas. In the evenings you'll join in on campfire sing-alongs, square dancing, and rodeos—just so you don't forget you're out West.

During the winter season guests take to skiing—cross-country on the 15 miles of trails maintained by the ranch and downhill at Winter Park and Silver Creek ski resorts, 25 miles away and accessible via the ranch's complimentary shuttle service.

But winter activities don't stop there. Enjoy horseback riding in the snow or in the 10,000-square-foot heated riding arena, or take a sleigh ride on an old-fashioned cutter and a world-class, $\frac{1}{2}$-mile sled run, or try dogsledding. Ride an inner tube down the tubing hill or behind a speeding snowmobile, and ice skate or play hockey or broomball on the groomed skating pond. Then snuggle in for hot drinks, the fireplace, Western dancing, and cowboy songs. Yippee-yi-ay! ≋

Club Med/Copper Mountain

50 Beeler Place
Copper Mountain, Colorado 80443
(970) 968–7000, (800) CLUB–MED
Web site: www.clubmed.com

Club Med's Copper Mountain village is in Summit County, famous for terrific downhill skiing and its Rocky Mountain powder. Seventy-five miles west of Denver, the village is surrounded by the Arapahoe National Forest, sits at 9,600 feet, and looks up to a glorious mountain with a summit elevation of 12,360 feet. Copper Mountain is open from early December to mid-April.

You might be thinking "Club Med and kids? It has a nice ring, but is this for real?" Yes, at certain Club Med destinations, the swinging singles image has

Photo courtesy of Club Med

been shed and whole families can partake in the attentive yet carefree spirit of a Club Med vacation. Mini-Clubs cater to the younger set and support the Club Med policy of "The children, don't leave home without them."

Accommodations: In four interconnecting buildings, five to seven stories high, lodging is provided in cozy rooms with twin beds. The views of the mountains and the valleys are truly beautiful. Club Med's "pay one price" philosophy relieves you of many hassles, including repeated searches for your wallet. A one-week stay runs $970 to $1,280 per person, depending on the season; there's a 25 to 40 percent discount for children three to twelve. This price covers accommodations, meals, the children's program, ski lessons, and lift tickets. There is no extra charge for cribs or rollaway beds. It's necessary to have a Club Med membership to vacation here. Annual dues are $50 per adult, $20 per child, and a one-time family fee of $30.

Dining: The main dining room, with its floor-to-ceiling windows (you don't want to miss those mountain views), is the setting for breakfast and lunch buffets and multicourse, table-service dinners. There's a more intimate restaurant on the lower level. The cuisine is French and is as elegantly presented as it is carefully prepared. Wine is served at lunch and dinner (free of charge). Located near the dining room is a large bar as well as a cozy fireplace where après-ski begins. For evening entertainment see the nightly show, drop by the disco, or perhaps find a good bridge game in the card room.

Children's World: The Mini-Club, directed by an experienced staff, offers organized activities for three- to twelve-year-olds. This optional, free program is available 9:00 A.M. to 9:00 P.M. Monday through Saturday during the ski season. Children can join the group or their parents at any time, depending on family plans.

Besides two hours of ski classes in the morning and the afternoon, kids go ice skating and sledding and have snow sculpture contests and arts-and-crafts classes. Don't worry about lunch and dinner; your child can enjoy the company of the counselors and other children at early mealtimes.

Recreation: Skiing at Copper Mountain just may lead to Rocky Mountain fever; with a 2,760-foot vertical drop, an average annual snowfall between 250 and 300 inches, and a season from early December to mid-April, it's not difficult to hit a skier's high. Fourteen chairlifts and seventy-six trails mean that long lift lines and crowded slopes are virtually unknown. The terrain offers beginner, intermediate, and expert runs, and Club Med's own ski school (two-hour classes mornings and afternoons) will guide you to improved downhill techniques whatever your level of ability. Classes are frequently videotaped, so be prepared for review and analysis with your instructor in the evening. For cross-country skiers, there are 16 miles of marked trails; however, no instruction or equipment is provided. Ice skating nearby on an outdoor pond is another favorite wintertime sport, as is snowboarding, with lessons for beginners.

Other activities include aerobics and stretch classes, jogging, and hiking. When the body grows weary, it may be time for pure relaxation in one of the Jacuzzis or saunas. The Copper Mountain organization has developed an athletic facility outside the Club Med property; for a small daily fee, Club Med guests have access to the tennis and racquetball courts, exercise equipment, swimming pool, saunas, and steam rooms there. ≋≋

Deer Valley Resort

P.O. Box 1525
Park City, Utah 84060
(435) 649–1000, (800) 424–3337
Web site: www.deervalley.com

Skiing for most folks means a little bit of the rugged outdoors—windburned cheeks, the raw natural beauty of mountain vistas, fresh tracks through pristine powder. Deer Valley has redefined skiing somewhat. It's all of the above but with an added twist. Instead of the Western flair you'd expect in Utah, there's a more sophisticated European atmosphere at Deer Valley. This is warm hospitality with a heavy dose of pampering—from the guest service attendants who help you unload your skis to the quite comfortable chairlifts to the signature food items in Snow Park Lodge.

Deer Valley, less than an hour's drive east of Salt Lake City, is actually four mountains: Bald Eagle Mountain, whose summit is 8,500 feet; Bald Mountain, which rises to 9,400 feet; Flagstaff Mountain, with the summit at 9,100 feet; and Empire Canyon, with a summit of 9,570 feet. The hubs of activity are Snow Park Lodge at the base of Bald Eagle Mountain and Silver Lake Lodge at midmountain. Silver Lake Village is in effect the midmountain point, for it is from here that lifts ascend to Bald Mountain's summit. Snow Park Lodge houses a restaurant and lounge, the ski school, the ski rental shop, the children's center, and a well-stocked ski shop. Silver Lake Lodge has three restaurants and a smaller ski shop.

Both lodges are very tastefully designed; inside the columns are natural tree trunks at least 2 feet in diameter, and wood accoutrements abound—from the handrails to the ceiling beams, from the facial tissue dispensers to the trash cans. You'll find no plastic chairs or Formica-topped tables in the dining areas here—no indeed! Understated elegance and tasteful attention to detail are hallmarks of Deer Valley, the first country club for skiers.

Accommodations: The Stein Eriksen Lodge, located at midmountain, is a Norwegian-style hotel built of stone and wood. There are 130 luxurious rooms and suites, starting at $450 a night in winter and $175 in summer. Shops, restaurants, a swimming pool, and a health club complement this lodge.

In addition, there are more than 500 units at the base of the mountain, along the trails, and near Silver Lake Lodge. The condominiums range from one- to five-bedroom units with fully equipped kitchens and living areas with fireplaces. Most have private Jacuzzis and individual decks or balconies; some include saunas and some feature ski-in/ski-out access. Daily maid service is available. There are substantial savings during value seasons, typically early December and early January, while rates increase during holiday periods. During the summer months rates range from $150 a night for a one-bedroom unit to $525 a night for a four-bedroom unit, with a minimum two-night stay. Contact Deer Valley Central Reservations for complete customized vacation planning.

Dining: Dining at Deer Valley is a gourmet experience. The Glitretind at the Stein Eriksen Lodge heads the list in elegance. The Snow Park Lodge and the Silver Lake Restaurant in the Silver Lake Lodge are "cafeterias." What misnomers! Though they're self-service, the lavish lunchtime displays (homemade breads and pastries, salads, quiches, deli sandwiches) are hardly typical of the standard quick bite between ski runs. In the evening The Seafood Buffet is offered at the Snow Park Lodge (mmm—iced shrimp and raw oysters on the half shell). The Mariposa at Silver Lake Lodge features table service for an elegant candlelight dinner. All these provide interesting alternatives to gourmet cooking in your condo.

Children's World: Deer Valley's Children's Center is a state-licensed facility providing indoor supervision and activities for nonskiing children. Located on the main level of the Snow Park Lodge, the center is open daily 8:30 A.M. to 4:30 P.M. during the ski season and can accommodate infants as young as two months of age. Prices for enrollment are as follows: two- to twenty-four-month-olds, $80 for a full day (with lunch); two- to twelve-year-olds, $70 for a full day (with lunch).

Recreation: There are eighty-eight downhill runs, nineteen chairlifts, and a vertical drop of 3,000 feet. Combine these with well-groomed trails and a restricted number of skiers on a daily basis—what more could a skier ask for? The mountains are beautiful, and the attention to them and to the skiers is high quality. Full- and half-day private and group lessons are available. Cross-country ski lessons are also offered nearby; trails roll over broad, open expanses and through aspens and evergreens.

If you don't have a sufficient workout on the slopes, maybe the exercise rooms will test your limits. Then relax your weary muscles in one of the saunas or Jacuzzis. Though primarily a winter wonderland, Deer Valley operates year-round. In warmer weather guests enjoy 50 miles of lift-served mountain biking, scenic chairlift rides, the Utah Symphony Series, and the Deer Valley Summer Adventure Camp. ≋

Flathead Lake Lodge

Box 248
Bigfork, Montana 59911
(406) 837–4391; fax (406) 837–6977
E-mail: fll@digisys.net
Web site: averill.com

M ix some city slickers with a few expert wranglers out in Montana horse country, toss in beautiful scenery and clear blue skies, and come up with quite a different vacation experience at Flathead Lake Lodge. On 2,000 acres in northwest Montana, just south of Glacier National Park, this dude ranch specializes in water sports and just about anything that has to do with horses, from riding them to shoeing them. The lodge is situated on the shores of Flathead Lake (15 miles wide by 30 miles long), and the surrounding timberland stretches up into the Rocky Mountains. The ranch is open from May 1 to October 1, and one- or two-week visits are standard.

Accommodations: The main lodge is the focus of activities and dining; in a warm and rustic setting, the old stone fireplace lures many guests to gather for cozy chats. There are guest rooms here and in the south lodge; some families find the two- and three-bedroom cottages particularly attractive. Many of the lodge rooms and the guest cottages have views of the lake. The weekly rate for an adult is $2,186; for a teenager, $1,624; for six- to twelve-year-olds, $1,463; for three- to five-year-olds, $996; and for infants and toddlers, $101. These rates include lodging, three meals a day, and recreation, including horseback riding, tennis, and use of the boats and sports equipment. Cribs are available at no additional charge.

Dining: Dining is a family affair, with good home cooking. Guests gather at the long tables in the lodge dining room or at the picnic tables out on the patio overlooking the lake. Everyone may sample buffalo or roast pig at an outdoor barbecue, along with homemade breads and pies. Children eat together before their parents, allowing grown-ups time to get acquainted and plan the next day's events. Sometimes adults meet in the Saddle Sore Saloon.

Children's World: The friendly staff—mostly energetic college students who can keep up with excited youngsters—guide children through the day's activities. They can swim, lend a hand with the daily chores, and learn to ride horses. Arts-and-crafts classes are offered from 10:00 A.M. to noon most weekdays. Children six years and older can join cowboys on the horseback-riding trails in

Photo courtesy of Flathead Lake Lodge

the mountains. You might want to bring along a sleeping bag for your child; there's a campout in tepees near the ranch. Baby-sitting is also available.

Recreation: The great outdoors awaits you. Horses are a way of life here; ride 'em, rope 'em, or test your nerve and verve in competition. Take an early-morning breakfast ride to work up a good appetite, then enjoy a breakfast cookout amid the tall pines. Old-fashioned Western rodeos are part of the evening activities.

Take a dip in the large swimming pool or the crystal clear waters of the lake. Sailing, canoe races, and waterskiing may fill your afternoons. Cruises on the lake are organized several times a week. Fish in the lake or the nearby streams, and add a trout to a cookout dinner or spin a good story about the one that got away.

It's easy to find partners for a game of tennis (four courts) and to organize table tennis or volleyball. You might take a stroll along the wooded trails and pick berries. You can schedule full- or half-day excursions for white-water rafting, river tubing, and wilderness fishing. The National Bison Range, only an hour away, attracts many visitors; seeing real live buffalo is a highlight for kids—and parents. ≈≈≈

Keystone Resort

Box 38
Keystone, Colorado 80435
(970) 468–2316, (800) 468–5004
Web site: www.ski-keystone.com

L ike many fine Western ski resorts, Keystone first attracted settlers in search of the rich minerals in its mountains. Today visitors flock here seeking light powdery snow and the mountain high for which the Rockies are known. At the base of Loveland Pass, 70 miles west of Denver, Keystone has ninety-one runs on three interconnecting ski mountains and a vertical drop of more than 2,300 feet. The resort remains open year-round, so when summer rolls around, many folks hang up their skis and head for Keystone's golf course (designed by Robert Trent Jones Jr.), the Keystone Tennis Center, and the Keystone Music Festival.

Accommodations: River Run Village at Keystone Resort is the largest ski area development project in North America. When finished, Keystone will have an estimated 4,560 residential units and lodge rooms. To date, two buildings have been constructed in River Run: Jackpine Lodge and Black Bear. Both buildings have ground-floor shops and restaurants, with three upper levels of mountain condominium homes. Upper-floor residential units total sixty-one. A third building, Arapahoe Lodge, includes thirty-six upper-floor condominium homes. Rentals are available. Prices are yet to be determined.

The Keystone Lodge is an elegant resort hotel with more than 150 rooms offering mountain views, most with a private balcony. Facilities here include an indoor/outdoor swimming pool, sauna, Jacuzzi, and three restaurants. Nightly rates during the summer are $190 to $230 for two people; during the ski season rates are $170 to $236 a night.

The Inn at Keystone is a six-story hotel with 160 rooms, just 200 yards from the lift. Rooms here are $130 to $170 during summer, $135 to $215 during ski season (from the end of November to the beginning of April). Children twelve and under stay free in the same room with their parents. Cribs are available.

In addition to River Run, 850 condominium units are arranged near the slopes, in the village, and bordering the lake; these studios to four-bedroom units have a fully equipped kitchen, and most have a fireplace. All complexes have a heated swimming pool, a sauna, or a Jacuzzi. In the summer one-bedroom units are $135 to $195 a night, and a four-bedroom unit for eight people is $265 to $360 a night. Winter rates are $140 to $360 for a one-bedroom and $370 to $960 for a four-bedroom unit. Package plans are offered for skiing, golf, tennis,

Photo courtesy of Keystone Resort

and music festival vacations. A shuttle-bus service winds through the village and connects the mountain bases.

Dining: From romantic gourmet dinners in a mountaintop restaurant more than 2 miles high to family picnic lunches carried by llamas, unique and award-winning dining choices set Keystone Resort apart from other mountain resorts. The resort features more than a dozen dining options that range from gourmet six-course meals to a Western family-style cookout and include Summit County's only AAA four-diamond-rated restaurants—The Alpenglow Stube and Keystone Ranch.

At the Keystone Lodge, the Garden Room features Continental cuisine and a Sunday brunch; the Edgewater is a casual restaurant open for breakfast and lunch. Among the numerous restaurants in the village, you'll find Pizza on the Plaza; Idabelle's, for Mexican fare; and Out of Bounds, for a sports bar/nightclub atmosphere. Lunch and dinner are served at both the Keystone Ranch and Alpenglow Stube. In the summertime you can hop a hayride to Soda Creek Homestead—in winter a sleigh ride takes you there—for a juicy steak dinner.

Children's World: At Keystone youngsters start skiing at age three. The Mini-Minor's Camp is a program of introductory skiing and sledding and indoor activities for four- and five-year-olds. Graduating from this, a child joins the Minor's Camp for six- to eight-year-olds; more ski instruction is integrated into the fully supervised day. The fee for all day, 8:30 A.M. to 4:00 P.M., is $72, including lunch.

The Children's Center is located at the Mountain House base area of the mountain and provides nursery care for little ones as young as two months. The fee for the day-care center is $46 a day.

During the summer Keystone's Children's Center provides attention for children two months to twelve years, 8:00 A.M. to 5:00 P.M., in age-appropriate activities. Little ones are amused with a stock of toys; preschoolers enjoy nature walks, picnics, pony rides, and arts and crafts; and older children go swimming, boating, hiking, horseback riding, fishing, and take rides in the gondola. The daily charge for the program is $54; lunch is included except when baby food and formula are required. Baby-sitting services are also available, at an hourly rate of $8.00.

Recreation: With three interconnected mountains—Keystone Mountain, North Peak, and The Outback—Keystone offers terrain for skiers and snowboarders of all levels. Keystone Mountain offers mainly beginner and intermediate terrain, with night-skiing operations that keep the mountain open until 9:00 P.M. North Peak challenges guests with more intermediate slopes and runs that plunge down mogul-filled terrain. The Outback features only intermediate and expert runs. Some of Summit County's best tree skiing is found on The Outback. Skiers can find deep powder in open bowls adjacent to The Outback. And the twenty-acre snowboard terrain park features two half-pipes. Nighttime lighting makes Keystone's terrain garden the largest night-snowboarding operation in Colorado.

The ski season opens at Keystone in mid-October (Colorado's earliest opening date) and continues into early May. Whether you're trying to figure out what a snowplow is or you're looking for perfection in powder skiing, the more than 350 ski and snowboarding instructors can guide you through the 1,749 acres of skiable terrain.

Other winter sports at Keystone include ice skating at the Skating Center in the village, cross-country skiing from the Keystone Cross-Country Center into Arapahoe National Forest (cross-country and telemark lessons are offered), snowmobile tours into the backcountry, sleigh rides, and indoor tennis.

Summertime at Keystone means golfing on the masterfully designed Robert Trent Jones Jr. course; eighteen holes with a Scottish flair respect the woodlands, meadows, and a nine-acre lake. The course is open from June to mid-October; golf pros offer private lessons and clinics.

Keystone is a haven for mountain-bike enthusiasts. The resort offers a special program called Dirt Camp, a series of instructional mountain-bike camps that provides intense riding retreats for "mud studs" and "wannabes." Even if you're a beginner and conquering single-track, Dirt Camp helps you hone your mountain biking skills.

Another important summertime attraction here is the Music Festival. Ranging from classical to pop, the National Repertory Orchestra and the Summit Brass carry the season from June through Labor Day.

At the Keystone Tennis Center, two indoor courts permit year-round play, and an additional twelve outdoor courts expand summertime possibilities. Ball machines, video analysis, and group and private lessons aid the tennis player in his game.

Fishermen take to the local haunts for rainbow trout; boaters sail on Lake Dillon (5 miles west of Keystone) or skim across Keystone Lake in a paddleboat or kayak. Bicyclists ride the paths along Snake River, and hikers plod along the trails through wildflowers and aspens into the national forest. Horseback ride from the Keystone Stables through the Snake River Valley (breakfast rides are specialties), tour the high country of the Arapahoe National Forest by four-wheel drive, go white-water rafting down the Colorado and Arkansas Rivers, be treated to a lunch of rattlesnake meat and buffalo, or enjoy the great outdoors and mountain scenery on a gondola ride to Keystone Mountain's summit.

Reservations and more information on these activities (including dining at Keystone's award-winning restaurants) can be arranged by the Keystone Activities and Dining Center well before a guest arrives, so that everything is already in place at vacation's start. The number to call is (800) 354–4FUN. ≋

Mountain Sky Guest Ranch

P.O. Box 1128
Bozeman, Montana 59715
(406) 587–1244, (800) 548–3392
E-mail: mountainsky@mcm.net
Web site: www.mtnsky.com

J ust turn me loose, let me straddle my own saddle underneath the Western sky." At Mountain Sky all guests (age seven and older) are assigned their own special horse. Careful matching of horse and rider according to the latter's age and skills ensures a compatible duo during a vacation stay. Under the guidance of experienced wranglers, you'll be swaggering like a Montana cowboy before the week is out.

Mountain Sky Guest Ranch has a rich history dating back to the mid-nineteenth century. This is no modern mock-up of Old West ranching. It was an active operation during the days of cattle empires and witnessed the excitement of the gold mining era. With its genuine Western flavor, Mountain Sky offers visitors a combination of "wide open spaces" and modern conveniences and comforts.

Photo courtesy of Mountain Sky Guest Ranch

Located just 30 miles north of Yellowstone National Park, Mountain Sky sits in Paradise Valley, in southwestern Montana. Surrounded by national forest and wilderness areas, the wooded mountainous landscape of Montana's high country is a beautiful vacation setting.

Accommodations: Guests are lodged in rustic but modern cabins; each one has a refrigerator. Rates are $2,380 to $2,660 a week for an adult, $2,030 to $2,450 for a child seven to twelve years old, and $1,575 to $1,820 for a younger child. These prices include accommodations, all meals, use of all recreational facilities, and a horse for each guest (except those six and younger). Cribs are available at no charge. During the summer the vacation week runs from Sunday to Sunday; within a couple of days, you'll make friends not only with your horse but also with the other guests.

Dining: Meals are served in the dining room of the main lodge and at barbecue cookouts. Understanding that the atmosphere of the great outdoors can generate healthy appetites, the chefs often prepare hearty as well as gourmet meals. Rugged attire (jeans, boots) is standard most of the time; Tuesday- and Saturday-night dinners are a bit more formal. For good conversation and evening cocktails, drop by the Mountain View Lounge.

Children's World: In summer trained counselors guide children of all ages in a program of activities. The youth schedule includes arts and crafts, nature walks, and swimming. There's even a small fishing pond reserved for children. Children ages seven and older learn horseback-riding skills with the Children's

Wrangler. With the exception of family cookouts, children can stay with their friends and counselors for evening meals. The game room for teens features table tennis, a jukebox, and a pool table. There is no additional charge for these activities; the supervised children's program is part of the weekly rate.

Recreation: Horseback riding is the primary sport at the ranch. Mounting your own horse and exploring hundreds of miles of trails can be as invigorating or relaxing as you want to make it. Besides morning and afternoon excursions, guests enjoy evening dinner rides.

In between take a dip in the heated swimming pool, play a game of tennis (two courts), or hike in the woods. Table tennis, volleyball, softball, and horseshoes are also popular games at the ranch. Anglers head to the mountain streams, where rainbow and brown trout are in plentiful supply. After active adventures, unwind in the hot tub or sauna. Capping off a fun-filled day, evening Western dances and campfire sing-alongs are frequently planned. ≋

Park City Mountain Resort

P.O. Box 39
Park City, Utah 84060
(801) 649–8111; (800) 222–7275 for lodging information
Web site: www.parkcitymountain.com

Park City was originally a mining camp in the nineteenth century. From the late 1860s to the 1930s, the wealth of silver in the mountains attracted miners with dreams of great fortunes. Today people flock to Park City not for the silver but for the incredible Utah snow.

As one local said, "Skiing is almost a religion here. People talk about when it snowed, how much it snowed, and what kind of snow it snowed when it snowed!" In the 1940s the potential of this snow was realized and the first runs were opened. By the 1960s the development known today as the Park City Mountain Resort had begun.

The town is at 6,400 feet, and summits rise to 10,000 feet. Just thirty-five minutes from Salt Lake City's airport and surrounded by the Wasatch Range of the Rocky Mountains, Park City is more than a mountain and luxury condominiums. Historic Main Street is lined with Victorian architecture containing shops, restaurants, and galleries and gives you a sense of what the Old West was all about. With a little imagination, you can just picture an old miner swaggering into a Main Street restaurant (it would have been a saloon in the old days), ready to make friends with some pretty dance-hall girl. The resort area is open year-round. A summertime calendar of events and activities can be obtained from the Park City Chamber of Commerce.

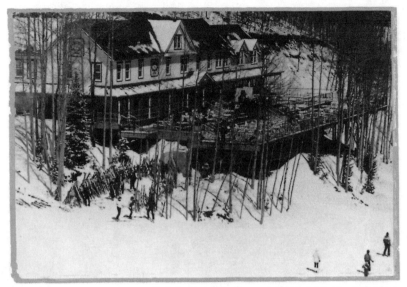

Photo by Hughes Martin, courtesy of Park City Mountain Resort

Accommodations: There are approximately 3,000 hotel rooms and condominium units in Park City at the mountain base, a couple of blocks from the runs, and throughout town. Prices vary depending on the proximity to the slopes and the amenities offered. The Park City Chamber of Commerce garners complete listings of accommodations in the area; call (801) 649–6100. A free bus connects all points in the town.

The Lodge at Mountain Village is at the base of the ski area and features ski-in/ski-out convenience. Surrounding the ice-skating rink and above the many shops and restaurants of the resort center, the accommodations range from studios at $239 a night to four-bedroom units up to $999 a night during the regular season (late January to early April). Package plans that include lift tickets are offered.

The Silvertown Lodge offers one- to four-bedroom condominiums, each with a fireplace and kitchen. It is a couple of blocks from the slopes, and prices range from $134 to $215 a night for a one-bedroom to $240 to $399 a night for a four-bedroom unit, depending on the season.

Dining: With a well-developed resort village at the mountain base and a historic Main Street, the dining facilities are numerous, to say the least. Though most people lodging in condominiums find cooking at home convenient, the many eating establishments will probably entice you for a few meals out.

At the resort center are several refreshment spots, from Rocky Mountain Chocolate Factory, with luscious bonbons and fudge, to Baja Cantina, with its generous portions of Mexican dishes. Moose's serves burgers, and Food for Thought has deli sandwiches and pastries. Legacy Lodge, a new 54,000-square-foot base lodge, offers food court–style dining, a coffee bar, and après-ski at Legends private club.

Three restaurants are on the mountain, one of which, the Mid Mountain Lodge, was built about 1898 and is one of the top twelve mountain restaurants in North America (as rated by *Ski* magazine). Enjoy a variety of entrees and sandwiches, either inside or outside on the 10,000-square-foot deck. Summit Smoke House & Grill, located at the top of the Bonanza chairlift, features smoked and authentic barbeque items in a table-service atmosphere. The Snow Hut, located at the base of the Silverlode chairlift, offers classic wintertime fare, including soups and chilli, daily specials, and grilled items.

Main Street opens up another realm of dining establishments: the Claimjumper, for steaks and prime rib; Cisero's, for chicken, seafood, and pasta dishes; and Texas Red's Pit Barbecue, for spareribs and beef brisket. At Prospector's Square the Grub Steak Restaurant features prime rib, steak, and seafood.

Children's World: All ages will enjoy skiing at Park City Mountain Resort. Specialists and indoor staffers assemble a day's worth of activities that blend fun and learning. Little Groomers (Level 1–2) is a unique way for your three- to five-year-old to learn how to ski. The Magic Carpet surface lift helps assure that your child's first time on skis will be safe and memorable. Bombardiers (Level 1–6) provides ski lessons for five- through twelve-year-olds with instruction tailored to individual abilities. Free-Riders (Level 1–5) groups snowboarding lessons for seven- through twelve-year-olds for a structured coaching environment. Reservations are required for all children's programs. All full-day lessons include lunch and lift ticket.

Teen Time, the workshop for teens, offers a safe, supervised environment that allows a group of teens with similar skills the opportunity to explore the mountain. Chaperones balance fun and safety with subtle coaching. For thirteen- to seventeen-year-olds (Levels 6–8 plus); skiers only. Cost includes lift ticket; parents provide lunch.

Recreation: With an annual average snowfall of 350 inches, a ski season from mid-November to the end of April, and 3,300 acres of skiable terrain, including one hundred runs and seven bowls, fourteen chairlifts, and 3,100 vertical feet, Park City is one of the largest Rocky Mountain ski resorts. Whether you ride the six-passenger high-speed chair, Silverlode, or the chairs up to Jupiter Bowl, you'll find runs to meet your whim and your expertise. Whether you ramble down gentle slopes past old mining buildings, take on the moguls between groves of aspen, or get knee-deep in powder, plenty of variety will keep you happy. Park City allows snowboarding, too, and there's even night skiing and riding, if you just can't bear to leave the slopes.

Ice skating is another fun wintertime sport, and with the rink, rentals, and lessons available in the resort village, it's a convenient diversion. The resort village, which includes several restaurants, is also the center for many shops: ski rental and repair, fashions and ski accessories, gifts, T-shirts, toys, and handcrafted items.

Though primarily a wintertime resort area, Park City is a destination for summertime vacations as well. The clean mountain air, the plentiful wildflowers, and the great outdoors beckon you. Hiking, horseback riding, tennis and racquetball (at specific condominium properties, the Athletic Club, and the Racquet Club), golf, and bicycling are favorite warm-weather activities. ≋

Snowbird Ski and Summer Resort

P.O. Box 929000
Snowbird, Utah 84092
(801) 742–2222; (800) 453–3000 for lodging and air reservations
Web site: www.snowbird.com

S nowbird's diverse terrain includes some of the most challenging skiing in the world. Yet surprisingly, the size of its intermediate, novice, and beginner areas is greater than the total terrain of many notable resorts. Every night more than half the slopes and trails are groomed, paving the way for beginner and intermediate skiers, while leaving the rest for those who seek the light, dry Utah powder. Whatever your proficiency and desire, Snowbird accommodates you with more than 2,500 acres of wide-open bowls, gladed tree runs, steep chutes, nightly groomed trails, and cruising boulevards. From the 500 acres of new terrain on Mineral Basin to the terrific novice and intermediate terrain off the Thunder Chair, you'll be amazed by the sheer excitement of skiing the "Bird."

Here are a few facts about Snowbird: vertical rise of 3,240 continuously skiable feet; 2,500-plus skiable acres; average annual snowfall of 500 inches; many lifts, including one aerial tramway, seven double chairlifts, and three high-speed detachable quads; a ski season extending from mid-November through late May; the longest descent, Gad Valley, at 3½ miles; the longest designated run, Chip's Run, at 2½ miles.

Snowbird enjoys one of the finest ski seasons in the world. Beginning in mid-November, the ski season regularly extends 200 days. In fact, skiers have even been known to celebrate the Fourth of July on the slopes.

Photo courtesy of Snowbird Ski and Summer Resort

Accommodations: A cozy slopeside pedestrian village, Snowbird harmonizes fittingly with the rugged, natural beauty of Little Cottonwood Canyon. Yet here you'll find all the services necessary to complete the perfect vacation. And everything at the resort—accommodations, restaurants, shops, skiing, and activities—is within easy walking distance.

Snowbird has three distinctive condominium properties: The Inn, The Lodge at Snowbird, and the Iron Blosam Lodge. Each offers homelike features, such as fireplaces and kitchens, with several different floor plans to suit your family's needs. Pools, saunas, exercise facilities, and other services are included or easily accessible. Snowbird's flagship accommodation, the Cliff Lodge, offers easy ski-in/ski-out access, full-service child care, shops, and a business center. It is adorned with the decorative luxury of North America's foremost Persian and Oriental rug collection. Three restaurants, two lounges, and the world-class Cliff Spa and Salon make it the perfect place to retire after an exhilarating day on the slopes.

Snowbird's 57,000-square-foot conference center includes fourteen meeting rooms and a 7,800-square-foot ballroom. These facilities, uncompromising services, and a professional staff are the reasons Snowbird has been awarded one of the industry's highest honors, *Meetings & Conventions* magazine's Gold Key Award.

Dining: The dining at Snowbird is diverse, with many restaurants and lounges to please a variety of tastes and styles. Snowbird dining offers everything from Niçoise-style striped sea bass to mountain-grilled burgers to coconut beer-battered shrimp. Live entertainment and other après-ski activities also complement Snowbird's winter season.

Children's World: Snowbird offers ideal family vacations. According to *Skiing* magazine, "Snowbird has come up with what might be the best family ski value at a major ski area." The resort has been awarded the Family Channel's Seal of Quality. From family ski zones to the Kids Park Mining Town replica, Snowbird is certain to please young skiers. So don't bring the kids just because they ski for free; bring them because Snowbird is one vacation they'll always remember.

Camp Snowbird, located in the Cliff Lodge, provides state-licensed infant and toddler care. Available services at Camp Snowbird include daytime supervision, meals, ski lessons, and, most of all, a good time. In-room baby-sitting is also available to lodging guests. Make reservations two weeks in advance.

Recreation: Snowbird's Mountain Host program offers free guided skiing tours every day to acquaint guests with the runs and lifts best suited to their skiing abilities. All you need is a lift ticket and a smile to join the group and get better acquainted with the incredible mountain. New this season, Snowbird and Little Cottonwood Canyon neighbor Alta will offer one lift ticket for both resorts. Made possible by Snowbird's second Mineral Basin chairlift, the Alta–Snowbird ticket provides two of the world's top resorts in one day of skiing.

Almost as famous as the snow, and every bit as great, is the ski school. More than 300 professional instructors offer all-day or by-the-hour private and group lessons. Or, if you want to take your vacation to new heights, try one of Snowbird's specialized seminars that address the specific interests and needs of women, seniors, snowboarders, and experts.

The Cliff Lodge and the Snowbird Center house shops and boutiques specializing in products unique to Snowbird. From children's clothing to jewelry, from a general store to a pharmacy, and from ski rentals to Snowbird's own signature clothing line, you're certain to find what you're looking for. ≋

Snowmass Village Resort Association

Box 5566
Snowmass Village, Colorado 81615
(800) 598–2006 for guest information;
(800) 598–2004 for reservations
E-mail: info@snowmassvillage.com
Web site: www.snowmassvillage.com

Aspen is one heck of a fine mountain. With more than 3,300 feet of vertical drop and exciting, challenging runs, it attracts very skillful skiers. But when talking Aspen skiing, you've actually got four mountains to consider: Aspen Mountain (sometimes called Ajax); Snowmass, 10 miles away; and Aspen Highlands and Buttermilk in between. A combined skiable terrain that totals more than 3,500 acres provides more runs and variety than you could possibly test in a two-week ski vacation. Lift passes are valid for all four mountains. Aspen is chic and supports an active night life; Snowmass is devoted to its motto "A Mountain of Family Fun." But who splits hairs when the best of both worlds is all within 10 miles? Though best known for skiing, both resort areas are open year-round.

Aspen's origins are rooted in the silver boom of the early 1880s. Many of the charming Victorian structures have been preserved and renovated; today they house boutiques, art galleries, hotels, and restaurants. Skiing in Aspen started in the 1930s and really took hold after World War II during conscientious development of the area as a winter resort. Aspen is just waiting to tempt you. Folks here boast that 70 percent of their visitors return every year and more than 90 percent come back sooner or later. So if you give it a shot, you may just have to plan on being hooked.

Accommodations: Whatever your preference in lodging, you should have no problem finding the perfect place to hang your hat in the Aspen and Snowmass area. From moderate to expensive, from quaint to modern, all the possibilities seem to be here. For the most part, lodgings in Aspen are in the village; at Snowmass they're slopeside with immediate access to trails. This is not, however, a hard-and-fast rule, and because shuttle buses always cruise the roads, there's no problem getting to the lifts and from one mountain to another.

The Aspen Club Lodge is at the base of Aspen Mountain and includes a swimming pool, Jacuzzi, saunas, and restaurant ($170 to $425 a night, higher for suites). Just across from the Little Nell Lift is Aspen Square, a complex of about one hundred condominium units that features a swimming pool and saunas; nightly rates range from $139 to $429, with a seven-night minimum for most of the season. The Hotel Jerome on Main Street is a Victorian building more than one hundred years old; room rates are $255 to $725 a night.

The Snowmass Lodge and Club in Snowmass Village combines hotel and condominium accommodations on 120 acres at the base of the mountain. The amenities include a restaurant and bar, indoor tennis courts (two), exercise equipment, swimming pools, and, for summer and fall holidays, eleven outdoor tennis courts and an eighteen-hole golf course. Double rooms start at $145 a night, going to $848 for a three-bedroom unit (depending on the date). There is a three-night minimum. Other hotels in Snowmass are the Wildwood Lodge, the Stonebridge Inn, the Pokolodi Lodge, the Mountain Chalet, and the Silvertree; among the more than twenty condominium complexes are Aspenwood, Shadowbrook, Crestwood, and Timberline. With close to one hundred hotels, lodges, inns, and condominiums in the Aspen area, it is indeed fortunate that the resort associations publish descriptive lists to help you sort through the possibilities. Inquire carefully about various pricing packages: five- or seven-day packages that include lifts and lessons, low-season rates, and family plans.

Dining: As with lodging arrangements, the dining possibilities seem almost limitless. Whether you've got a hankering for pizza, quiche, fresh veggies and salads, a juicy steak, spicy Szechuan or Northern Italian cuisine, you'll find the right spot among the more than one hundred restaurants in and around Aspen. La Cocina Su Casa and the Cantina serve Mexican dishes; steaks and prime rib are typical fare at the Steak Pit. And, of course, restaurants and refreshment stops are at the mountain bases and on the mountains. For sweets you can stop by the Paradise Bakery or Cafe Ink.

Among the twenty restaurants in Snowmass are The Stew Pot, featuring wholesome family fare; the Mountain Dragon, featuring Chinese food; and the premier restaurants, La Bohème and Cowboys.

Children's World: Even the youngest traveling companion will not keep you from days on the slopes. From 8:30 A.M. to 4:00 P.M., Snow Cubs entertains eighteen-month to three-year-old children in a play program filled with puppet shows, stories, arts and crafts, snowman building, some skiing, and sledding; four- to six-year-olds participate in ski lessons as well as indoor and other outdoor activities in the Big Burn Bears program. The program is $78 daily or $360 for five full days and includes lunch and lift tickets. Late-afternoon and evening baby-sitters are also available through Snowmass Ski School. Family activities are scheduled all season long.

Powder Pandas is Buttermilk Mountain's ski school for three- to six-year-olds, 8:30 A.M. to 4:00 P.M. Snowpuppies Ski School is Aspen Highlands' version of ski lessons and fun for ages three and a half to six, 9:30 A.M. to 3:30 P.M. The daytime programs include lunch and snacks at each of these locations and cost $72 at the Highlands and $78 at Buttermilk.

The children's classes at the Snowmass Ski School organize seven- to twelve-year-old skiers from 9:30 A.M. to 3:15 P.M.; the cost is $65 per day. Also at the Snowmass Ski School, a special teen program is designed to bring together by age and ability skiers thirteen to nineteen years old; besides skiing, picnics, races, and sled parties are planned. The cost is $60 per day.

Operating a summer program (June through August) for five- to twelve-year-olds, Camp Snowmass emphasizes a healthy, active outdoor schedule of fishing, hiking, swimming, nature walks, horseback riding, visits to the nature preserve, and picnics. Overnights are planned during the season. For a day's events from 7:45 A.M. to 4:00 P.M., Monday through Friday, the fee is $50 (lunch is provided for an additional $5.00). Five- and ten-day packages are available for additional savings. Snowmass also offers free daily activities for kids and adults all summer long.

Recreation: From the end of November to mid-April, skiing is on everyone's mind, and regardless of your skiing ability you'll have plenty of runs to schuss down. Aspen's reputation as a mecca for advanced skiers is well earned, with 30 percent of the runs down Ajax ranked as expert, 35 percent advanced, and the remaining 35 percent intermediate. But beginners and intermediates should not grow faint in the face of overwhelming ventures, for the other mountains accommodate the not quite so adept. Aspen Highlands is 50 percent intermediate and 25 percent each in expert and beginner categories; the total vertical drop is 3,635 feet. The vertical rise at Snowmass is almost 4,400 feet, and more than 60 percent of the runs are intermediate. Buttermilk with 2,000 vertical feet caters more to novices, with almost half of its runs designated for beginners. A teaching staff that totals more than 1,000 ski professionals can introduce a beginner to the slopes (except at Aspen Mountain) as well as help an expert perfect techniques in mogul skiing, snowboarding, and telemarking. At Buttermilk and Snowmass, look for special three-day, first-time-on-skis or -snowboard packages.

Wintertime fun continues with ice skating at the Aspen Ice Gardens and the Silver Circle, dogsled rides at Krabloonik Kennels, snowshoe tours, cross-country skiing, sleigh rides at Snowmass Stables and T Lazy 7 Ranch, snowmobiling, and hot-air ballooning (yes, even in winter!). Many of the lodging complexes have swimming pools and exercise equipment. The tennis and athletic clubs also provide opportunities for indoor workouts. Evening entertainment includes films, concerts, plays at the Wheeler Opera House, and classical music at Harris Hall.

Though skiing is practically synonymous with Aspen, this place does not turn into a ghost town when the snow melts. During the summer, the hills are alive with cultural events. The Aspen Music Festival, nearly fifty years old, runs from the end of June to the end of August and is complemented by the Aspen Community Theater and the Jazz Aspen Snowmass Music Festivals. The Anderson Ranch Arts Center in Snowmass has a summer program of classes in photography, ceramics, painting, and printmaking.

You can just about have your pick of outdoor activities: horseback riding, hiking, jogging, rafting, kayaking, fishing, hot-air ballooning, and jeep tours. There is also lift-served mountain biking at Snowmass Ski Area. An eighteen-hole golf course is located on the west perimeter of Aspen; another is in Snowmass. Tennis courts at condominiums and racquet clubs dot the valley. But even in summer you have to take at least one gondola ride—to the top of Aspen Mountain for a spectacular view of this bit of the Rockies. ≋

Vail/Beaver Creek Central Reservations

P.O. Box 7
Vail, Colorado 81658
(800) 525–2257

Lots of folks talk of Vail and Aspen in practically the same breath. Usually these are people who have never visited either one. Granted, several similarities between the two come to mind: Both rank right at the top in excellent skiing, both are high in the Rockies west of Denver, both are chic and sophisticated, and to both have been appended newer developments that are more upscale and remote—Beaver Creek at Vail and Snowmass at Aspen.

Unlike Aspen's history as an old mining town, Vail grew up in the 1960s. The modern-day careful planning and systematic development give Vail its atmosphere; it is a well-laid-out, Alpine-style village designed with the pedestrian in mind (it's so nice that so few cars spoil the scenery). Actually, there are three village areas at the base of Vail Mountain—Golden Peak, Lionshead, and Vail Village—each with its own lodging, restaurants, and facilities, and each within walking distance of base lifts. In practical terms, though, since each abuts the next, most folks think of the tripartite as one friendly town. While Vail is 100 miles west of Denver, Beaver Creek is just 10 miles farther down the road. Opened in 1980, Beaver Creek, too, has been planned around a pedestrian village; in addition to the accommodations in the village, some lodges and condominiums are tucked among the grand spruce trees on the mountain. Shuttle-bus lines service the Vail Valley, within each village and between mountain bases. A year-round resort area, the Vail Valley also boasts of its summer beauty and offers art and music festivals, hiking, mountain biking, and more from April through October.

Accommodations: Lodging at Vail can be right at the mountain base a couple of skips from the chairlift and dripping with amenities, or back a couple of paces and not so overloaded with extras. Of course, the options are reflected in the rates. The Lodge at Vail, just steps from two chairlifts, has a heated swimming pool and a sauna, and some of its rooms feature a fireplace, balcony, and kitchen; daily rates for a one-bedroom condominium during the regular season, early February to early April, are $730 to $775 per night. At the Lion Square Lodge, located at the lower terminus of the gondola, a one-bedroom condominium (regular season) is $395 to $445 a night; this complex has a heated swimming pool, sauna, and whirlpool and some accommodations include a kitchen, fireplace, and balcony. The Landmark faces the pedestrian area at Lionshead and rents a two-bedroom condo for $375 to $695 a night; the facil-

Photo courtesy of Vail Valley Tourism and Convention Bureau

ities include two outdoor hot tubs and a heated outdoor pool, and the rooms have a balcony, fireplace, and kitchen.

Within walking distance of Beaver Creek Village is the Charter at Beaver Creek, a ski-in/ski-out lodge and condominium property with balconies and indoor pool; daily rates range from $195 to $340. Beaver Creek Lodge is slopeside and the only all-suite property in Vail Valley; its rates are $285 to $365. The Hyatt Regency at Beaver Creek is also ski-in/ski-out; in addition, it offers the Camp Hyatt children's program for ages three to thirteen. Rates are $380 to $470 ($290 to $355 in the summer). The cost of the children's program is $7.00 an hour; winter hours are Monday through Sunday, 9:00 A.M. to 10:00 P.M.; summer hours are 9:00 A.M. to 4:00 P.M. Sunday through Wednesday and 9:00 A.M. to 10:00 P.M. Thursday though Saturday.

The rates quoted are in effect during the regular season (early February to early April); Christmastime rates are higher. Summer rates can be as much as 50 percent lower than the winter rates. The January value season represents approximately a 20 percent savings over regular rates; further savings can be realized during late November to the third week of December and in April. Discounts for children are just about universal. Some package plans include lodging, lift tickets, and group lessons. The options are numerous, and fortunately, the resort associations at Vail and Beaver Creek publish detailed, descriptive accounts of their accommodations and packages. Cribs are available at most facilities upon request.

Dining: Hungry for a hamburger? Eager to savor a juicy steak? Or is Mexican fare your idea of the perfect après-ski dinner? In the Vail Valley all this is possible, plus Italian, Chinese, French, and German food. With more than 110 restaurants and bars, there is lots of variety. Many restaurants are right in the lodges, such as the Lodge at Vail, Lion Square Lodge, the Landmark, and the Charter at Beaver Creek. Others, like McCoy's and the Coyote Cafe, are in the villages at the base of the lifts or in the pedestrian areas.

More are on the mountains: Cook Shack at Vail and Spruce Saddle and Rafters at Beaver Creek. These are not just quick, cafeteria-style mountainside rest stops; some hit gourmet standards. Whenever weather permits, outdoor barbecues are planned at the midmountain points. Many of the restaurants have children's menus—just ask.

Children's World: Even a two-month-old can comfortably visit Vail Valley. At Beaver Creek and at Golden Peak in Vail, the Small World Play School entertains little ones two months to six years old from 8:00 A.M. to 4:30 P.M. daily. The toddlers and preschoolers enjoy games, songs, crafts, and indoor and outdoor play in a schoolhouse atmosphere. Separate playrooms for ages two to eighteen months, nineteen to thirty months, and preschoolers offer closer supervision. The cost is $57 a day.

The Children's Skiing Center operates out of three locations—Lionshead, Golden Peak, and the Village Hall at Beaver Creek (so convenient no matter where you're staying!)—and divides children into two groups (three- to six-year-olds and six- to twelve-year-olds) for daily lessons from 8:00 A.M. to 4:30 P.M. Both groups have some indoor activities as well as skiing; the older children's schedule concentrates more on skiing. These programs average $75 a day, including lunch.

In summer from early June to late August, five- to ten-year-olds can join Camp Vail, sponsored by the Town of Vail Recreation Department. On weekdays from 8:00 A.M. to 5:00 P.M., kids gather for mountain hiking, gymnastics, swimming, arts and crafts, films, and nature studies. The daily fee is $38 a child. More information is available by calling (970) 479–2292.

Recreation: The name of the game is skiing, and the Vail Valley has all the ingredients for an excellent ski holiday. In the middle of the White River National

Photo by Jack Affleck, courtesy of Vail Associates, Inc.

Forest, Vail Mountain rises to 11,250 feet; at Beaver Creek the summit is 11,440 feet. The vertical drop is more than 3,150 feet at Vail and close to 3,350 feet at Beaver Creek. An average annual snowfall between 300 and 350 inches (and an artificial snowmaking system) accounts for a season lasting from late November to mid-April.

Vail and Beaver Creek skiable terrain totaling 5,641 acres (lift tickets for the two mountains are interchangeable) provides variety for all levels of skiers, from gentle beginner slopes to challenging intermediates to exciting mogul and bowl skiing. At Vail the runs are ranked 32 percent beginner, 36 percent intermediate, and 32 percent advanced; at Beaver Creek the breakdown is 19 percent beginner, 43 percent intermediate, and 38 percent advanced.

So that you can cut tracks through the Rocky Mountain powder in style, a very large ski school (1,200 instructors!) can assist you. In addition to the typical group and private lessons for all ability levels, the Vail/Beaver Creek Ski School offers free Meet the Mountain introductory tours: a morning of skiing with guest services staff who acquaint you with the area's history and topography, classes with videotaped analysis, and high-powered workshops in mogul and powder skiing. Or enroll in lessons in cross-country skiing, which is so refined here that distinctions are made between backcountry skiing, telemark skiing, and track skiing.

Other wintertime sports include ice skating at Dobson Ice Arena or Nottingham Lake, snowmobiling at Piney Lake, and ice fishing. An evening outing in a horse-drawn sleigh may be the right way to finish off a perfect day. Indoor evening entertainment includes nightclubs and movie theaters; favorite haunts for kids are the video arcades and the Vail Youth Center.

Even after the last skier comes down the mountain in late spring, fun in the Vail Valley continues. As in the winter, summertime activities focus on the beautiful outdoors. Hiking through stands of aspens along the trail systems up Vail Mountain and Beaver Creek Mountain, biking on paths through wildflowers, and fishing in mountain streams get you back to nature. Ride horseback at Eagle Ranch, Beaver Creek Stables, and Piney River Ranch, or muster your courage for river rafting with Timberline Tours or Nova Guides.

Of the five eighteen-hole championship golf courses in the valley, one was designed by Jack Nicklaus and one (the Beaver Creek Course) by Robert Trent Jones Jr.; the clear mountain air and spectacular scenery lead to invigorating play. In Vail the twenty tennis courts, where clinics and lessons are scheduled, are located near Lionshead and Gold Peak; another twenty courts are scattered throughout the valley. And for purely taking in the scenery, ride the gondola or a chairlift. ≋

WEST

California

Idaho

Nevada

Oregon

Washington

The Alisal Guest Ranch

1054 Alisal Road
Solvang, California 93463
(805) 688–6411, (800) 4–ALISAL
Web site: www.alisal.com

I n the Santa Ynez Valley of southern California is a real working cattle ranch—The Alisal (from the Spanish word meaning "grove of sycamores"). Some things just don't change—cattle have been grazing here for almost 200 years. Fifty-two years ago the current owner's father, a cattleman himself, decided to open the ranch to guests. Today visitors enjoy the atmosphere of an active ranch and the facilities of a great resort on this 10,000-acre spread. Only forty minutes from Santa Barbara and two hours from Los Angeles, The Alisal is a welcome haven to harried city-dwellers. It is open year-round.

Accommodations: Decorated in classic California ranch design, seventy-three cottages accommodating up to 200 guests are clustered near the swimming pool and tennis courts or overlooking the golf course. All have a wood-burning fireplace, and front porch or garden areas. Based on a modified American plan, rates range from $335 to $455 a night, double occupancy; children three through five years are $40, and those ages six and older are $65 a night. Connecting suites are available for larger families.

Dining: The Ranch Room serves breakfast (a lavish buffet or a la carte) and gourmet dinners from a five-item menu that changes every evening. Jackets are required for gentlemen (ties optional), and ladies and children dress appropriately for fine dining. Parents with small children are encouraged to have dinner at 6:30 P.M., before the peak hours of 7:15 to 8:15 P.M. Lunch (not included in the room rate) can also be ordered from the Chuckwagon Grill (poolside snack bar) and at the Ranch Course Grill (open from 8:00 A.M. to 3:00 P.M.) on the golf course. The River Grill is open daily from 7:00 A.M. to 8:00 P.M. for all meals. Once in a while you can saddle up early for a breakfast ride or join a poolside steak fry. The Oak Room Lounge, an inviting room with a large fireplace, is decorated with warm colors, rustic Western artifacts, and Native American–style rugs. Cocktails and complimentary appetizers are served and stories of the day's activities or tall tales are shared. It's adults-only after 8:00 P.M., with live entertainment and dancing that begins at 6:30 P.M. During the summer and holidays, The Waggin' Tongue Lounge by the pool is open daily from 11:30 A.M. to 5:00 P.M.

Children's World: All summer long and at holiday times, counselors conduct an active schedule of arts and crafts, scavenger hunts, volleyball, hikes, croquet, and other outdoor games.

From age seven and up, children can participate in horseback riding on the trail rides or in private lessons. Younger children get corral rides and equestrian-care lessons. Everyone learns more about ranch animals at the on-site petting zoo. Children also love the private lake, where they can participate in fishing, boating, or canoeing. Summer evenings may include campfires with sing-alongs and stories, which are always better at the lake setting. Kid's Mini Rodeo is staged weekly in the summer—this is every kid's dream of being a cowboy come true. After watching wranglers perform, they get to participate in branding (on leather or wood), roping, and rodeo-style games; a Western barbecue completes the evening. In the summer the children's program (no charge) runs seven days a week, all day. Evening events may include a movie, storytelling, or a talent show. During the winter, supervised arts and activities go from 10:00 A.M. to 2:00 P.M., with golf, tennis, and horseback riding lessons filling in the other times. Although the program is free, some things such as lessons and horseback riding do have a charge. Check the daily program.

The summertime activities for teens involve their favorite things: eating, music, and sports.

Recreation: Be sure to saunter over to the barn to be matched with the perfect mount for the twice-daily trail rides ($50 per ride). A breakfast ride is offered three times a week in summer, twice a week during the rest of the year. More than 50 miles of trails meander through oak and sycamore groves in the rolling hills and along the lake. Wranglers are happy to share a bit of advice about riding, information about the ranch, or maybe even some tall tales along the way.

But the fun doesn't stop at the end of a ride. The gently rambling fairways of two eighteen-hole golf courses are graced with eucalyptus as well as oak and sycamore trees and occasionally a deer or two. Each of the two championship golf courses, The River Course and The Ranch Course, has distinct characteristics shaped by its unique terrain. The driving range, putting green, and practice trap can keep you so busy you'll ride off into the sunset on a golf cart rather than a horse! The resident pro and the pro shop can help with anything from lessons to new equipment. On the tennis courts (seven in all, located in one of the most scenic areas of the ranch) you're likely to find a good game from 8:00 A.M. to 5:30 P.M., or the resident pro conducting lessons (private and groups).

If your interests are more wet-and-wild, you might swim in the large outdoor heated pool or head to the lake and hop aboard a sailboat, rowboat, paddleboat, canoe, or kayak. Even beginners find lots of enjoyment in the sailing and fishing lessons offered. The lake—man-made, but mature and encompassing more than ninety-five acres—is stocked with bass, bluegill, and catfish, much to the delight of every angler.

After riding, golfing, playing tennis, swimming, sailing, and fishing, you can always jog, join a guided nature walk, play volleyball, badminton, horseshoes, shuffleboard, croquet, or archery, or take on the new challenge course. Tired yet? Indoors you might play pool or table tennis in the recreation room or relax in the library with a good book or board game by the fireplace. Be sure to save energy for the evenings, filled with square dancing, cookouts, and movies as well. ≋

Coffee Creek Ranch

HC 2, Box 4940
Trinity Center, California 96091-9502
(530) 266–3343, (800) 624–4480
E-mail: ccranch@tds.net
Web site: www.coffeecreekranch.com

C offee Creek Ranch is located in northern California, approximately 300 miles north of San Francisco. Surrounded by the Trinity Alps Wilderness Area, the ranch covers 127 acres along Coffee Creek and is home to wranglers and dudes alike. Whether you are an old pro at horseback riding or a greenhorn mounting up for the first time, the ranch hands will ensure that your horse and your excursion match your abilities. You can roam this territory all day long or ease into your new cowboy lifestyle more slowly with a half-hour lesson or a two-hour trail ride.

Accommodations: The fifteen cozy, secluded cottages (one or two bedrooms) are scattered among the trees. Weekly rates during the summer are $1,034 for an adult, $920 to $940 for a teenager, $820 to $840 for a three- to twelve-year-old child, and $300 for little ones under three. Cribs, playpens, and high chairs are provided at no extra charge. Besides lodging, these prices include three meals a day and all recreational activities. Horseback riding is priced separately for the summer but is included in the lower rates for spring and fall.

Dining: Recognizing the healthy appetites that fresh air and exercise can generate, the main dining room serves up hearty, nutritious meals with fresh fruit and vegetables, Black Angus beef, and homemade bread. Outdoor barbecues and poolside cookouts are friendly evening events. Beer and wine are served in the Pony Room.

Children's World: In the summer months the youth program, a complimentary service operating 9:00 A.M. to 5:00 P.M., Saturday through Thursday, attracts children ages three to seventeen. On its fun-filled schedule are pony rides, archery, nature walks, pedalboating, gold panning, games, and crafts. For children under three the weekly rate includes baby-sitting while you're out on the trail. If additional baby-sitting is required, you can make arrangements for $6.25 an hour.

Recreation: Saddle up and head into the wilderness for an all-day ride or a two-hour ride. You'll venture up into the mountains and go through the wooded landscape along a clear fresh stream; maybe you'll spot a deer or a bear. Even novice cowpokes with a few lessons soon experience the friendly spirit of a trail ride.

When taking a break from riding, you might swim in the pool or in the creek; play volleyball, table tennis, badminton, shuffleboard, and horseshoes; or hop aboard a hayride. Locals say that Coffee Creek yields up some mighty fine trout, so an afternoon with rod and reel may turn into a fresh fish supper. Perhaps you'll test your keen eye at the archery range, the rifle range, and the trapshoot, or save your energy for evening square or line dancing. ≈≈≈

Forever Resorts

Lake Mead National Recreation Area
Callville Bay Marina
Lake Mead, Nevada
(800) 255–5561
Web site: www.foreverresorts.com

If you are looking for a unique vacation experience, houseboat rentals from Forever Resorts at Callville Bay on Lake Mead may be just what you are looking for. Created by the completion of Hoover Dam in 1935, Lake Mead is one of the largest man-made lakes in the world. The lake's contours vary from the expansive Boulder and Virgin Basins to countless small coves along the shoreline. The desert terrain surrounding it ranges from wide sandy beaches to dramatic canyon walls towering high above the water.

Everyone—novice or expert—renting a houseboat from Forever Resorts is given a "shakedown cruise" to learn how to operate the craft. Comforts uncommon to houseboating are included, even a complete kitchen. The finest equipment and friendly, professional service are what make a few days or a week at one of the Forever Resorts marinas a vacation to remember . . . forever.

Accommodations: Houseboats vary in size but standard features include a stove and oven, two built-in ice chests, two refrigerators (electric and gas), an electrical generator, a gas grill, five queen beds, one and a half baths, a captain's flying bridge, central air-conditioning and heat, a microwave, linens/pillows, and

Photo courtesy of Forever Resorts

even a water slide. The 65-foot VIP Houseboat boasts a larger living area in the front salon, a hot tub on the upper deck, two full baths, trash compactor, a dishwasher, a wet bar with refrigerator and ice maker on the upper deck, a canopy on the upper deck, and an intercom from the lower to upper helm. Rates range from $995 to $6,295 per package, depending on the type of houseboat engaged, the season, and the number of days.

Dining: Culinary feasts are limited only by your imagination, as each kitchen is fully equipped to make mealtime preparation a breeze.

Children's World: The lake behind Hoover Dam provides recreation for millions of people annually. Your child is sure to enjoy swimming, powerboating, houseboating, scuba diving, beach camping, sailing, windsurfing, fishing, rock climbing, hiking, and photography. If outdoor activities wear you out, you can always use the TV and VCR for movies or video games.

Recreation: The complete houseboat experience includes a tag-a-long powerboat, so termed because the boat is tied to the back of the houseboat while cruising. The tag-a-long is used for exploring, tubing, fishing, and just plain enjoying the lake, thus making the houseboat home base a movable floating resort. ≋

The Inn of the Seventh Mountain

18575 Southwest Century Drive
Bend, Oregon 97702
(541) 382–8711, (800) 452–6810
E-mail: reservations@7thmtn.com
Web site: www.7thmtn.com

A vacation in the woods and mountains of the great Pacific Northwest, the serenity of hiking in the forest, and the excitement of exploring the Deschutes River whisk you away from city life and everyday routines. The Inn of the Seventh Mountain, located in the Cascade Mountains of central Oregon, is a year-round family resort that boasts a cool forest setting and warm hospitality. The recreation department at the inn plans activities for every member of the family, concentrating on water sports, swimming, tennis, and raft trips on the river in the summer and ice skating, cross-country skiing, and sleigh rides in the winter. Wintertime also means the thrill of downhill skiing at nearby Mount Bachelor (only 14 miles from the inn).

Accommodations: You can choose from a variety of accommodations, from a lodge room to a full condominium apartment, depending on the size of your group. Most of the lodge rooms have a private balcony; the condominium units have one to three bedrooms, fireplace, kitchen, and balcony. Some of these units can sleep up to ten people. The architecture is modern and rustic, the natural-wood facades blending well with the wooded landscape. Prices range from $59 to $299 a night, depending on the size of the accommodation and the season (summer and fall are slightly higher than winter and spring). Cribs are available at no extra charge.

Dining: The Poppy Seed Cafe serves homestyle breakfast and lunch. Josiah's, open for dinner only, features seafood specialties and Northwest cuisine. For a light lunch or dinner, pick up a sandwich or salad at the Mountain Market. The lounge is open every night.

Children's World: In addition to individual baby-sitting, which the staff can help you arrange, events are scheduled all day long for your child's enjoyment. In summer and winter the recreation office publishes a flyer, *This Week at the Inn,* to help you keep track of all the activities. At Camp 7, a supervised play program for children ages four to eleven, a daily charge of $25 buys lunch, arts-and-crafts classes, movies, and more from 9:00 A.M. to 4:00 P.M. each day. Your child might also participate in a tennis clinic, take a hayride or a sleigh ride, search out treasures on a scavenger hunt, or hop aboard the children's storybook train. For some events, no fees are charged; others are priced individually (for example, $6.00 for a half-hour swimming lesson). There are also two playgrounds and a wading pool.

Photo courtesy of The Inn of the Seventh Mountain

In season the Mount Bachelor Ski School (541–382–2607) offers lessons for youngsters. The Children's Ski School, called Mountain Masters, is for ages four to twelve. Divided by age (four to six and seven to twelve) and also by level of ability, several options are available. A full day, including lunch, is $45 for the younger children, $55 for the older group. Rentals are $5.00 extra. Morning or afternoon sessions (two and a half hours each) cost $32 for ages four to six years and $42 to $47 for ages seven to twelve. Teens join the adult lessons for $30 to $40. Reservations are recommended.

The West Village Main Lodge, at the base of the mountain, has a day-care center for little ones six weeks to six years old; activities are planned from 8:30 A.M. to 4:30 P.M. The fee is $31.00 a day or $7.50 an hour. Lunch is an additional $5.00. Sunrise Lodge has child care available. Rates and hours are the same.

Recreation: In summer you just have to discover the beauty of the Deschutes River. Take a relaxing canoe ride and get back to nature, or join a moonlight raft trip. For the more daring souls, there are guided white-water raft trips through the rapids. If you prefer to take in the scenic river from land, horseback riding is a great alternative; group trail rides run along the river and into the Deschutes National Forest. The National Forest is also a picturesque haven for hikers and joggers. For the fisherman the recreation office arranges trips to the favorite spots with a naturalist guide. Spend an afternoon in sailboarding or waterskiing classes.

Back at the inn take a dip in one of the two pools, rent a bicycle, play a good game of tennis on one of the four Plexipave courts (group clinics and private lessons are offered), work out in an aerobic exercise class, try your talents in an arts-and-crafts class, go rollerskating, or get lucky in a bingo game. The rec office organizes all sorts of ball games—softball, volleyball, football, lacrosse, and soccer. Join a hayride, complete with a stop for a marshmallow roast, play table tennis, take in a poolside movie, or head to the video-game room. Then relax in the sauna or one of the hot whirlpool baths.

The Oregon High Desert Museum, just 6 miles south of Bend, discloses the natural and cultural history of this region. The museum makes for a fun as well as educational afternoon.

This part of Oregon experiences beautiful Indian summers, so activities continue well into the fall. During the winter months the inn's special events include ice skating, sleigh rides, cross-country skiing (with lessons for novices), and horseback riding through the snow-covered landscape.

The inn is the closest lodging facility to the Mount Bachelor ski resort and provides daily transportation to the mountain base. With 3,100 vertical feet, forty runs, double and triple chairlifts, and plenty of dry powder, Mount Bachelor means excellent downhill skiing for all levels of ability. The five lodges at the mountain have restaurants for breakfast, lunch, snacks, and cocktails; ski shops; and the ski school, which offers group lessons for all ranges of expertise as well as private lessons. The season lasts long here, attracting many visitors late into spring. The summit season even extends into the summer. ≈≈≈

Konocti Harbor Resort and Spa

8727 Soda Bay Road
Kelseyville, California 95451
(707) 279–4281, (800) 660–LAKE
Web site: www.konoctiharbor.com

K onocti Harbor Resort and Spa is a lakeside resort in northern California, approximately two and a half hours from San Francisco. If you're driving from the city or other points south, your vacation begins with a tour of the Napa Valley wine country on your way to Konocti. Open year-round, the inn sits beneath the 4,300-foot peak of Mount Konocti (an extinct volcano) on the southern shore of Clear Lake, which stretches 25 miles by 8 miles. All this clear blue water of California's largest lake provides the setting for much of Konocti's recreation: swimming, boating, and fishing. Although today you'll find just happy, active visitors heading to the water, a romantic Indian legend tells of a saddened princess whose many tears formed the lake.

Accommodations: Hotel rooms, apartments, and beach cottages make up the 266 guest units at the Konocti. All have different features, but families like the beach cottages for their convenient location and kitchen, open-air porch, and space. Some rooms include a private balcony, and most afford views of the lake. The locations of some make the marina easily accessible, while others are near the tennis courts. Sixteen deluxe apartments are situated near the spa. The apartments and cottages have complete kitchens and living rooms, and many have been recently renovated.

During the high season (May through October), a double room is $49 to $85 a night, and the apartments and cottages for four are $135 to $175 a night. Lower rates are in effect the rest of the year. Children eighteen years and younger staying in their parents' room are accommodated free of charge. Rollaway beds and cribs are available for $10 a night. Tennis, fishing, spa, and golf package plans are offered.

Dining: For a relaxing evening meal, try the Classic Rock Cafe, which is open for breakfast, lunch, and dinner. Adjacent to the two pool areas are snack bars so that you don't have to interrupt a lazy day of sunning for refreshments. For evening entertainment The Full Moon Saloon beckons.

Children's World: Kids at Konocti practically live in the water, with hours spent at the lake swimming, boating, and fishing. They also take hikes and nature walks, play horseshoes, and putt around the eighteen holes of peewee golf. Little ones particularly like the two wading pools and the playground equipped with a slide, swings, and monkey bars, while those a bit older head to the recreation center for table tennis, pool, and video games. The children's programs are open only in the summer and the fee is $15 for each session. The events start at 10:00 A.M. Monday through Friday, break at 4:00 P.M., and pick up again from 5:00 to 10:00 P.M. for a night camp. Baby-sitting in the evening runs about $5.00 an hour.

Recreation: With Konocti's full-service marina, you can take your pick of water sports. Dock your own boat here or rent a paddleboat, Wave Runner, motorboat, or sailboat for an adventure on the lake. Go fishing in these waters where the rewards are many: largemouth bass, trout, crappie, and catfish. There's even a bass-fishing pro to advise you. Water-ski across the lake, or board the *Konocti Princess,* a nostalgic paddle wheeler, for an afternoon excursion. Swim in the lake waters from the small sandy beach, or do laps in one of the two Olympic-size pools overlooking the lake.

The Dancing Springs Health Spa is designed to pamper you a bit. This facility features an indoor pool and capable personnel who will help you relax with a massage, facial, or herbal body wrap. Take a fitness class or work out with free weights or cardiovascular equipment if you're feeling more energetic.

The eight tennis courts are lighted for evening play, and lessons with the tennis pro are available. After a good practice session with a ball machine, reward yourself with a new accessory from the tennis shop.

Five area golf courses, all within 20 miles, honor Konocti's golf packages. Round up a fast-paced game of softball, basketball, volleyball, or table tennis, or slow down to a more relaxing tempo with horseshoes and shuffleboard. While jogging and hiking, explore the scenic, hilly terrain that borders the lake. ≋

La Costa Resort and Spa

2100 Costa del Mar Road
Carlsbad, California 92009
(619) 438–9111, (800) 854–5000
Web site: www.lacosta.com

L a Costa is a luxurious resort and a serious spa. In fact, it was the first establishment to revive the spa regimen as Americans became more health-conscious in the 1960s. Today you can pursue a program of exercise and sound nutrition, redefining your lifestyle after years of sedentary executive matters; or you can indulge in a program of sheer pampering, relieving the stress and tensions of the business world.

Located in Carlsbad, just thirty minutes north of San Diego and ninety minutes south of Los Angeles, La Costa enjoys lovely Southern California weather and a picturesque setting of rolling hills.

Accommodations: Rooms, suites, and private homes number 479. They are situated around courtyards, near the tennis facilities, adjacent to the spa, and along the golf courses. Room rates are $345 to $520 a night; one- and two-bedroom suites are $570 to $2,400 a night, and the two- to five-bedroom executive homes are $1,400 to $2,000 a night. Children under eighteen staying in their parents' room are free; cribs are provided without charge. Be sure to inquire about the spa, golf, and tennis package plans.

Dining: La Costa's three restaurants offer variety in cuisine and ambience. For a casual atmosphere Brasserie La Costa is open for breakfast, lunch, and dinner. Besides tempting fare such as eggs Benedict and grilled veal chops, the Brasserie has a selection of spa-menu items, just as tasty but low in calories and fat. For more elegant dining, Pisces specializes in fresh seafood, and Ristorante Figaro is devoted to Northern Italian cuisine. Both are open for dinner only.

Children's World: Camp La Costa is active year-round and operates from 9:00 A.M. to 4:00 P.M. daily. For five- to twelve-year-olds, the fun includes golf and tennis lessons, swimming, kite flying, and arts and crafts. The fee is $65 a day and includes lunch. In the evenings Camp La Costa at Night takes over with dinner and entertainment from 6:00 to 10:30 P.M.; the fee is $45 a night. Individual baby-sitting can be requested through the concierge.

Recreation: The spa programs and facilities are extensive. Facials from deep cleansing to mud packs, massages of the shiatsu and Swedish variety, herbal wraps, body scrubs, exfoliation, and hydrotherapy baths are just some of the methods utilized to revive weary guests. Exercise facilities include swimming pools, a weight room, a cardiovascular room, and a jogging track. You can join one of the many exercise classes offered throughout the day or, with an exercise physiologist, you can devise a personalized fitness program. Individualized analysis also extends to dietary counseling and menu planning.

Golf enthusiasts find their exercise on the two eighteen-hole championship courses. At the Golf School the latest technology is used to scrutinize and improve your game. Tennis players have twenty-one courts at their disposal and can choose grass, clay, or hard-court surface. Clinics are held daily, and private instruction is easily arranged. The golf and tennis pro shops offer a wide range of equipment and apparel. Five heated swimming pools complete the picture of exercise potential at La Costa. ≈≈≈

Northstar-at-Tahoe

P.O. Box 129
Truckee, California 96160
(530) 562–1010, (800) GO–NORTH (466–6784)
E-mail: northstar@boothcreek.com
Web site: www.skinorthstar.com

Tahoe has long been known for the clear deep waters of a 200-square-mile lake, the majestic mountain peaks of the Sierra Nevada range, and its proximity to the entertainment and nightlife of Nevada casinos. Northstar-at-Tahoe enables vacationers to partake of all of these. Open year-round, it is a 2,420-acre mountain resort just 6 miles from Lake Tahoe that offers winter and summer family sports activities. With the Nevada state line only 7 miles away, side trips to gambling casinos are manageable excursions for grown-ups.

Accommodations: The lodging facilities include hotel-type rooms, condominiums ranging in size from studios to four-bedroom units, and three- and four-bedroom homes. With the exception of the lodge rooms, all have a fully equipped kitchen and fireplace; many units have a private balcony overlooking

Photo courtesy of Northstar-at-Tahoe

the wooded landscape and the mountains. The wooden facades and rustic designs of the buildings blend well with the natural setting.

Prices range from $99 a night in the summer and $178 a night in the winter for a hotel room to $339 a night, summer, and $489 a night, winter, for a four-bedroom, two-bath condominium. Package plans are available throughout the year. The on-site transportation system is complimentary for Northstar guests. Cribs are provided at no additional charge.

Dining: The six restaurants at Northstar mean time off for the family cook. Timbercreek Restaurant serves dinner in the winter and summer. The Martis Valley Grille specializes in family-style dining, while Pedro's Pizza Parlor is a casual spot for lunch and dinner; the Martis Valley Grille and Pedro's are open only in winter. The two restaurants on the mountain are the Lodge at Big Springs, open for breakfast and lunch, and the Summit Deck and Grill, open for lunch. Each offers an informal atmosphere and allows skiers to get back on the slopes quickly. The Clubhouse offers breakfast and lunch, indoors or outdoors, in summer only. The Village Food Company, in the Village Mall, is open year-round; with a deli, gourmet groceries, espresso bar, and video rentals, it also provides the supplies for a picnic or snacking in your condo.

Children's World: The Minors' Camp Child-Care Center is fully licensed and accepts children as young as two years old (must be toilet trained). In the winter it is open daily from 8:30 A.M. to 4:30 P.M. Under the guidance of an experienced staff, two- to six-year-olds paint, learn songs, listen to stories, play in the snow, and take walks; with snacks and a hot lunch, the full-day fee is $56.

At three years little ones can join the Ski Cubs Program; in addition to the nonskiing activities, these children receive one and a half hours of ski instruction during the day. The fee for child care plus skiing (equipment included) is $68 a day. Four- to six-year-old Super Cubs receive two and a half hours of ski instruction in addition to indoor activities at a daily rate of $78. When not with the other Cubs, a child under five years skis free with a ticketed adult.

The Star Kids Program is designed for five- to twelve-year-olds. The $78 daily fee covers five hours of lessons, lifts, and lunch.

The highlights of the summer program (mid-June to Labor Day) for children ages two (must be toilet trained) to ten are swimming lessons, nature walks, tennis, arts and crafts, and horseback riding. Day camp is in session Monday through Saturday, 9:00 A.M. to 5:00 P.M. You can reserve a slot for your child for $33 per half day or $55 all day (includes lunch). A free half-day is provided with more than two nights' lodging.

Recreation: For downhill skiing at Tahoe, you can look forward to 2,200 vertical feet. The Northstar Village is at the base of Mount Pluto, which rises to a summit of 8,600 feet. There are seventy runs and fifteen lifts, and locals boast of sunshine 80 percent of the season. The ski school, with its 200-plus instructors, offers lessons for beginners through experts to help all visitors meet the variety of this mountain. Forty miles of groomed trails attract cross-country skiers; lessons, guided tours, and snowshoe rentals are available at the Cross-Country Center.

Après-ski activities may mean taking a sleigh ride or a trip to the Swim and Raquet Club, where you'll find saunas, spas, an adult lap pool, a fitness center, and a teen center, or enjoying a stroll through the Village Mall, which houses shops, restaurants, and bars.

During the summer other activities lure visitors outdoors to the sunshine and clean mountain air. Enjoy golf on an eighteen-hole course that wanders over meadows, past mountain streams, and through groves of tall pines and aspens. The Golf Course Clubhouse includes a pro shop and a restaurant. To work on improving your game, check with the resident pro for tips, or practice solo on the driving range and putting green.

Play tennis on one of the ten courts, take a swim in the adult lap pool or junior Olympic-size pool, or just soak up the sunshine on the poolside deck. The Northstar stables provide well-groomed horses for riding the mountain trails and offer lessons and guided trail rides. Hiking and biking are also favorite sports in High Sierra country. For adventures in boating and fishing, the clear blue waters of Lake Tahoe await you. And music fills the air every summer Sunday afternoon with free outdoor concerts. ≋≋

The Rancho Bernardo Inn

17550 Bernardo Oaks Drive
San Diego, California 92128
(619) 487–1611, (800) 542–6096
Web site: www.jcresorts.com

L isten up, weary travelers. It is still possible to vacation in the classic style and relaxed atmosphere of an old California ranch. Set in the San Pasqual Mountains of Southern California, The Rancho Bernardo Inn is just thirty minutes north of San Diego. Here, on 265 acres, the inn revives the elegance and charm of the early rancheros' way of life, capitalizes on the California sunshine and balmy weather, and adds fine sporting facilities as well—all to provide the perfect holiday for you. The inn is open year-round.

Accommodations: As you might expect of an old Southwestern ranch, the architecture reveals a Spanish influence reminiscent of the area's heritage. The eight red-tiled haciendas house 287 rooms and suites. These are decorated in warm earth tones, highly polished wood, and local art. Double room rates start at $239, with suites going up to $578. Special promotional discounts and offers are available by visiting Web site www.ranchobernardoinn.com and are often available on holidays and selected Sunday-through-Thursday-night stays. Packages are available that include meals, activities for both parents and children, and local San Diego attractions at substantial discounts. Children stay free. Cribs are provided at no additional charge.

Dining: El Bizcocho is the elegant French restaurant of the inn. This mission-style dining room is open for evening dinner and Sunday brunch, for which gentlemen should wear jackets. Of the many tempting menu selections here, you might try the roast duckling in Calvados. More casual and open for breakfast, lunch, and dinner, the Veranda Room will lure you with its fresh seafood dishes, such as tiger shrimp Provençale. The Sports Grill serves sandwiches and snacks on its patio, near the ninth hole. Tea, tasty sandwiches, and pastries in the Music Room make a perfect afternoon interlude to tide you over between a lovely lunch and a delicious dinner. For evening entertainment La Taberna features a piano soloist, and La Bodega offers dancing.

Children's World: An active, fun-filled Kids Camp is offered from 9:00 A.M. to 9:00 P.M. on many holidays, summer weekends, and the month of August. Children ages five to eleven play tennis and miniature golf, swim, bake cookies, make kites, and go on scavenger hunts. Arts-and-crafts classes, croquet, movies, track meets, and cookouts are also on the schedule. Older children, up to age seventeen, can enjoy tennis, golf, basketball, swimming, and biking activities, as well as an evening luau or carnival. Options are offered for half- or full-day participation. Photographic mementos of Kids Camp participants are offered, and rate discounts are available for second and third children in a family.

Recreation: Golf and tennis players are well cared for at Rancho Bernardo. Three nine-hole executive courses will whet your appetite for the eighteen-hole championship golf course. Planted with sycamore, eucalyptus, pine, and olive trees, the lush green fairways roll down the foothills to the valley. With five resident pros, individual and group lessons, clinics, tournaments, a driving range, and a well-stocked pro shop, you've got every chance in the world of polishing your game.

Tennis players are found on the twelve outdoor courts, four of which are lighted for nighttime play. The Tennis College has a twenty-plus-year history of providing programs to players of all skill levels. Stroke development, teamwork, and strategy are just some of the topics covered in the two- to five-day sessions. Private instruction is also available.

When you've run out of energy and are ready to relax, head to the newly expanded, full-service Buena Vista Spa. You can enjoy an indoor or outdoor massage, facial, or other relaxing treatment; have a tempting, healthy spa lunch; and unwind in the steam or sauna room. Stop at the spa or gift shop and take your experience home with one of the spa's exclusive, custom-blended skin and haircare products. Have a pleasant dip in one of the two swimming pools, or bicycle and jog around the carefully tended grounds. Because of the sunny Southern California weather, these sports continue year-round.

All of San Diego's attractions are twenty to thirty minutes away. The famous San Diego Zoo, SeaWorld, the Aerospace Museum, and a Wild Animal Park beckon. Enjoy a picnic in Balboa Park, or shop at Horton Plaza, a fabulous "mall" like no other. You can even take a quick trip to Mexico—it's an easy forty-five-minute train ride from downtown San Diego to Tijuana—for great bargains. ≈≈≈

Port Ludlow Resort and Conference Center

200 Olympic Place
Port Ludlow, Washington 98365
(360) 437–2222, (800) 732–1239
E-mail: resort@portludlowresort.com
Web site: www.portludlowresort.com

Salmon fishing and timber from the hardwood forests first drew settlers to this area of the Northwest. Today visitors are lured by the clear deep waters of Puget Sound and the spectacular scenery presided over by the majestic mountains of the Cascade and Olympic ranges. Open year-round, the Resort at Port Ludlow is situated on a bit of land jutting out into Puget Sound, and with this prime location it's no wonder that water sports are favored here. The Olympic National Park and National Forest are practically in Port Ludlow's backyard (less than 15 miles away), which makes this a good spot for those who want the peace and serenity of a back-to-nature vacation. The weather here is mild, so many outdoor activities (such as golf) continue through the winter.

Accommodations: For lodging you may choose a traditional bedroom/bath combination (many with lovely views) or a one- to four-bedroom condominium, depending on the size of your party. The condominiums have living room, kitchen, fireplace, private deck, and water views. Sit on your balcony at night to catch a whiff of the clean, pine-scented air. There are 185 units in all, arranged in nineteen wooden town house structures; surrounded by beautifully landscaped grounds and bordering on wooded areas, these accommodations afford a sense of being close to nature.

Rates for a room alone start at $110 a night. A condominium starts at about $160 a night. Children twelve and under stay free in their parents' room; cribs are available at no charge. Rates are lower in fall, winter, and spring.

Dining: The Harbormaster Restaurant, which serves breakfast, lunch, and dinner, overlooks Puget Sound and grants visitors views of sun-sparkling waters and sailboats tacking in the breeze. The house specialties are steak and fresh seafood; maybe you'll have the Ludlow clam chowder, followed by a tasty crab or shrimp entree. The children's menu features fried chicken and fish-and-chips. The Wreckroom Lounge provides quick, light meals like hamburgers, sandwiches, salads, and thirst quenchers, with nightly entertainment, and views of the marina.

Children's World: While no specific children's activities are planned at Port Ludlow, there are many facilities available for leisure-time fun, including a game room with table tennis and pool tables, year-round swimming, tennis courts, and water activities of many kinds. Also available are games of softball, volleyball, basketball, or horseshoes. Children are welcome and will enjoy the playground area, with jungle gym equipment, located near the main building.

Recreation: The twenty-seven-hole championship golf course, designed by Robert Muir Graves, dips past ponds and edges around tall fir trees; during a challenging game you're rewarded with beautiful views of the water. For practice sessions head to the driving range and the putting greens. The pro shop can meet your needs for equipment, accessories, and clothing. If you don't want to bring along your own clubs, rentals are available and the golf pro is on hand to give you pointers on your swing.

For tennis enthusiasts, two Plexipave courts are located near the Beach Club. The Beach Club also houses the squash court, year-round swimming pool, sauna, and game room with table tennis and pool tables.

Beautiful Puget Sound is the focal point of many activities. The 300-slip marina handles both power- and sailboats. If you sail your own boat up the coast, this is the perfect place to dock. If not, you might want to rent a kayak and go exploring. Clamming, crabbing, and beachcombing along the shore are favorite pastimes here. With bicycling (rentals available) and hiking, you can get your exercise and see the scenery, too.

Nearby Port Townsend, a fine example of a Victorian seacoast town, is a great diversion for a day. You can join a guided tour, which includes entrance into a few of the old homes, or you can discover the restaurants, shops, and interesting architecture on your own. ≋

San Ysidro Ranch

900 San Ysidro Lane
Montecito, California 93108
(805) 969–5046, (800) 368–6788
E-mail: reservations@sanysidroranch
Web site: www.sanysidroranch.com

E legant yet rustic is the best way to describe San Ysidro. A quiet charm pervades the property. From the many lovely gardens—the Citrus Garden, the Herb and Vegetable Garden, the Hacienda Garden, the Wedding Garden—to the trails into the Los Padres National Forest, a respect and appreciation for nature are apparent. One comes here to relax, to rejuvenate the soul as well as the body.

Once a way station for Franciscan monks as they conducted their missionary work in the late 1700s, San Ysidro Ranch opened as a resort more than one hundred years ago. Today guests discover 550 acres of wooded countryside in the foothills of Montecito. Views extend into the Santa Ynez Mountains and down to the Pacific Ocean. San Ysidro Ranch is 3 miles south of Santa Barbara and just a ninety-minute drive north of Los Angeles.

Accommodations: Thirty-eight rooms and suites are arranged in twenty cottages. Each has a wood-burning fireplace and a private terrace; some have an outdoor whirlpool. The cottages have been christened delightful names, such as Creek, Outlook, Eucalyptus, and Acacia, each evoking the special milieu of its position. Room and suite rates range from $350 to $3,000 a night.

Dining: The Stonehouse Restaurant is developing a reputation as one of the finest in the Santa Barbara area. With culinary creations such as tortilla soup, lobster mushrooms in huckleberry vinaigrette, and salmon in chive sauce, it's easy to understand the appeal. Even the low-calorie spa dishes are hard to resist. Casual dinners and live jazz are the offerings of the Plow and Angel Pub, which dates from the time of the original resort (it was built in 1893). Outdoor dining at poolside is yet another option.

Children's World: Summertime at San Ysidro has much to offer the vacationing family. Along with their own facilities, which include tennis, swimming, boccie, and hiking trails, the resort can also recommend several local parks and attractions.

Recreation: Hiking on this terrain is a favorite among guests. The tennis courts (two) are situated on the highest plateau of the grounds; enjoy a rousing match along with panoramic views of the mountains and the ocean. Private instruction is available with the tennis pro. Work out at the health facility, with its weights and cardiovascular equipment; you might even schedule an appointment with a personal fitness trainer in order to devise a personal regimen. Or take your exercise in the outdoor heated pool.

The full spa and beauty treatments may be the highlights of your visit here. Aromatherapy facials, massages, herbal body wraps, reflexology, and stress-relieving treatments will add up to a new you. Some programs are combined with yoga lessons to maximize your revitalization. ≋

Schweitzer Mountain Resort

10,000 Schweitzer Mountain Road
Sandpoint, Idaho 83864
(208) 263–9555, (800) 831–8810
E-mail: ski@schweitzer.com
Web site: www.schweitzer.com

Way up in the northern part of Idaho's panhandle, just 60 miles from the Canadian border, is Schweitzer Mountain Resort. Set high in the rugged Selkirk Mountains, the skiing terrain sprawls over 2,500 acres. As it is a one-and-a-half-hour drive from Spokane and seven hours from Seattle, Schweitzer may not be the easiest resort to get to, but you rarely have to worry about the crowds. It is open year-round.

Accommodations: The Selkirk Lodge is at the base, and numerous condominiums supply ski-in/ski-out access. Rates range from $95 to $165 a night for hotel rooms; one- to three-bedroom condo units are $180 to $300; summer rates are lower. Additional condominiums are a bit of a walk to the lifts, and still other lodging facilities are in Sandpoint, 10 miles from Schweitzer. Many properties offer a "children ski and stay free" program, which applies to children twelve years and younger. Cribs are available at no charge.

Dining: The Chimney Rock Grill, located in the Selkirk Lodge, is slopeside at Schweitzer, and specializes in steaks, seafood, and daily specials. But if you can't bear to take out much time from skiing, stop in the Outback or the Cafe for a quick lunch. Or you can rustle up meals in your condo.

Children's World: The Mogul Mice program delights young skiers from seven to twelve years. Skiing and lunching with new friends and an instructor fill the hours. The fee is $60 for a full day, $40 for a half day. Kinderkamp, a day-care center, is a suitable alternative for nonskiers (infants to six-year-olds). In the summer months children and their parents can rent mountain bikes, take chairlift rides, and enjoy Western-style barbecues and picnics, too.

Recreation: Schweitzer has a lot of skiing terrain and a lot of variety, from the open bowls, demanding good performance of advanced skiers, to gentle beginner runs. Two expansive bowls and fifty-eight runs with 2,500 skiable acres ensure that you won't get bored. Add to this 2,400 feet of vertical drop and more than 300 inches of snowfall annually and you've got the full picture. The season starts up at the end of November and continues to early April. After skiing you might take a sleigh ride through the woods.

During the summer months visitors to Schweitzer turn to hiking along the mountain trails, mountain biking, horseback riding, attending concerts, and riding chairlifts. ≋

Squaw Valley USA
P.O. Box 2007
Olympic Valley, California 96146
(916) 583–6985, (800) 545–4350

S quaw Valley—the name itself is synonymous with skiing. From the earliest days (would you believe 1949?), the sunny California weather combined with six high alpine peaks and 4,000 acres of lift-served terrain have made this a world-class ski area. Mother Nature deposits an average of 450 inches of snow between mid-November and April. The Sierra Mountains and Lake Tahoe provide a spectacular backdrop, and the vastness of the area contributes to a wide variety of skiing. Open year-round, Squaw Valley is located near the north end of Lake Tahoe.

Accommodations: A central reservation office (888–SNOW–321) will work with you to find the most appropriate lodging for your family and your needs. Hotels, motels, lodges, and condominiums all have various rates and package plans. Among the closest to the slopes are Squaw Valley Lodge, a ski-in/ski-out condominium ($160 to $310), and the PlumpJack Squaw Valley Inn ($180 to $495), located next to the tram, with sixty rooms. The Resort at Squaw Creek is a full service resort and hotel with a deluxe conference center, a full service spa, and its own lift ($179 to $475), plus a Robert Trent Jones Jr. golf course.

The Olympic Village Inn is a European-style condominium complex about 2 blocks from the lift ($165 to $225).

Dining: You will find many food options from pastries, sandwiches, salads, ice cream, and pizza—even tacos. Some of these, such as Dave's Deli, Mother Barklays', Salsa Bar and Grill, Le Chamois, and the Sundeck Tavern, are found at the base facility, the Olympic Plaza.

Up on the mountain head to Alexander's for panoramic views and light lunches of soups and salads. In the evening the vistas take on a different glow and the dining becomes more sophisticated. The Poolside Cafe is a casual, friendly dining spot. At the Resort at Squaw Creek, Glissandi is an elegant restaurant featuring French cuisine, while the Cascades Restaurant offers regional American fare.

The casinos and showrooms of Nevada are readily accessible for dining and evening pleasures. If you want to stay in the neighborhood, however, try the après-ski at Bar One, Le Chamois, or the Plaza Bar, where you'll find entertainment after a strenuous day of skiing.

Children's World: Toddler Care is a program for children ages two to three years. Registration begins at 8:30 A.M. weekdays, 8:00 A.M. weekends and holidays. The center offers a full day of care and activity for $74 and a half day for $54. Four- to twelve-year-olds take to the joys of skiing in the Children's World. Full- and half-day programs are available. Lessons as well as other fun-in-the-snow activities keep this group occupied. Call (530) 581–7166 for reservations. Open winter season.

The Resort at Squaw Creek runs its own year-round program for children. Mountain Buddies, designed for three- to thirteen-year-olds, concentrates on sports, nature hikes, and arts and crafts. Teens join forces in the Mountain Adventure program.

Recreation: The definite wintertime focus of Squaw Valley is skiing. Imagine yourself on an uncrowded run. The sun is shining and you kick up some powder as you stop to check out the scenery. Take off your goggles and look out over glistening white snow to the blue waters of Lake Tahoe. Seventy percent of the runs are for beginner/intermediate skiers. Moreover, Squaw Valley is one of those rare places where this group is not confined to the lower elevations but can ski all day above 8,000 feet in the sunny, sheltered bowls. The vertical drop is 2,850 feet, and challenging slopes for expert skiers are not lacking. In fact, the 1960 Winter Olympics were held here. Squaw's six peaks are interconnected by thirty lifts that include a new 110-passenger cable car, a new twenty-eight-passenger Funitel (the first of its kind in North America), four high-speed detachable quads, and three six-passenger chairs. The ski school organizes classes and clinics for all levels, from beginners to racing competition. A coin-operated race course allows skiers to perfect their racing styles (and keeps them off the regular slopes!). Cross-country skiing, offered at the Resort at Squaw Creek, augments the snow diversions of Squaw Valley.

In the summertime the cable car operates for scenic tours, hiking, ice skating, swimming, full-moon hikes, stargazing, mountain biking, and many more events. The surrounding resorts focus on tennis, fishing, biking, horseback riding, and nature trails. Golf is top-notch here, with an eighteen-hole Robert Trent Jones Jr. course that weaves its way through mountains and meadows. Swimming pools, exercise spas, and racquetball/squash courts round out the pleasures. ≋

Sunriver Resort

Sunriver, Oregon 97707
(541) 593–1000, (800) 547–3922
E-mail: reservations@sunriver-resort.com
Web site: www.sunriver-resort.com

Nestled in the pines between the towering Cascade Mountains and the high desert, Sunriver Resort encompasses 3,300 acres and enjoys nearly 300 days of sunshine each year. Sunriver offers three championship golf courses—including Crosswater, chosen by *Golf Digest* as "America's Best New Resort Course"—and one of the most complete lists of recreational activities to be found. Experience more than 30 miles of bike paths, white-water rafting, canoeing, tennis, and organized children's, teen, and family programs. In the winter enjoy cross-country skiing, sleigh rides, a covered ice skating rink, an assortment of shops and restaurants, and world-class skiing at nearby Mount Bachelor. Sunriver Resort has its own shuttle to the mountain that will have you on the slopes within minutes.

Accommodations: Accommodations at Sunriver Resort include deluxe rooms and suites, featuring stone fireplaces and private decks; the suites accommodate two to six people and have a kitchen and dining/living room. Rates are

$115 to $225 per night, depending on the size and the season. Cribs are provided for a one-time charge of $7.00.

Approximately 260 private homes and condominiums can be rented on a short-term basis. With one to five bedrooms, these can easily sleep up to ten people comfortably. All include a well-equipped kitchen, living and dining areas, charming fireplace, and private deck. They are strategically located along the golf course, tucked in among the pines, facing the Cascade Mountains, or overlooking the Deschutes River. Prices range from $154 to $495 per night, size and season being the determining factors; summer and Christmas are the high seasons. The architecture is warm and rustic, modern yet compatible with the surroundings.

Dining: The Meadows at the Lodge specializes in Northwest cuisine and is open for breakfast, lunch, and dinner daily. The Merchant Trader Cafe, located on the lower level of the lodge, features snacks and lighter fare for breakfast and lunch, and is open daily. The Grille at Crosswater Club is open during the summer months for lunch and dinner, and in the winter for lunch on Saturdays and dinner Thursday through Saturday evenings. Open daily during the summer months are The Turn at Crosswater and McDivot's Café at the Woodlands golf course, both offering lighter fare and refreshments for golfers.

In addition, Sunriver's Village Mall has a number of restaurants and a grocery store. Whether you cook in or dine out, the variety from quick sandwiches to gourmet fare satisfies almost any mood. For late-night fun, the Owl's Nest Pub in the lodge offers cocktails nightly and live entertainment every Friday and Saturday night.

Children's World: Kid Klub gives children ages three through six and seven through ten a chance to develop new skills, interests, and friendships, as they create, discover, and experiment in Sunriver's unique environment. Each session revolves around a theme, including nature study, adventure, crafts, and games. Both day and evening sessions are offered daily from mid-June through Labor Day and over the Christmas holidays, and on weekends only the rest of the year.

Guided Adventures is designed for preteens and teens (ages eleven through fifteen) and is held during the summer months. Teen Time, offered year-round, gives young adults (ages thirteen to nineteen) the opportunity to meet other teens. Reservations are required for all youth programs, and costs vary by session.

In addition, youth summer activities include bicycle riding, swimming lessons, canoe or white-water raft rides, games, and tennis. The resident naturalists at the Sunriver Nature Center introduce children to the magic and mystery of the local environment and animals; the Nature Center is open year-round. In winter the rink at the Sunriver Village Mall makes a great spot for ice skating. Wintertime also means that all the services of Mount Bachelor are available.

Recreation: Sunriver Resort is proud to offer fifty-four holes of outstanding championship golf. Set amid rivers, meadows, wetlands, pine forests, and spectacular Cascade Mountain views, the Sunriver golfing experience offers incredible variety. Crosswater was designed by Robert Cupp and John Fought and offers play exclusively for resort guests and Crosswater Club members. The Woodlands was designed by renowned architect Robert Trent Jones, Jr., and consistently ranks among the top twenty-five resort courses nationwide. The Woodlands' tree-lined fairways, seven lakes, and strategically placed sand traps have earned Sunriver Resort the distinction of a *Golf* magazine Silver Medal Award. The Meadows, newly redesigned by Crosswater codesigner John Fought, opened in the summer of 1999. Playing to more than 7,000 yards, it has four sets of tees, meticulously prepared bent grass greens, and spectacular Cascade Mountain views. The Meadows is also home to the Sunriver Resort Golf Learning Center.

With twenty-eight Plexipave tennis courts, rimmed by tall pines and with blue skies overhead, who could possibly have a bad game of tennis? But if your serve needs some polishing, you can always sign up for lessons. Sunriver Resort offers Reed Anderson Tennis Schools, with classes ranging from one to five days, plus Tennis Express (one-hour programs) and Junior Tennis for ages four through eighteen.

Two swimming centers each have a heated Olympic-size pool, a diving pool, and a wading pool providing plenty of variety. The south pool also has a water slide and hot tubs. Also available are the Lodge Village pool and three outdoor spas.

The Deschutes River provides hours of enjoyment for fishermen, who snag brookies, rainbows, and German browns. The Sunriver Marina offers canoe, raft, and kayak float trips down the scenic and calm Deschutes. Marina staff will pick you up downriver and bring you back to the marina; the trips are offered mid-April to mid-October, weather permitting. For the more adventurous, local outfitters offer half-day and full-day white-water rafting trips down more turbulent portions of the Deschutes, leaving from the resort daily during the summer months.

For landlubbers in your party, rental bikes are available for excursions on the 35 miles of paved paths; guides at the Sunriver stables are ready to show off the scenery in rides along the river; the wilderness beckons interested backpackers. Trails past meadows and through the woods await joggers and nature lovers. Surrounding Sunriver Resort is the Deschutes National Forest, offering additional opportunity for back-to-nature serenity and elbow room. The Sunriver Nature Center has been offering extremely comprehensive, very reasonably priced programs for more than twenty-five years. Many nature walks, lectures, and programs are free; there are also archaeology tours, combined biking/bird-watching excursions, spelunking in Lava River Cave, and much more.

The Sunriver Racquet Club is a nearby sports facility with five racquetball courts, three indoor tennis courts, a swimming pool, an exercise room, a spa, and saunas. Use of these facilities is free for guests staying in Lodge Village rooms and suites; some private homes and condos have guest privileges at the Racquet Club as well, so check when you make reservations.

Sunriver Village has restaurants and interesting shops and boutiques. The Sunriver Music Festival takes place in August; orchestral programs are presented in the Great Hall, originally constructed as an officers' club when what is now Sunriver Resort was Camp Abbot, a U.S. Army Engineer Replacement Training Center for the Corps of Engineers during World War II. The Great Hall is composed of 511 logs, totaling 150,000 board feet of lumber. Completely restored to its original beauty, it serves as Sunriver's most popular ballroom and can accommodate approximately 350 people for dinner or meetings.

The High Desert Museum (8 miles from the lodge) is a terrific educational introduction to the cultural and natural history of the Northwest, and it is a big attraction for kids and adults alike. The otter pond, where you can watch playful otters preparing their food, is a favorite highlight, as is watching the birds of prey in action.

At Sunriver you'll find a dozen ways to enjoy winter. Mount Bachelor is one of the West's top-rated ski areas. You'll find breathtaking views, plenty of deep powder, and slopes to challenge skiers and snowboarders of all abilities—from beginners to Olympic champions. You can head cross-country on miles of groomed forest trails or break your own path through snowy meadows. Trek the mountain outback by snowshoe, snowmobile, or dogsled, or take a leisurely tour in a horse-drawn sleigh. And at day's end back at the resort, slip into a steaming outdoor spa for a relaxing soak. ≋

Sun Valley

Sun Valley, Idaho 83353
(208) 622–4111, (800) 786–8259
E-mail: reservation@sunvalley.com
Web site: www.sunvalley.com

Just the name Sun Valley calls to mind fantastic downhill skiing, beautiful powder, and gorgeous sunshine. Located in south-central Idaho, Sun Valley is a Tyrolean-style village perched on 2,054 acres of skiable terrain high in the Sawtooth Mountains. With a ski season that runs from late November to early May, spectacular scenery, and mountain air, Sun Valley is indeed a skier's paradise. Founded as a ski resort in 1936 by W. Averell Harriman, then chairman of

the board of Union Pacific Railroad, to draw rail travel west, Sun Valley immediately became the playground of Hollywood stars, introduced the world's first
chairlift, and began the long-running affair between Americans and skiing.

Winter activities include downhill and cross-country skiing, ice skating, and
sleigh rides. In summer tennis, golf, hiking, and fishing move to center stage. The
village, whose hub is the Sun Valley Lodge, supplements these activities with
restaurants, lounges, shops, movies, a game room, saunas, and a playschool for
children.

Accommodations: The Sun Valley Lodge is a full-service hotel with accommodations from standard and deluxe rooms to suites. The lodge also houses
restaurants, a glass-enclosed swimming pool, a game room, massage facilities,
and a sauna. Nearby is the Sun Valley Inn, another hotel, with its own restaurants

Photo courtesy of Sun Valley Resort

and glass-enclosed swimming pool. In addition, there are 575 condominium units scattered in clusters about the village. They are studios and one- to four-bedroom units with kitchen; many have a wood-burning fireplace and private balcony. They may be near the tennis courts, the lake, the riding center, or the golf course.

Nightly rates at the lodge and the inn start at $110 and run to $285 for a deluxe suite. In the condominiums studio rates are $110 a night, and four-bedroom units (sleeping up to eight people) are $280 a night (graduated prices for one-, two-, and three-bedroom apartments). Package plans are available except from just before Christmas through January 1. Summertime rates are $75 to $175 a night in the lodge and the inn, $100 a night for a studio, and up to $220 a night for a four-bedroom condominium. Children under fifteen ski and stay free, except during certain weeks of the year. There is no additional charge for cribs.

Dining: Twelve restaurants in the village please almost any mood from fancy to family style. Though many families cook meals in their condominium units, occasional nights dining out mean a real vacation for the family chef too!

Open for breakfast, lunch, and dinner, Gretchen's, in the lodge, is a family restaurant featuring an American menu; the Konditorei, in the village, specializes in sandwiches, pastries, and ice cream; and the Continental Cafe, in the inn, is a cafeteria. Also at the inn, the Ram Dining Room (open evenings only) serves steak, seafood, and cheese and chocolate fondues.

For an unusual adventure in dining, take a horse-drawn sleigh ride to a rustic cabin nestled in the woods; at the Trail Creek Cabin, enjoy prime rib or Idaho trout near a warm fire. Or you can spend an elegant evening at the Lodge Dining Room sampling French cuisine. On Sunday the dining room also serves a sumptuous buffet brunch of omelettes, crepes, fresh fruit, and pastries. For après-ski refreshment or a nightcap, try the Boiler Room or the Duchin Room, where you'll find evening entertainment.

Skiers intent on not losing time on the slopes can stop in for meals and snacks at one of the four mountainside restaurants. They serve soup, salads, and sandwiches cafeteria style.

Children's World: While Mom and Dad are schussing down Bald and Dollar Mountains, children are not left out of the fun in this winter wonderland. The Sun Valley Ski School starts three- and four-year-olds in introductory classes at $32 an hour. Four- to twelve-year-olds enjoy a full day of activity (8:30 A.M. to 4:00 P.M.), which includes four hours of lessons. The fee is $69 a day.

The Sun Valley Playschool entertains nonskiing little ones six years old and younger (even infants). The school is equipped with games and toys and a nap room for tots who grow weary of all the excitement. There are opportunities for ice skating and an outdoor playground for romping in the snow. The basic fee for the school is $55 a day per child; $65 a day for toddlers; and $85 a day for infants six months to óne year.

In summertime, school activities for the six-and-under group turn to swimming, hiking, arts and crafts, boating, and hayrides; the same fees are charged in summer as in winter. The Sun Valley Day Camp is designed for ages six to fourteen. Horseback riding, tennis, golf, fishing, and backpacking are scheduled for these age groups. The fee is $50 a day, excluding lunch.

Recreation: Suitable terrain for all levels of skiers is provided at Sun Valley. With its wide-open spaces and gentle trails, Dollar Mountain is favored by beginners and those who want a few warm-up runs. Bald Mountain is a challenge and caters to intermediate and expert skiers. Combined, these mountains offer seventy-eight runs, seventeen chairlifts, and 3,400 vertical feet. Sun Valley prides itself on lots of good skiing from well-groomed terrain to unpacked powder and short lift lines—the combination every downhill skier seeks. A complimentary bus service (operating continuously throughout the day) shuttles guests to the base of both mountains.

The Nordic and Snowshoe Center grooms 40 kilometers of well-marked trails for cross-country skiers through aspen trees, along the creek, and over sloping meadows. There are also 6 kilometers of designated snowshoe trails. Sun Valley was a pioneer in providing Nordic skiing specifically for children. Machine-set tracks designed for a child's stride cover 3 miles of the Nordic Ski Center and in some places parallel adult tracks, allowing an easy family cross-country-skiing experience. Backcountry skiers can tour the mountain from yurt to yurt (Siberian-style huts), finding a warm, welcoming meal and bed at each.

Private and group lessons are available in both downhill and cross-country skiing at beginner, intermediate, and advanced levels. At the ski shops you can rent equipment or purchase all the accessories necessary for either undertaking. Another favorite wintertime sport has become a year-round one here. Ice skates can be rented, and just behind the lodge is an Olympic-size skating rink where such greats as Sonja Henie, Peggy Fleming, and Dorothy Hamill have practiced. Saturday night ice shows are presented throughtout the summer.

Another year-round activity is swimming; there are two indoor heated pools (one at the lodge and one at the inn) and one outdoor Olympic-size pool. Relax in the sauna or the Jacuzzi, or make an appointment with the masseur in the lodge to ease your overworked muscles. The game room in the lodge offers pool tables, video games, and bowling alleys; or perhaps you'd like to take in a movie at the Opera House. The shops in the village might tempt you with their selections of books, gifts, fashions, jewelry, pottery, and toys.

Summer brings music festivals, parades, antiques and crafts fairs, bicycle races, and much more. Tennis and golf enthusiasts are in their heyday, for there are eighteen outdoor tennis courts, as well as clinics and private lessons with videotaped analysis. An eighteen-hole championship golf course, redesigned by Robert Trent Jones, Jr., rolls over gently sloping terrain. Two nine-hole courses provide another option. At the pro shop, you can arrange for lessons and pick up extras in equipment and clothing.

Fishing in Silver Creek makes a pleasant afternoon for novice fishermen as well as experienced anglers; Sun Valley Lake is stocked with trout. The mountain trails are open to you for horseback riding and hiking in the wooded wilderness. Archery and trap and skeet shooting (instruction available) are also popular with summer visitors. Take a rowboat or paddleboat out on the lake, line up rentals at the bike shop, or plan a white-water raft trip. Whether winter or summer sports beckon you, you'll be captivated by the majestic mountains and the warm, friendly atmosphere of Sun Valley. ≈≈≈

The Westin Mission Hills Resort

71333 Dinah Shore Drive
Rancho Mirage, California 92270
(760) 328–5955, (800) WESTIN–1
E-mail: ranch@westin.com
Web site: www.westin.com

The 360-acre Westin Mission Hills Resort, located near elegant Palm Springs, is also adjacent to the Mission Hills Country Club, the site of world-class golf. The lush landscaping, verdant golf courses, and abundance of water belie its desert location, but the surrounding mountains and canyons, which reflect the sun and shadow and the clear starry nights, are stark and wondrous reminders of what lies beyond the resort's boundaries.

Accommodations: Southwestern adobe mixed with classic Moroccan design provides a distinctive architectural achievement. Blue domes reflect the cloudless skies; warm brown arches repeat themselves down a long pathway, framing the desert palms and mountains. The 512 guest rooms are scattered in sixteen low-rise pavilions interspersed with meandering walks, gardens, lagoons, and waterfalls. Guest rooms are of generous size, and most feature a private patio. January to April is the high season, when rooms range from $450 to $495; from June through mid-September, the rates drop to $179 to $229. The remaining months are a midrange of $340 to $385. Children under eighteen stay free in their parents' room.

Photo courtesy of The Westin Mission Hills Resort

Dining: Bella Vista features California cuisine for breakfast, lunch, and dinner. Typically Californian, it blends a sunlit atrium with palm trees. Indoor/outdoor dining is available. Each of the three swimming pools has a cabana serving breakfast, lunch, snacks, and cool beverages; you need never leave the sun. For evening cocktails the elegantly casual Lobby Lounge offers drinks and hors d'oeuvres (inside or on the patio with its circular firepit), or relax and imbibe poolside at Las Brisas if you can't tear yourself or the kids out of the water. Westin has prepared a nice list of family restaurants in the area for those who want to venture out.

Children's World: Westin Kids Club is a basic program at all Westin resort properties, designed to make family travel safe, convenient, and enjoyable. Children get special age-appropriate gifts upon check-in; parents get a safety kit, if desired (electric-outlet covers, adhesive strips, ID bracelets, and local emergency numbers); and the room is ready with cribs, potty seats, or bed rails if needed. Jogging strollers, high chairs, and bottle warmers are complimentary, meals can be ordered in advance from a children's menu so that they are ready upon arrival at the restaurant, and a lot of information about local things of interest to families is available. It's a really comprehensive approach, and during the summer special rates and "Kids Eat Free" promotions are generally available.

The Cactus Kids program at Mission Hills bills itself as "the coolest thing in the desert." Operating daily year-round from 8:00 A.M. to 5:00 P.M., it costs $40 per four-hour session or $12 per hour. Lunch is additional. Reservations are requested at least one day in advance, and the program will be run for even one or two children. Activities include arts and crafts, volleyball, lawn games, movies, nature walks, and bicycle riding.

Recreation: Two championship golf courses, two practice ranges, and six greens and sand traps keep golfers happy. The Pete Dye Resort Course has his trademark deep bunkers and undulating fairways, while the Gary Player Signature Course is a mosaic of waterfalls, ravines, and lakes. Take lessons from the resident pros, or sign up for a Golf Digest School. Play tennis in the cool of the evening on the seven lighted tennis courts, or join the Reed Anderson Tennis School. Forget something? The pro shops have everything you need. Las Brisas is the largest of the three swimming pools; it was made to resemble the surrounding canyons and has a 60-foot water slide, two whirlpools, and spacious sundecks. Treat yourself to massage, herbal wraps, and facials at the new spa at Mission Hills; work out at the fitness club; or follow a more leisurely pace with traditional lawn games such as croquet and shuffleboard.

If you need more action, Oasis Waterpark is nearby as well as Camelot Park, where you can enjoy miniature golf, bumper boats, go-carts, or batting cages. Take the Palm Springs Aerial Tramway 8,516 feet to the Mountain Station for a bird's-eye view, and hike through Mt. San Jacinto Wilderness State Park. Weather permitting (meaning when there is snow), Nordic skiing operates from November to April. At the opposite end of the environmental spectrum, explore the desert by four-wheel drive with experienced guides who can show you the secret life of the desert, or have a real Old West experience in a two-hour covered-wagon tour. As a contrast to all this nature, any teenagers in your party might gravitate toward the Palm Desert Town Center, the area's largest indoor shopping mall. ≋

CANADA

Alberta

British Columbia

Ontario

Quebec

Deerhurst Resort

1235 Deerhurst Drive
Huntsville, Ontario
Canada P1H 2E8
(705) 789–6411, (800) 461–4393; fax (705) 789–5204
E-mail: inso@deerhurst.newcastlehotel.com
Web site: www.deerhurst.on.ca

The Muskoka region is Ontario's most popular holiday area. With its clear lakes and beautiful woodlands, it attracts visitors in summer and winter. Deerhurst Resort encompasses 800 acres on the shores of Peninsula Lake and allows guests to experience all the beauty of the area.

The original lodge at Deerhurst was opened in 1896 by Charles Waterhouse, with just eighteen guest rooms. Three generations of Waterhouses oversaw the expansion of the property and today it is one of the largest resort complexes in Canada.

Deerhurt is two and a half hours by car north of Toronto, or only forty minutes by air from Toronto to the resort's private airstrip.

Accommodations: Today's accommodations are a far cry from the lodge rooms (without baths) of the early days. The thirty-five guest rooms and suites are well appointed and comfortable and are grouped in condominium-style buildings with views of the lake, woods, pools, and golf course. Rates range from $66 (U.S. dollars) a night for a standard room to $494 a night for a premier three-bedroom suite. Children under eighteen stay free when occupying their parents' room. For an extra $43 per person per night, you can add a modified American plan meal package.

Dining: In the Lodge Dining Room, the chef displays his talents with regional bounty; venison, fresh fish, wild mushrooms, and wild berries are often featured in his creative dishes. The Lodge Dining Room is open for breakfast as well as dinner. The Pub in the Pavilion is casual and well suited for families; soups, sandwiches, pastas, and salads are typical fare here. Steamers Restaurant has a hearty menu and is open seasonally. The Poolside Deck, with views of the lake, serves barbecue favorites in the summer. Evening entertainment at the resort is lively, with a critically acclaimed musical stage show as well as dancing in the Cypress Lounge.

Children's World: Daily through the summer season, during school holiday periods, and on weekends throughout the year, Deer Club operates from 9:00 A.M. to 5:00 P.M. Children ages four to twelve swim, hike, make crafts, and enjoy the playground. The fee, including lunch, is $28 for a full day and $14 for a half

Photo courtesy of Deerhurst Resort

day. Younger children, ages six months to three years, join the Bambi Club, which has its own premises especially suited to little ones. The cost is $40 full days and $20 half days.

Recreation: The eighteen-hole Deerhurst Lakeside Golf Course was built in 1966 and redesigned in 1988 with many enhancements. Built in 1991, the top-rated Deerhurst Highlands is a magnificent eighteen-hole course winding atop a ridge above the lake, resulting in a combination of challenging play and beautiful scenery. A driving range, practice tees, and target greens make up the seven-and-a-half-acre instructional facility. A team of professionals direct private lessons and group clinics.

The Pavilion, a complete sports complex, consists of two indoor tennis courts, a racquetball court, three squash courts, a fitness room, a pool, and a whirlpool. Also available here is an Aveda Concept Spa, where you can relax in the steam and sauna rooms or schedule a massage, facial, body wrap, or hair-styling service.

If you prefer to exercise in the open air, three more swimming pools await you, and eight more tennis courts are outdoors (tennis lessons are available). Water sports on the lake abound: sailing, waterskiing, kayaking, fishing, and sailboarding. And don't forget to hike and jog along the nature trails in the beautiful Muskoka Woods. Or try one of the resort's unique 4-by-4 off-road driving adventures.

In the winter guests turn their energies to cross-country skiing, ice skating, snowmobiling, and dogsledding (quite an unusual sport!). ≋

The Fairmont Chateau Lake Louise

111 Lake Louise Drive
Lake Louise, Alberta
Canada T0L 1E0
(403) 522–3511, (800) 441–1414
Web site: www.fairmont.com

The Fairmont Chateau Lake Louise is located 100 miles west of Calgary in spectacular Banff National Park, Canada's oldest and largest national park. The hotel sits at the edge of beautiful Lake Louise, 1½ miles long by ¾ mile wide. Views from the hotel across this magnificent glacier-fed lake are truly breathtaking, as the eye takes in the expanse of the lake's turquoise water, the blue ice of the Victoria Glacier, and the majestic peaks of the Canadian Rockies, which form the Continental Divide. The mountains provide excellent opportunities for skiing in winter and endless exploration into the wonders of nature in summer.

Original accommodations on this site, built in 1890 by the Canadian Pacific Railway, were rather modest, welcoming a mere dozen adventurous guests at a time during summer only. Following two devastating fires, which left only the Painter wing standing, the main structure of the current hotel was built in 1925. An additional wing was created as part of a $65 million dollar renovation in the late 1980s. Today the resort is open year-round. From the elegant lobby to the helpful staff, careful attention to the needs of guests is evident everywhere.

Accommodations: The resort's 489 rooms, ranging from standard bedrooms to suites, are all comfortably and pleasantly decorated. Some offer the luxury of a private Jacuzzi. Rooms facing the lake are preferable, but it is difficult if not impossible to find a bad view anywhere. During the regular ski season (February 1 to early April), a six-night, five-lift ticket package with a lakeside room is $660 per person, based on double occupancy, and $580 for a room on the opposite side of the hotel. (At the beginning and end of the ski season, rates run approximately $170 less for the same ski package.) High season is June, July, and August, and rates increase significantly; for example, a bed-and-breakfast package in June would be $300 to $400 per night (per room, double occupancy), depending on the size and location of the room. Christmas is considered peak ski time at Lake Louise and rates are more than double the regular season rates.

Dining: The Fairmont Chateau Lake Louise offers nine restaurants and lounges for a wide variety of dining experiences. For fine dining at its best, try the gracious and elegant Edelweiss Dining Room, which presents a lovely selection of Alberta beef, lamb, and fish dishes as well as a wine list that includes wonderful British Columbia wines and many choice selections from around the world. For lighter fare enjoy the quick and easy Chateau Deli for sandwiches, soups, and salads. The Poppy Room is a casual family restaurant with buffets ranging from East Indian to Italian and an a la carte menu as well. The Walliser Stube features fondue and raclette along with steak and seafood. The Victoria Dining Room, open only in summer, recaptures the charm and opulence of the early twentieth century. For the Old West at its best, try the Glacier Saloon for light meals, drinks, and dancing. Both the Lakeside Lounge and the Lobby Bar afford splendid views as guests sip a cocktail or glass of wine. Off-site from the hotel is the Brewster Dance Barn, known for its roast beef dinners and dancing; open winters only, the fun starts with a sleigh ride from the resort.

At the mountain, two base lodges and two lodges on the slopes offer warmth and good food in typical cafeteria or restaurant style.

Children's World: The Children's Playroom at the hotel is for youngsters two and older; the Playroom will also arrange baby-sitting for all ages. Children's programs at the base of the mountain happily accommodate little ones from infancy on up. Children begin skiing at age three and can join a full day of indoor and outdoor fun in Chocolate Moose Park, with one-hour ski lessons in the morning and afternoon; the cost is $28. Five- to twelve-year-olds graduate to a more rigorous program and can spend all day with their instructors for lessons and lunch; the cost is $34. Snowboarding days are offered for seven- to twelve-year-olds at the same rate, $34.

Recreation: Lake Louise boasts more than 4,000 skiable acres with a vertical drop of almost 3,400 feet and a summit of 9,000 feet. Since this resort is located so far north, snow is abundant. Average annual snowfall is a respectable 200 inches, and snowmaking supplements the snowfall on 20 percent of the runs. There are more than one hundred runs (the longest is 5 miles), with almost half rated intermediate. Whether on a long run from the top of the mountain or in the middle of acres and acres of open bowls, everyone in the family will find his or her cup of tea.

Cross-country is a big feature at the resort, with a wide variety of picturesque trails leading right from the hotel. Ice skating on Lake Louise, snowshoeing, dogsledding, and horse-drawn sleigh rides add to the wintertime picture.

In May the hotel sponsors a wine and food festival. In summer the interpretive hiking and mountaineering programs are truly special. Excursions that range from four to eight hours, with professional mountain guides, reveal the nature and history of the Canadian Rockies in a national park that is home to elk, bighorn sheep, moose, and mountain goats. Canoeing on the lake and biking the many trails open up to visitors the natural splendors of this region.

The resort has an indoor swimming pool, a hot tub, and a well-equipped exercise room. Several shops fill your needs for souvenirs, clothing, and jewelry. ≋

Fairmont Le Château Montebello

392 rue Notre-Dame
Montebello, Quebec
Canada J0V 1L0
(819) 423–6341, (800) 441–1414
Web site: www.fairmont.com

You don't have to travel all the way to Europe for a vacation in a French château. Fairmont Le Château Montebello is a luxury resort in a peaceful woodland setting located on the shores of the Ottawa River between Montreal and Ottawa.

Built of massive cedar logs by a team of craftsmen in 1930, Fairmont Le Château Montebello served as an exclusive private club for forty years. In 1970

it became a resort open to the public year-round. Today the Château's old-world charm and contemporary elegance come together as a lovely holiday destination, with the distinction of being the world's largest log structure.

Accommodations: The château has four wings radiating from the center, affording the guest rooms outlooks to the river and the forests. For the 211 well-appointed rooms, rates begin at $130 (U.S. dollars) a night. The summertime family package starts at $225 per adult for two nights, based on double occupancy; it includes breakfast and dinner, pontoon riverboat cruise (one hour), bicycle rental (three hours), canoeing (half day), and various other sports. With this package, two children age twelve and younger stay and eat free when occupying a room with their parents. Each additional child age thirteen to seventeen is $105.

Dining: Aux Chantignoles is the elegant gourmet dining room of the resort. This is also the venue for Sunday brunch. The Golf Club House is popular for lunch; the Igloo is an outdoor barbecue restaurant, ideal for lunch or dinner. Light snacks and refreshments are served at the Golf Terrace and the Seignory Bar.

Children's World: The Kid's Centre, presided over by Monte the Beaver, is open from 9:00 A.M. to noon daily from July to September, and weekends year-round. For children ages three and up, the cost is $17 per day. Toys, games, and arts and crafts are mixed with outdoor activities such as swimming, hiking, and group games based on the ages and number of children in the program. While the Kid's Centre is not open all day, the hotel often arranges special things such as treasure hunts. Special events for children and families are usually planned for holiday periods and weekends throughout the year.

Recreation: The resort offers something for everyone. Built in 1929, the eighteen-hole golf course has been totally renovated, resulting in a more challenging and more scenic course. The golf school provides lessons and organizes clinics. The course is rated "Double Platinum" by *Canada's Golf Course Ranking Magazine*.

At the Health Club and Sports Complex, you can work out in the exercise room, play squash or tennis, swim laps in the indoor pool, or relax at the Spa in the saunas or whirlpools. The outdoor pool is a beautiful setting for relaxing, sunning, and swimming. Referee the kids in volleyball and badminton games, then round up the whole crew for bike riding or miniputt.

The Spa offers professional services, including full-body massage, facials, body wraps of mud or algae, body exfoliation and polishing, and therapeutic baths using either relaxing pine and rosemary milk or stimulating mineral salts. What a treat after a full day of activity! Other activities include water sports, cruises, jet-skiing, and horseback riding.

The whole family can discover the beauties of Fairmont Kenauk, a 100-square-mile plant and wildlife preserve within 6 miles of the resort, with scores of activities—bird-watching, picnics, hikes with or without a naturalist, mountain biking, or fishing. Explore White Fish Lake by rowboat or canoe, float down the Kinonge River, or rent a motorboat at the marina. It's a great place to laze away summer days enjoying nature. Omega Park provides a slightly different approach to nature. Drive along a 10-kilometer road through 1,500 acres of a woodland corral where native animals small (raccoons, wild boar, and deer) and large (bison, black bears, and wild sheep) roam free.

Snow brings enchantment to the woods and hills and is the focus of wintertime fun. The familiar activities of ice skating, ice fishing, sleigh rides, and snowmobiling compete with the more exotic: dogsledding, curling, snowshoeing, broomball, and deck hockey. More than 27 kilometers of cross-country ski trails beckon, or you may prefer just a walk in the snow and curling up with a good book in front of the huge six-sided fireplace in the château. ≋

Gray Rocks Resort

Mont-Tremblant, Quebec
Canada J0T 1Z0
(800) 567–6767; fax (819) 425–9156
E-mail: info@grayrocks.com
Web site: www.grayrocks.com

Just 75 miles northwest of Montreal, in the Laurentian Mountains, you will find a charming four-season, four-star lakeside family resort with a French flavor. Although it's right in the middle of French-speaking Canada, Gray Rocks welcomes American visitors and English is spoken here routinely. You might choose to take the opportunity to brush up on your French, but rest assured that your interests uttered in English in the dining room, on the tennis courts, or during a ski lesson will be well received with warm French-Canadian hospitality.

Since its beginning in 1906, Gray Rocks has developed into a renowned ski, golf, and tennis resort with hotel and condominium accommodations for all tastes. The hotel, with dining room, fitness center, convention center, and bar, sits on the shores of Lac Ouimet. Gray Rocks' own ski mountain, Sugar Peak, rises right behind the hotel; beautiful views of Mont-Tremblant are also impossible to miss. Golf was the first sport in this area, followed by skiing. Today recreational pastimes also include tennis, water sports, horseback riding, mountain biking, or nature hikes.

Accommodations: Lakeside rooms with a private balcony are available in the hotel's Pavilion and Chalet Suisse. Fifty-six one-, two-, and three-bedroom condominiums are tucked in among the trees ¾ mile from the hotel, with free shuttle-bus service. In summer hotel packages include accommodation, buffet breakfast, table d'hôte dinner, access to the fitness center with indoor pool, use of the private beach and marina, daily activities, nightly entertainment, Kids Club supervised morning activities, and gratuities. Twice a week, guests can choose to eat a sunset barbecue dinner on the lakeside terrace by the beach; dinner is followed by a family party, games, music, and a bonfire. Rates vary from $72 (U.S. dollars) for a regular room during value season (June 22 to July 12 and August 26 to September 3) to $99 for a Pavilion room with private balcony in summer season (July 13 to August 25). A full American plan is available. One-bedroom, fully equipped, four-person condominium rates start at $102 per night. A meal plan is also offered to condominium guests.

In winter guests enjoy a getaway similar to the summer hotel package, with free skiing at Gray Rocks or nearby sister resort Mont Blanc. The most popular winter package is the all-inclusive ski or snowboard week. For approximately

$792 per person (U.S. dollars), double occupancy, you will enjoy six nights of lodging; eighteen full-course meals; twenty hours of ski instruction or ten hours of snowboard instruction with the renowned Snow Eagle Ski School; video critique; seven-day lift ticket; races and awards; complete social program for adults, teens, and children; and access to the fitness center with indoor pool. Gray Rocks' ski week is considered one of the best ski vacation values in North America. Other options: the ski or snowboard week with condominium accommodation (no meals), at approximately $395 per adult; the ski week with a Snow Eagle instructor at nearby Mont-Tremblant ski area; and the American Thanksgiving package. A children-stay-for-less plan (seventeen and under; kids five and under eat and stay free) makes Gray Rocks family friendly in summer as well as in winter.

Dining: The main dining room located at the hotel, with its fireplace and picture windows overlooking the scenic landscape, provides a pleasant ambience during meals. Continental and French-Canadian cuisines are featured. Cozy lounges with fireplaces and lake views are perfect to relax and mix with old and new friends. There's also a cafeteria at the ski chalet, located midmountain and accessible by car, shuttle bus, or skis. Both golf courses have a club house with restaurant and lounge area.

Children's World: In summer, from June 23 to August 26, the children's activity program is in high gear. Youngsters join other children their own ages for supervised morning and afternoon events. Preschoolers ages three to five head to the playground, go on treasure hunts and hayrides, or frolic on the private beach. Kids ages six to nine go swimming and horseback riding, try their talents in arts and crafts, and join hayrides. Preteens (ten to twelve) and teens (thirteen and older) enjoy volleyball, tennis, hiking, canoeing, sailboarding, fishing, and various excursions.

For the aspiring tennis or golf pro, there's a famous junior camp. Gray Rocks' Matchpoint Junior Tennis Camp or Eagle Junior Golf Camp offer a great program for eleven- to sixteen-year-olds. Two-week sessions include lakeside accommodations, all meals and snacks, five hours of instruction per day, round-the-clock supervision, and a complete social program for approximately $1,104 (U.S. dollars) per child (one week session: $564 per child).

In winter Gray Rocks' philosophy is to put children on skis as much as possible. Given that the resort's own gentle mountain is just out the back door, this philosophy is easily practiced. The children's ski classes are divided along age lines as well as ability; heaven forbid your first-time thirteen-year-old skier should be in a class with four-year-olds! Camaraderie in a peer group is important in the learning experience. Children and teens can also meet their friends

Photo courtesy of Gray Rocks Resort

in a variety of après-ski activities, such as cookie baking, face painting, treasure hunts, arts and crafts, table tennis tournaments, parties, movies, water polo, and sleigh rides or bingo with Mom and Dad. You want to have some fun with your kids, too!

Day-care service is available for ages six months to two years as well as private baby-sitting. In winter a Ski 'n' Play program combines day care and one hour of ski instruction per day for three- to five-year-olds. The rate is $179 (U.S. dollars) per child, with the hotel/meals package free.

Recreation: Think of Gray Rocks as a university for sports. Its qualified ski, golf, and tennis instructors combine expertise with a sincere enthusiasm for teaching. Improvement of skills and self-confidence go hand in hand, and both are better achieved with ample doses of encouragement and humor. Since 1951 more than 250,000 ski weekers have enjoyed Gray Rocks' unique teaching methods in a safe, uncrowded ski environment.

The Snow Eagle Ski School has a fine reputation (rated by *Ski Magazine* as one of the top-ten ski schools in North America) and more than fifty years of experience. Skiing is a major wintertime activity. The resort boasts a number of third-generation families who have learned to ski on these slopes and continue to return for their winter holidays. Though Gray Rocks has a modest 620-foot vertical drop, there's variety and, if not long, then challenging runs. Snow-making facilities cover 95 percent of the slopes, ensuring a ski season from

Thanksgiving through early April. Mont-Tremblant ski resort is less than 5 miles from Gray Rocks, so intermediate and advanced skiers can seek additional challenges there. The ski boutique can meet your needs for rentals, repairs, fashions, and accessories. Cross-country skiing is a growing favorite at Gray Rocks. Nearby Domaine St. Bernard offers well-maintained trails through the woods, next to the river. A tour around the area is a lovely way to spend a winter morning, and a sleigh ride with the kids caps off a perfect day.

Summertime opens another whole realm of outdoor sports and activities. There's a private sandy beach along a section of the lake. This is Canada, but summers are hot, so swimmers will be happy. The complete marina near the beach offers opportunity for canoeing, sailboarding, sailing, taking out a paddleboat, or enjoying an afternoon of fishing.

A classic eighteen-hole golf course (La Belle) will take you through lush fairways over diverse terrain framed by the rugged beauty of the Laurentians. Three learning holes are reserved for Eagle Golf Academy players. The combination of time-proven teaching strategies and small class ratios helps players take strokes off their game and turns newcomers on to the joys of the sport. Gray Rocks recently opened an eighteen-hole championship course (La Bête) designed by renowned golf architect Graham Cooke. The course winds its way along Devil's River, offering superb views of the surrounding mountains. With bent grass tees, greens, and fairways, four sets of tees to choose from, and eighteen distinct and challenging holes, you will leave knowing you have played one of Canada's best courses.

Tennis buffs enjoy the largest outdoor complex in Canada with twenty-two Har-Tru courts (ten near the hotel and twelve at the golf club). Tennis lessons with videotaping can help you isolate the improvements necessary for a good game. Gray Rocks' golf and tennis academies offer acclaimed two- and five-day clinics.

Jogging along the lake or hiking and horseback riding in the hills are excellent ways to explore the countryside and revel in the clean mountain air. You can enjoy a nice afternoon next to the beach playing lawn games, or get in shape at Le Spa fitness center. Le Spa features an indoor swimming pool, an exercise room, hot tubs, a sauna, and a professional massage service. Many activities are offered free of charge; some, such as golf, tennis, and horseback riding, carry additional fees.

Gray Rocks provides the area's only resort-based pet kennel. You can now travel with the entire family! ≋≋

Inn on the Park

1100 Eglinton Avenue East
Toronto, Ontario
Canada M3C 1H8
(416) 444–2561, (877) 644–4687 (United States and Canada)
E-mail: iotp@idirect.ca
Web site: www.innontheparktoronto.com

If you're in the mood for a slightly different vacation experience from that offered by most of the resorts we've listed, this is the place. Inn on the Park has the distinction of being a city hotel in a resort setting: Situated on 500 acres of parkland, it's right in the middle of Toronto, one of Canada's liveliest cities. It's the best of both worlds, with shopping, art galleries, and museums offset by the green grandeur of the surrounding park.

Accommodations: A twenty-two-story high-rise with 268 rooms in one tower allows views of the city, the park, or the inner courtyard. Nonsmoking floors, twice-daily maid service, complimentary parking, shoe polishing, and terry-cloth robes are some of the amenities offered, and the hotel prides itself on excellent service. Guest rooms are classified deluxe ($110 to $175, U.S. dollars, per night); differences in size, location, and view determine the rating. Some superior rooms have a patio leading directly to the pool area. Deluxe rooms overlook the city and park. If you like more space, one-bedroom suites are $225 to $250. Children under nineteen stay free in their parents' room.

Dining: The Harvest Restaurant is casual, with a children's menu of those all-time favorites—grilled cheese sandwiches, hamburgers, and spaghetti. During the summer months the Cabana serves light snacks by the pool. The Terrace Lounge has buffet or a la carte lunches and late-night snacks, when you can also enjoy a piano bar. What child doesn't adore room service? Here it's available daily. And all the wonderful restaurants of Toronto are at your doorstep, waiting to be discovered.

Children's World: Innkidz is a very popular and highly organized program that is complimentary for hotel guests. Geared to children ages five to twelve, the program is available from 9:30 A.M. to 4:00 P.M. daily during the summer. Children gather at the Innkidz Centre on the first floor of the Tower for such activities as puppet making, outdoor games and swimming, and making crafts or clay art. Special treats are a picnic on the helicopter pad and making cookies with the chef in the hotel kitchen. Counselors are art students and teachers, so the experience is very creative. Children under five are welcome if parents remain with them. Lunch can be ordered from the Harvest Room menu and charged to the room. Cribs and high chairs are available.

Recreation: At the hotel you can work out in the fully equipped health club and then relax those muscles in the sauna or whirlpool; or try your hand at badminton, volleyball, or shuffleboard. Decide between the indoor and outdoor pools, then decide between swimming and lounging. Window-shop the boutiques and gift shop, get your hair fixed, or stop by the games room.

Toronto holds many treats for families. Kids like to wander through Ontario Place, by the harbor. Shops, eateries, an IMAX theater, and changing exhibits of dinosaurs or gemstones intrigue everyone. Go to the top of the C.N. Tower, the largest freestanding tower in the world; or check out the planetarium at the Royal Ontario Museum. Let the kids pick out a postcard in the gift shop, then try to find the original in the museum. The Ontario Science Museum has a lot of hands-on exhibits, and the Toronto Zoo is a nice excursion on a pretty day. ≋≋

Severn Lodge

Box 250
Port Severn, Ontario
Canada L0K 1S0
(705) 756–2722, (800) 461–5817; fax (705) 756–8313
E-mail: info@severnlodge.on.ca
Web site: www.severnlodge.on.ca

Severn Lodge is beautifully located in the midst of the Georgian Lakelands of Ontario, only 90 miles from Toronto. Georgia Bay forms the northeastern part of Lake Huron and is named in honor of England's King George IV. The area's piney woods, fine fishing, and clear waters attract many vacationers. And the Severn Lodge, on the shores of Gloucester Pool, adds to the natural features with its warm pride of being "owned and operated by the same family for families since 1937." The lodge is open from mid-May to mid-October only.

Accommodations: Severn Lodge dates back to the late 1800s. Its early-twentieth-century ambience remains preserved in the many white clapboard buildings, log crisscross railings, and cobblestone sidewalks. All accommodations and facilities, however, are very modern.

Grouped in about a dozen individual buildings set among the trees and along the lake, the accommodations feature small living rooms, large windows for enjoying the lake views, and ample space for a crib or rollaway bed (for which there is no charge). Rates range from $69 to $111 (U.S. dollars) a day per person, double occupancy, and include three meals a day and all the planned activities, entertainment, and recreational facilities (except motorboats) of

Photo courtesy of Severn Lodge

the lodge. Two-bedroom suites and some rooms with Jacuzzis and fireplaces also are available. When sharing a room with their parents, children under two years are free; two to five years are charged $37; six to twelve, $45; and thirteen to eighteen, $57. Two- to seven-day package plans are offered. During special family weeks in the summer season, rates for children twelve and younger are reduced 20 to 50 percent or more. Several housekeeping cottages are available nearby, and they share some of the facilities of the Lodge.

Dining: The charming, elegantly rustic dining room has a woodbeamed ceiling and many large windows that capture the views. The Canadian cuisine is accompanied by freshly baked breads and pastries. Picnic lunches can be prepared for guests who are off hiking or canoeing during the midday meal.

Children's World: The activities program for children, which runs from mid-June to Labor Day, includes hikes, crafts, volleyball and baseball games, swimming, diving and boating lessons, picnics, and movies. Add waterskiing, Indian Night, Talent Night, a Fish Derby, corn roasts, and bonfire sing-alongs and you know you have happy kids. No additional charges are applied for these events, and children of all ages are welcome to participate.

Every effort is made to include even very young guests, but when your little one is just not able to keep up with the group, a supervised toddler activity program will provide pint-size fun. Specially designed indoor and outdoor play areas for two- to five-year-olds are open daily. The program is complimentary and includes arts and crafts, sand-castle building, and other beach and playground activities. The lodge staff can also arrange an individual baby-sitter for an extra cost. Favorites among the younger set are the sandy beach; the playground, with its swings, slide, sandbox, and climbing equipment; and the dock, for "just fishin'."

Recreation: Water sports are an important part of Severn Lodge. Wonderful swimming can be had either in the lake or in the heated swimming pool; perhaps you'd like to try the whirlpool spa at the deepwater dock. Maybe you would prefer to stay on top of the water in a fishing boat reeling in walleye, bass, muskie, and northern pike. Also on top of the water (with any luck, you *will* stay on top) is the complimentary waterskiing instruction offered several times a week. Free use of the lodge's sailboats, paddleboats, kayaks, and canoes can make an afternoon lazy or exciting, depending upon your skill. The resort has a unique collection of antique runabouts and motor launches. Rental fees are charged on a daily or weekly basis for outboard boats, motors, and Jet-Skis; the lodge offers free cruises and live evening entertainment during summer.

On land you can jog or hike on the trails around the lodge's one hundred acres or play a game of tennis. The recreation building, with its library and large stone fireplace, is quite inviting if relaxing is a favorite pastime; here you will find table tennis, a wide-screen TV, card and board games, and a pool table. Nearby sight-seeing (15 to 20 miles) takes you back in history; Sainte-Marie among the Hurons, a Jesuit Mission, and the Huron Indian Village are reconstructions of seventeenth-century settlements. You will also find horseback riding, golf, live theater, museums, casino gambling, and fabulous shopping in nearby lakeside villages. ≋

Sunshine Village

Box 1510
Banff, Alberta
Canada T0L 0C0
(403) 762–6500, (800) 661–1676
E-mail: reservations@skibanff.com
Web site: www.skibanff.com

High in the Canadian Rockies in Banff National Park is Sunshine Village, one of the best ski destinations in Canada. Perched along the Continental Divide, the peak elevation at Sunshine is 9,200 feet. Located only 85 miles west of Calgary and just 10 miles from the town of Banff, Sunshine is a three-mountain ski resort. More than $9 million in improvements await you at Sunshine, Banff's most visited ski resort.

Accommodations: The only accommodation on the mountain is the Sunshine Inn. A three-story complex consisting of eighty-five rooms and suites, the inn affords its guests ski-in/ski-out access. Rates start at $65 (U.S. dollars) per person per night. A five-night package, including lodging, lift ticket, and daily ski lessons, costs $350 per person, based on double occupancy during the value season (from November to mid-December, from the second week of January to mid-February, and from late April to closing). The powder season is defined as the week before Christmas, the week after New Year's, and mid-February to late April, when the package costs $450. During Christmas week this package is $500.

Dining: The inn's dining room, the Eagle's Nest, offers fine dining, from rack of lamb to fantastic sirloin steak. The Chimney Corner is a lounge offering cocktails and entertainment in the evenings. In the Daylodge, the Deli and the Cafeteria offer soup and sandwiches; the new Mad Trappers Saloon, located in the original 1928 Sunshine Lodge, is the place to go for drinks and burgers.

Children's World: For young skiers and snowboarders, Wee Angels (ages three to six) and Young Devils (ages six to twelve) provide a great time, with snow games, skiing, and other fun activities. Divided not only by age but also by ability, the kids set the pace for the day—how much they want to ski, and where. The 10:00 A.M. to 3:00 P.M. program costs $26 and includes lift ticket, lunch, and lessons. A day-care center, Sunshine Kids Kampus, is open from 8:00 A.M. to 5:00 P.M. for children nineteen months to six years. Full-day cost is $23, and half-day is only $15.

Recreation: Sunshine Village is located on the Continental Divide, where you can ski the provinces of both British Columbia and Alberta off the same run. The top elevation at Sunshine is more than 9,000 feet and the base elevation is 5,440 feet, yielding skiers more than 3,500 vertical feet. Mother Nature drops more than 360 inches of snow here each year, which results in good skiing from mid-November through the end of May. Of the eighty-nine runs currently open, 50 percent are intermediate; the remainder are split evenly between beginner and expert. Many of the runs are above the treeline, giving skiers that top-of-the-world feeling. Sunshine Village boasts North America's largest new ski terrain, Goat's Eye Mountain (elevation 9,200 feet), offering extreme-expert-only (Double Black Diamond) chutes and glades.

When not skiing, you may want to pursue less rigorous activities in the family games room or relax your weary muscles in the sauna or the Sunshine Inn's giant outdoor hot pool, rated Canada's best by *Ski Canada* magazine. ≈≈

Whistler/Blackcomb

Tourism Whistler
4010 Whistler Way
Whistler, British Columbia
Canada V0N 1B4
(604) 664–5625, (800) 944–7853
Web site: www.tourismwhistler.com

If you're lucky enough to hear the whistling call of the indigenous marmots, you'll easily recognize how Whistler Mountain got its current name. Originally known as London Mountain, on the old Caribou Gold Rush Trail, this area saw its first settlers in 1914, an adventurous couple who built a fishing lodge on the shores of Alta Lake. Though still attracting fishermen in the summer, Whistler is famous today as an outstanding ski destination.

Skiers first schussed these slopes in the mid-1960s, and the early 1980s witnessed considerable expansion and development, primarily the opening of Blackcomb Mountain. The two mountains, Whistler and Blackcomb, are serviced by three base facilities. In the Coastal Mountains, Whistler/Blackcomb is just 75 miles north of Vancouver.

Accommodations: Hotels and condominiums are found throughout Whistler Resort. The larger facilities are the Fairmont Château Whistler at the base of Blackcomb, with 558 units, indoor and outdoor swimming pools, a health club, and indoor tennis courts; the Delta Mountain Inn in Whistler Village, with 288 rooms, an outdoor pool, and two all-season tennis courts; and the Crystal Lodge, also in the Village, with 137 units and an outdoor pool and Jacuzzi. But a smaller complex, such as the Hearthstone Lodge, Powderview, Whistler Resort and Club, or Whiski Jack Condos, might also be the perfect choice for your family. There's also Marriott Residence Inn, with 184 units, slopeside on Blackcomb Mountain. Contacting Central Experience at (800) WHISTLER is the first step in sorting out all these choices. You might want to consider one of the available packages. The Early Riser, at $246 per person, includes three nights' accommodation, three days' lift tickets, and one Fresh Tracks breakfast ticket. Truly Canadian, at $492 per person, features five nights' accommodation, three days' lift tickets, dogsledding, a two-hour snowmobile tour, and one Fresh Tracks breakfast. The Extreme Experience, at $1,086 per person, provides seven nights' accommodation, five days' lift tickets, four runs of heliskiing, and a three-hour snowmobile tour with fondue dinner.

Contact Whistler/Blackcomb directly for other rates and packages.

Dining: With more than sixty restaurants and cafes, you'll never have trouble indulging your palate's whim, whether you crave French, Italian, Japanese, Mexican, or Greek cuisine. Three restaurants on Whistler and six on Blackcomb serve hearty soups and stews, burgers, pizza, and pasta to skiers reluctant to leave the slopes for very long. Some of the restaurants favored by families are Black's Restaurant, The Old Spaghetti Factory; Monk's at Blackcomb; and Hoz's Cafe, Boston Pizza, and Dusty's at Whistler Creek.

Children's World: Whistler Kids has 500 instructors dedicated to making the mountains a kids' playground. The instructors are highly trained ski and snowboard professionals, specializing in kids' needs. The children's programs are designed for children up to twelve years old, with youth programs providing activities for children ages thirteen through seventeen. Kids Adventure Camps and Kid's Night Out are always great fun.

Instructors will design a program for one to five children for private skiing or snowboarding lessons (contact Whistler for rates). Whistler Kids offers a broad range of programs catering to kids as young as three months; kids first take to skis at three years of age. Teaching more than 140,000 kids every winter, Whistler Kids is Canada's premier recreational operation for children. No wonder the kids keep bringing their parents back!

While Whistler/Blackcomb has no formal summertime program, there's lots going on. Whistler/Blackcomb Mountain can provide contacts for privately run ski and snowboarding camps offered in June and July. The Meadow Park Recreation Center has an indoor swimming pool as well as an ice rink for those who miss winter. And with glacier skiing, winter sports last through August, side by side with hiking, biking, and swimming.

Recreation: Get introduced to Whistler/Blackcomb in a morning or afternoon guided tour (free) and you'll begin to appreciate their more than 7,000 acres of skiable terrain and more than 5,200 feet of vertical drop. More than 200 trails, twelve bowls, and three glaciers provide all the variety any skier could hope for. Choose chutes filled with powder, steep runs through trees, broad trails perfectly groomed, or mogul monsters. The average annual snowfall of 360 inches is complemented by sophisticated snowmaking capabilities. Both mountains open in late November, and skiing continues to late April on Blackcomb and to mid-June on Whistler. Blackcomb opens again in mid-June for glacier skiing through August. You can book private and group lessons or join a camp specializing in skiing bumps or powder.

When taking a break from skiing, try ice skating and snowmobiling, or organize a sleigh ride. Cross-country skiers take to the 10 miles of track-set trails through the forest and valley. For less strenuous exercise stroll through the village to discover its 207 shops.

In summer golf is the premier sport, with four eighteen-hole courses, each with fine credentials. The Whistler Golf Course was designed by Arnold Palmer, and the Château Whistler Course was designed by Robert Trent Jones Jr. Jack Nicklaus was responsible for Nicklaus North, which opened in 1994, and the Big Sky Golf and Country Club was designed by Robert Cupp.

Hiking and biking across the Alpine terrain are favorites with summertime visitors. The five lakes provide fishermen, swimmers, and boaters with ample fun. A variety of festivals and special events are available throughout the year. ≈≈≈

ndexes

Alphabetical Index to Resorts

Schweitzer Mountain Resort, Sandpoint, Idaho, 237

Seabrook Island Resort, Seabrook Island, South Carolina, 79

Severn Lodge, Port Severn, Ontario, Canada, 264

Shangri-La Resort and Country Club, Afton, Oklahoma, 173

Shanty Creek, Bellaire, Michigan, 150

Sheraton El Conquistador Resort and Country Club, Tucson, Arizona, 174

Skytop Lodge, Skytop, Pennsylvania, 59

Smugglers' Notch Resort, Smugglers' Notch, Vermont, 34

Snowbird Ski and Summer Resort, Snowbird, Utah, 208

Snowmass Village Resort Association, Snowmass Village, Colorado, 210

South Seas Resort, Captiva Island, Florida, 119

Squaw Valley USA, Olympic Valley, California, 238

Stratton Mountain Resort, Stratton Mountain, Vermont, 38

Sugarloaf/USA, Kingfield, Maine, 41

Sun Valley, Sun Valley, Idaho, 243

Sunriver Resort, Sunriver, Oregon, 240

Sunshine Village, Banff, Alberta, Canada, 266

Tanque Verde Guest Ranch, Tucson, Arizona, 175

Taos Ski Valley, Taos Ski Valley, New Mexico, 177

The Tides, Irvington, Virginia, 82

TradeWinds Island Resorts, St. Pete Beach, Florida, 120

The Tyler Place Family Resort on Lake Champlain, Highgate Springs, Vermont, 44

Vail/Beaver Creek Central Reservations, Vail, Colorado, 214

The Westin Innisbrook Resort, Palm Harbor, Florida, 123

The Westin Mission Hills Resort, Rancho Mirage, California, 247

Whistler/Blackcomb, Whistler, British Columbia, Canada, 268

Whitney's Inn, Jackson, New Hampshire, 46

Wild Dunes Resort, Isle of Palms, South Carolina, 84

Classic Resorts

The Arizona Biltmore, Phoenix, Arizona, 156

The Balsams Grand Resort Hotel, Dixville Notch, New Hampshire, 18

The Breakers, Palm Beach, Florida, 94

The Broadmoor, Colorado Springs, Colorado, 188

The Cloister, Sea Island, Georgia, 103

Fairmont Le Château Montebello, Montebello, Quebec, Canada, 256

The Greenbrier, White Sulphur Springs, West Virginia, 64

The Grove Park Inn Resort, Asheville, North Carollina, 67

The Homestead, Hot Springs, Virginia, 72

Country Inn Resorts

Resorts with Golf

Stratton Mountain Resort, Stratton Mountain, Vermont, 38

Sun Valley, Sun Valley, Idaho, 243

Sunriver Resort, Sunriver, Oregon, 240

The Westin Innisbrook Resort, Palm Harbor, Florida, 123

The Westin Mission Hills Resort, Rancho Mirage, California, 247

Whistler/Blackcomb, Whistler, British Columbia, Canada, 268

Wild Dunes Resort, Isle of Palms, South Carolina, 84

Resorts with Horseback Riding

The Bishop's Lodge, Sante Fe, New Mexico, 158

C Lazy U Ranch, Granby, Colorado, 191

Coffee Creek Ranch, Trinity Center, California, 222

Flathead Lake Lodge, Bigfork, Montana, 198

Flying L Guest Ranch, Bandera, Texas, 161

Golden Acres Farm and Ranch, Gilboa, New York, 50

Mountain Sky Guest Ranch, Bozeman, Montana, 203

Rocking Horse Ranch, Highland, New York, 54

Tanque Verde Guest Ranch, Tucson, Arizona, 175

Lakeside Resorts

The Balsams Grand Resort Hotel, Dixville Notch, New Hampshire, 18

Bluewater Bay Resort, Niceville, Florida, 93

Deerhurst Resort, Huntsville, Ontario, Canada, 252

Eagle Ridge Inn and Resort, Galena, Illinois, 128

Flathead Lake Lodge, Bigfork, Montana, 198

Grand Geneva Resort and Spa, Lake Geneva, Wisconsin, 132

Grand View Lodge, Nisswa, Minnesota, 136

Gray Rocks Resort, Mont-Tremblant, Quebec, Canada, 259

Highland Lodge, Greensboro, Vermont, 21

The Homestead, Glen Arbor, Michigan, 139

Inn of the Mountain Gods, Mescalero, New Mexico, 168

Konocti Harbor Resort and Spa, Kelseyville, California, 227

The Lodge of the Four Seasons Championship Golf Resort and Spa, Lake Ozark, Missouri, 142

Ludlow's Island Lodge, Cook, Minnesota, 144

Marriott's Tan-Tar-A Resort and Golf Club, Osage Beach, Missouri, 145

Mohonk Mountain House, New Paltz, New York, 52

Ruttger's Bay Lake Lodge, Deerwood, Minnesota, 149

Seaside Resorts

Spa Resorts

Resorts with Skiing

Gray Rocks Resort, Mont-Tremblant, Quebec, Canada, 259

The Inn of the Seventh Mountain, Bend, Oregon, 225

Keystone Resort, Keystone, Colorado, 200

Killington Ski and Summer Resort, Killington, Vermont, 23

Mount Snow, Mount Snow, Vermont, 27

Northstar-at-Tahoe, Truckee, California, 230

Park City Mountain Resort, Park City, Utah, 205

Schweitzer Mountain Resort, Sandpoint, Idaho, 237

Shanty Creek, Bellaire, Michigan, 150

Smugglers' Notch Resort, Smugglers' Notch, Vermont, 34

Snowbird Ski and Summer Resort, Snowbird, Utah, 208

Snowmass Village Resort Association, Snowmass Village, Colorado, 210

Squaw Valley USA, Olympic Valley, California, 238

Stratton Mountain Resort, Stratton Mountain, Vermont, 38

Sugarloaf/USA, Kingfield, Maine, 41

Sun Valley, Sun Valley, Idaho, 243

Sunriver Resort, Sunriver, Oregon, 240

Sunshine Village, Banff, Alberta, Canada, 266

Taos Ski Valley, Taos Ski Valley, New Mexico, 177

Whistler/Blackcomb, Whistler, British Columbia, Canada, 268

Resorts with Tennis

Amelia Island Plantation, Amelia Island, Florida, 90

Callaway Gardens, Pine Mountain, Georgia, 97

Club Med/Sandpiper, Port St. Lucie, Florida, 106

Gray Rocks Resort, Mont-Tremblant, Quebec, Canada, 259

Kiawah Island Resorts, Kiawah Island, South Carolina, 75

La Costa Resort and Spa, Carlsbad, California, 229

The Lodge of Four Seasons Championship Golf Resort and Spa, Lake Ozark,
    Missouri, 142

Marco Island Marriott Resort and Golf Club, Marco Island, Florida, 113

The Rancho Bernardo Inn, San Diego, California, 233

The Resort at Longboat Key Club, Longboat Key, Florida, 117

Sheraton El Conquistador Resort and Country Club, Tucson, Arizona, 174

South Seas Resort, Captiva Island, Florida, 119

Stratton Mountain Resort, Stratton Mountain, Vermont, 38

Sun Valley, Sun Valley, Idaho, 243

The Westin Innisbrook Resort, Palm Harbor, Florida, 123

Wild Dunes Resort, Isle of Palms, South Carolina, 84

About the Authors

JANET TICE grew up in Oklahoma City and lived for twenty years in New York City. She earned an M.S. in Psychiatry from New York University, owned a travel agency for many years, and, in 1986, founded Families Welcome!, a tour company specializing in family travel. She currently resides in Chapel Hill, North Carolina, with her daughter, Fabiana, and travels extensively, "but never enough!"

JANE WILFORD was born and reared in New Orleans, Louisiana. She earned a B.A. in Art History and History from Duke University and an M.S. in Library Service from Columbia University. In 1986 she moved to London, where she currently resides with her husband, D. Sykes Wilford, and sons, Sykes and Paul, and daughter, Sarah. The Wilford family has traveled extensively throughout the United States and Europe.

About the Editor

BECKY DANLEY has roots deeply tied to the Midwest, growing up in central Iowa and later relocating to southern Iowa. An entrepreneur with a successful small business, she enjoys traveling with her retired husband, Dennis. Although sons, Cory and Caleb, are now grown and traveling on their own, her most enjoyable memories are the many, many trips they have taken together over the years. Traveling the United States from north to south and east to west, they never tire of the new vistas and excitement around each corner!

High Hampton Inn & Country Club

P.O. Box 338 • Cashiers, NC 28717
Phone: 828–743–2411 • Fax: 828–743–5991
www.HighHamptonInn.com
info@HighHamptonInn.com
Reservations: 1–800–334–2551